American Obsession:

Race and Conflict in the Age of Obama

Copyright © Seth Forman 2011

Hardcover ISBN: 978-1-60910-231-9
Paperback ISBN: 978-1-61434-263-2

All rights reserved. No part of this publication may be reproduced, stored in a retrieval system, or transmitted in any form or by any means, electronic, mechanical, recording or otherwise, without the prior written permission of the author.

Published in the United States by Booklocker.com, Inc., Bangor, Maine.

Printed in the United States of America on acid-free paper.

Booklocker.com, Inc. 2011
First Edition

American Obsession:

Race and Conflict in the Age of Obama

Seth A. Forman

For my mom, Edith Forman, of blessed memory

Acknowledgements

I'd like to thank Ms. Diane Burman for suggesting I write about this topic. David Gelernter's gracious help and support was instrumental to this project, as was the help of Abigail Thernstrom, Stephen Thernstrom, Dinesh D'Souza, Irving Louis Horowitz, Jonathan B. Imber, and Lee E. Koppelman. Finally, anything written about the Obama presidency that doesn't draw deeply from Charles Krauthammer's ocean of insight is not worth reading. Similarly, anything written in the field of social science that doesn't draw deeply from Thomas Sowell's body of work is not worth reading. Both men are national treasures.

About the Author

A native Long Islander, Seth Forman received his doctorate in American history from the State University of New York (SUNY) at Stony Brook in 1996. He holds a bachelor's degree in political science and a master's degree in public administration, both from SUNY at Albany. Prior to this book, Dr. Forman co-authored *Fire Island National Seashore: A History* (with Lee E. Koppelman, State University of New York Press, 2008), was the author of *Blacks in the Jewish Mind: A Crisis of Liberalism* (New York University Press 1998), and co-edited the anthology *Great Jewish Speeches Throughout History* (Jason Aronson 1994). Dr. Forman blogs at www.mrformansplanet.com and www.opinion-journal.com and has written articles and reviews for such publications as *The Weekly Standard, American Thinker, American Enterprise, Academic Questions, Gotham Gazette, Partisan Review, Newsday, The American Scholar, American Jewish History, American Outlook, American Historical Journal, Long Island History Journal,* and *Midstream.*

Dr. Forman teaches government and public policy at Stony Brook University and at Suffolk County Community College. He also serves as Chief Planner of the Long Island Regional Planning Council.

American Obsession: Race and Conflict in the Age of Obama

Table of Contents

LIST OF FIGURES AND TABLES XIII

INTRODUCTION: THE CHALLENGE OF AN AFFIRMATIVE ACTION PRESIDENCY 1

CHAPTER 1 - OBAMA'S PROBLEM WITH AMERICA 19

CHAPTER 2 - OBAMA AND THE POLITICS OF RACE 86

CHAPTER 3 - THE RACIALIZED BLACK VOTE 107

CHAPTER 4 - THE DERACIALIZED WHITE VOTE 121

CHAPTER 5 - "OBAMA EUPHORIA" AND BLACK PARANOIA 171

CHAPTER 6 - OBAMA'S RADICALISM AND THE DAMAGE TO NATIONAL UNITY 198

CHAPTER 7 - AMERICA THE ORDINARY, OBAMA THE GREAT 215

CHAPTER 8 - E PLURIBUS PLURIBUS: OBAMA AND THE HISPANIC FACTOR 245

CHAPTER 9 - CONCLUSION: WHAT WAS LOST 263

INDEX 273

NOTES 281

List of Figures and Tables

Figures

FIGURE 1 - Black Voter Turnout for President 2004 vs. 2008

FIGURE 2 – Increase in Number of Voters in Presidential Elections by Race 2004 vs. 2008

FIGURE 3 – Black Elected Officials in the United States

FIGURE 4 – How They Voted: Voters Who Said "Race Was the Most Important Factor in Deciding How to Vote"

FIGURE 5 Change in Number of Non-white Voters vs. Change in Number of Non-white Votes for Democrat

FIGURE 6 - Obama's Vote Margin Over McCain vs. Obama's Increase in Non-White Voters Over John Kerry in 2004

FIGURE 7 – Percentage Vote for Obama by Race

FIGURE 8 - Percentage of White Vote John Kerry in 2004 vs. Obama in 2008

FIGURE 9 - Percentage Vote of White Evangelicals Democratic Candidate vs. Republican Candidate 2004 vs. 2008

FIGURE 10 - Percentage Vote of White Evangelicals Aged 18-29 John Kerry in 2004 vs. Obama in 2008

FIGURE 11 - Percentage Vote of Households with Over $200,000 Annual Income

FIGURE 12 - Percent Who Think of Themselves as An American Before They Think of Themselves as a Member of a Particular Race

FIGURE 13 - "I Am Very Patriotic"

FIGURE 14 - Percent of Hispanic Children Living in Married Couple Families

FIGURE 15 - Percent of Hispanics Who Say an Immigrant Has to do each of the Following to Be a Part of American Society

Tables

TABLE 1: Presidential Vote Breakdown by Race 2004 vs. 2008

TABLE 2: Presidential Voter Breakdown by Church Attendance 2004 vs. 2008

TABLE 3: Presidential Voter Breakdown by Household Income 2004 vs. 2008

Introduction

THE CHALLENGE OF AN AFFIRMATIVE ACTION PRESIDENCY

Platitudes concerning the racial and civic utopia that will spring forth from the election of Barack Obama to the U.S. presidency began early. The day after the election of the first black president, the *Washington Post's* E.J. Dionne -- practicing his own form of wedge politics -- wrote, "Yes, it is time to hope again. Time to hope that the era of racial backlash and wedge politics is over."[1]

Newsweek magazine, which by August of 2008 had featured Obama on its cover no less than ten times, compared the not yet single term U.S. senator and president-elect to none other than Abraham Lincoln, while Jon Meacham temporarily, one hopes, transformed himself from the magazine's editor into its party planner: "We're celebrating a moment as much as a man, I think," Meacham told Howard Kurtz of the *Washington Post*. In keeping with the festive mood, the magazine's quadrennial election volume was given the judicious title *A Long Time Coming: The Historic, Combative, Expensive and Inspiring 2008 Election and the Victory of Barack Obama,* while its commemorative issue -- "Obama's American Dream" -- Kurtz reports, was "filled with

Introduction

so many iconic images and such stirring prose that it could have been campaign literature."[2]

Not to be denied a tenor spot in the pro-Obama chorus, NBC News, on November 10th, announced the release of a special DVD on Barack Obama's life story, using Obama's own campaign slogan for the title -- "Yes We Can!" -- accompanied by the following description: "DVD extras include footage of the full inspiring speeches which were the most pivotal and memorable ones of his two year campaign."[3]

Joining the herd of independent minds, *Time* magazine named Obama "person of the year" in a cover piece that included this remarkable, though indecipherable, ode to Obama: "His genome is global, his mind is innovative, his world is networked, and his spirit is democratic." The piece breathlessly explained why Obama was awarded the coveted title: "for ushering the country across a momentous symbolic line, for infusing our democracy with a new intensity of participation, for showing the world and ourselves that our most cherished myth -- the one about boundless opportunity -- has plenty of juice left in it."[4] The months following Obama's election did not dampen *Time's* enthusiasm for the President. In late April 2009 *Time* featured Obama on its cover for the thirteenth time in a twelve month period.

And in the rush to prevent an event of global significance from passing him by without claiming paternity, the characteristically understated *New York Times* columnist Thomas Friedman declared nothing less than the end of the Civil War: "And so it came to pass that on Nov. 4th, 2008, shortly after 11 p.m. eastern time, the American Civil War ended, as a black man . . . won enough electoral votes to become president of the United States."[5]

The punditry can be forgiven its preening. It is right about the historical significance of Obama's election, and it is genuinely proud of how thoroughly involved they were in bringing it about. Besides, other more measured critics also saw cause for hope. Fox News and former National Public Radio commentator Juan Williams pointed out that with this election "the market has irrevocably shrunk for Sharpton style tirades against 'the man' and 'the system.'" Even conservative critics -- including some of the most doctrinaire adherents to color blind principles -- reacted with uncharacteristic exuberance. Writing in the *New York Post*, historian and U.S. Commission on Civil Rights Vice Chair Abigail Thernstrom opined that "by unleashing imagination and energy, dreams come true. Already, Barack Obama is changing black America." Columnist Jonah Goldberg called Obama's election "a bipartisan racial success story," writing in *National Review* that "if ever there were a wonderful consolation prize in politics, shattering the race barrier in the White House is surely it." Representatives from Obama's predecessor President George W. Bush's inner circle could count themselves among the impressed. Michael Gerson, Bush's head speechwriter, wrote that "simply by mounting the platform as

Introduction

America's first ever black president, Mr. Obama will be sending a message of change and reconciliation."[6]

Even the conservative firebrand and academic freedom crusader David Horowitz, author of the 1999 volume *Hating Whitey and Other Progressive Causes*, argued that Obama's election by itself produced much good. "It means that the race card has been played out and America can once again see itself -- and be seen -- for what it is: a land of incomparable opportunity, incomparable tolerance, and justice for all."[7]

Given this surfeit of unbridled optimism, it was shocking how quickly the proposition that Obama's election laid waste to the "race card" was debunked. If "playing the race card" means the cynical use of white racism by a black person for the sake of personal gain, Obama's own Attorney General (and the nation's first black AG), played it immediately. During his senate confirmation hearings, Eric Holder attempted to divert attention from his prior role in backing President Bill Clinton's pardon of international fugitive Marc Rich by lambasting the first majority white country in history to elect a man of African dissent its president as a "nation of cowards" on all matters racial. And Holder finished second behind former Black Panther and Illinois congressman Bobby Rush in the race to use black victimization to secure a public prize. Rush implored Illinois Governor Rod Blagojevich to appoint a black person to fill the U.S. senate seat left vacant by Obama's election because, you see, "there presently is no

African-American in the U.S. Senate, and I don't think that anyone, any U.S. senator who is sitting right now, would want to go on record to deny one African-American from being seated in the U.S. Senate."[8]

Attorney General Holder and Congressman Rush were joined in their invocation of racial injustice to exact a wage from white guilt by the first black governor of the nation's third most populous state. In the face of approval ratings in the twenties, a ballooning state budget deficit, a much derided appointment to replace the departing Hillary Clinton in the U.S. senate, and an $8 billion tax increase for 2009-2010, New York Governor David Paterson blamed a racist media for trying to push him out of the 2010 election. The appointed successor to scandalized governor Eliot Spitzer in 2008, Paterson became vulnerable to a primary challenge after an unprecedented stalemate in the New York State senate in the summer of 2009. But Paterson believed his problems had other causes. On a morning radio show he made the following points: that "certain media outlets have engaged in coverage that exploits racial stereotypes," that Massachusetts Governor Deval Patrick, the country's only other black governor at the time, was also under fire because of his race, and that "The reality is the next victim on the list -- and you can see it coming -- is President Barack Obama, who did nothing more than trying to reform a health care system . . . We're not in the post-racial period."[9]

But for sheer racial demagoguery perhaps nothing matched the crass exploitation of America's civil rights legacy by the Congressional

Introduction

Black Caucus (CBC) during the battle over the 2010 health care overhaul. This was to be, of course, wholly expected. The only racially exclusive caucus in the U.S. congress and the beneficiary of racial gerrymandering schemes that guarantee lifelong tenure for its members, the CBC maxed out its race card long ago. In 2006, for example, the CBC rallied around fellow black congressman William Jefferson (D-LA), who was videotaped receiving a $100,000 bribe which the FBI subsequently found stashed in his freezer. In Jefferson's defense, CBC chairman Melvin Watt of North Carolina told reporters that some black voters might ask why punitive action was sought against "a black member of Congress." Later, in 2010, when CBCer Maxine Waters (D-CA) faced charges of steering $12 million in federal "bailout" money to a bank partially owned by her husband, another CBC member anonymously told *Politico.com* that "There's a dual standard. One for most members and one for African-Americans." The Waters investigation transpired at roughly the same time that CBC elder statesman Charles Rangel (D-NY) was being asked by house leadership to resign rather than face a trial over thirteen violations of house rules. A year earlier Rangel had stepped down from his chairmanship of the powerful ways and means committee due to the fallout over a corporate sponsored junket to the Caribbean he led for four other CBC members. Still, Rangel chose the last refuge of scoundrels to defend himself against the pending charges. "I think that the numbers look odd in terms of the number of African-Americans that have been brought before the [House Ethics] committee," he told CNN.[10]

So while the cries of racism emerging from the CBC during the 2009-2010 debate over health care reform were not unique, the health care reform law itself, passed by congress on March 22, 2010, represented several historic firsts: it was the first federal mandate on citizens to purchase a commodity or service; it was the first time a piece of legislation expanding the annual federal budget by 10 percent or more was passed strictly along party lines. Not a single opposition party legislator voted for the bill (20 percent of the majority party also voted against it); and it was the first time a law of such magnitude was passed without the support of the voting public. At the time of its passage, a CNN/Opinion Research poll showed that 59 percent of the public opposed the health care law and 40 percent favored it. The average of all national polls during the month the legislation was passed showed 52.4 percent of those surveyed opposed the law and 40.4 percent favored it. In the past, every piece of legislation with the financial or political heft of health care reform succeeded only upon condition of popular support. A Gallup poll from 1965, for example, showed that Medicaid had 63 percent popular support when it passed. Sixty percent of the public favored the Civil Rights Act when it passed in 1964. In 1996, 68 percent of Americans favored welfare reform. In 2000, before Bush's $1.3 trillion tax cut was introduced, 63 percent of Americans thought they were paying too much income tax; by the

Introduction

spring of 2001, 56 percent favored Bush's proposed cuts. In 2003, 52 percent supported the second round of Bush tax cuts. "In every one of these contentious national debates," Democratic consultant Mark Penn wrote before health care reform passed, "public support was solidified as a pre-condition to final passage . . . But, for better or worse, this is not the dynamic in health care today."[11]

President Barack Obama meets with House Speaker Nancy Pelosi, House Majority Leader Steny Hoyer, and House Education and Labor Committee Chair Rep. George Miller, in the Oval Office, May 13, 2009.

Nevertheless, two days before the law's adoption the CBC, which counted as members some of the most ardent supporters of health care reform, staged a cynical manipulation of America's racial sensitivity to increase support for the bill. In an attempt to demonize the bill's most vocal opponents, caucus members decided to walk slowly and provocatively through a peaceful but animated (and mostly white) "Tea Party" demonstration on Capitol Hill. There was no obvious reason for the black representatives to slog through the throng of anti-tax and spend demonstrators other than to elicit an offensive response: the most commonly used path between the house office buildings and the capitol are the underground tunnels that lie between them, not the above ground area playing host to the protestors. The black caucus members claimed they were merely enjoying the first day of spring when they were accosted by demonstrators shouting racial epithets at them. But none of the thousands of recording devices on the scene -- professional audio and video equipment, and tens of thousands of handicams, BlackBerrys and iPods -- captured anything discernably racist. The event was shown repeatedly on television stations and internet sites around the world, which did nothing to either validate or debunk the charges of racial hectoring. But that did not prevent Congressman Andre Carson (D-Indiana) from insisting that "the 'N' word, the 'N' word, [was chanted] fifteen times." Another black caucus member claimed he was spit at, one of several serious accusations the veracity of which was impossible to verify.

What is clear is that the black caucus members were not taking a spontaneous spring jaunt through the capitol grounds: they walked separately from other white members of congress, and were followed by the reviled House Speaker Nancy Pelosi (D-California), who carried

Introduction

an oversized gavel and a triumphant grin through the crowd. Despite the paucity of evidence, the "racism" of the anti-Obama Tea Party movement became a permanent feature of the black racial narrative in the Obama era: several months after the event, the National Association for the Advancement of Colored People, citing "racial slurs . . . hurled at members of the Congressional Black Caucus as they passed by a Tea Party health care protest in Washington, DC," passed a resolution "condemning the racist acts of Tea Party protesters." In May 2010, Obama himself told guests at a private White House dinner that race was probably a key component in the rising opposition to his presidency from the Tea Party. When one of those in attendance suggested that the Tea Party was created to stir up anger at having a black president, Obama agreed that there was a racially biased, "subterranean agenda" in the anti-Obama movement.[12]

Not only has Obama's election failed to hasten the demise of the "race card" in American politics, it has not even stopped it from migrating to the Republican National Committee, whose black chairman Michael Steele played it to dislodge himself from a spending scandal. Asked on ABC's *Good Morning America* if he thought he was being criticized unfairly because he's black, Steele took the bait, responding that "the honest answer is, yes." Steele added, in a remarkable attempt to make common cause with the president he had been charged with defeating, that because he is black "Barack Obama has a slimmer margin. A lot of folks do. It's a different role for me to play and others to play and that's just the reality of it." Steele failed to explain what his race had to do with the reimbursement of a contributor by the committee he ran for $2,000 spent at a West Hollywood bondage themed lesbian nightspot.[13]

Leaving aside, for the moment, that black public figures have refused to forfeit the cudgel of racial grievance to enhance their power or position, in broader terms the euphoric pundits seem to have overlooked the role that racial favoritism played in Obama's election, how identity politics benefited Obama, and how electing a president on the basis of race could be disastrous for America. As the rest of this book makes clear, if Obama were not black he would not have won the Democratic primary for president and the presidency itself. This is troubling on a number of levels, not the least of which is the harm it may have already done to the office of the U.S. President, the only nationally elected office (along with that of Vice President) and historically a unifying force for the nation. The president is elected by the entire country, and because of this is endowed with great symbolic importance. A U.S. senator may be "California's junior senator" and a congressman can be part of a "black caucus" or a "blue dog" Democrat. But even the most vicious partisan calls the president "our president." If, as seems likely, enough American voters judged Obama not by his character, but by the color of his skin, we will have shrouded America's most powerful public institution in the obsessive racial awareness that has led to endless contention elsewhere. In the future, in

Introduction

light of America's increasing diversity, if presidents are selected even partially because they are members of a politically favored racial or ethnic group, it won't be long until the president becomes "their president" and not "our" president. In more general terms, the trouble with electing a president on the basis of race begins with what Thomas Jefferson knew when he wrote in the Declaration of Independence that "all men are created equal": it is impossible to know the substance of an individual's character by any inherited physical characteristic. This is as true of presidential candidates as it is of insurance brokers or policemen. If Obama's view of the United States, its position in the world, and how it should be governed was relegated to second tier status in evaluating his fitness for office, disappointment, alienation, and bitterness await large swaths of the electorate.

President Barack Obama: Inauguration Day 2009.

Many people who voted for Obama, particularly his white supporters, did so because his blackness offered a chance at absolution, proof that America, and perhaps they themselves, were still worthy and exceptional. In return, voters agreed to overlook much about the candidate that would have been unacceptable if he were white: the fact that Obama himself does not view America as either particularly virtuous or exceptional; his membership in a racist church whose preacher was central to his life; his support of black nationalism; his association with political radicals like William Ayers and radical outfits like Chicago ACORN (Association of Community Organizations for Reform Now); his positions on issues ranging from allowing illegal immigrants to obtain driver's licenses to conditionless dialogue with Iran, a nation actively engaged in armed combat against U.S. forces; his accusations that U.S. armed forces in Afghanistan were "just air-raiding villages and killing civilians"; his feeble estimate of America's moral authority in the world; and his overall lack of experience. Such was the need of so many Americans to feel good, to try a new course after a bitter and acrimonious eight years, and to quell the vitriol served up by a media fairly deranged by hatred of George W. Bush, that many decided Obama's being the first black president had more to offer than his policies could ever possibly cost.

All of this is not to discount the importance -- even the primacy -- of the financial crisis of 2007-2008 and an unpopular sitting president in determining the election outcome. Nor is it to deny Obama's considerable skill and formidable political operation. It is merely an acknowledgement that Obama's blackness was necessary for *him* -- someone with his background and political viewpoint -- to be elected and an observation, in the words of Hoover Institute race expert Shelby Steele, that "something extremely powerful in the body politic, a force quite apart from the man himself, has pulled Obama forward."[14]

Introduction

The things about Obama that were ignored by large numbers of voters matter, and their costs may be higher than many voters believed when they voted him into office. They reflect the character and world view of the person and suggest how he will govern. It is one thing to be disappointed in a president after voting for him. That happens often enough. It is quite another to be disappointed in a president after voting for him on the basis of assurances -- in this case made by both Obama and a reverential media -- that the candidate's past is irrelevant, and that it does not reflect his world view or how he will govern. In the vernacular preferred by both the late Malcolm X and Obama during the 2008 presidential campaign, many voters were "hoodwinked" into believing that Obama was a centrist "post-racial" candidate for whom race and identity politics meant nothing, and whose view of America's place in the world and the role of government in their lives was very much in line with their own. Judging from Obama's career and life, this is demonstrably false. Like anyone else, politicians can change. Many "grow" or "evolve" in the offices they hold. Obama's predecessor George W. Bush, after all, spent much of his first presidential campaign warning against the perils of "nation building" before embarking on just such a mission in Iraq in the wake of the terrorist attacks of September 11th, 2001. The fabulous complexity of America's political system creates convoluted paths of causation, curious combinations of policy and effect, and often unanticipated modes accountability. But if no serious transformation takes place with Obama, it will become clear to increasing numbers of voters that Obama does not share their view of America and its governance, that he is not a mainstream pragmatist, that he is, at the very least, extremely ambivalent about American power, wealth, and influence in the world, and that his viewpoint derives very much from the politics of racial identity that he has been immersed in for much of his life. As a result, the raw ideological differences among American voters, now manifest most clearly in racial identity, have been stripped bare for all to see. This book, in short, lays out in detail the following about President Obama from the available evidence:

1) Obama's race made his election possible. Large and important segments of the media, the voting public, various interest groups, and even some of Obama's political opponents operated within the confines of a racial double standard that overlooked actions, beliefs, and past experience that would not have been acceptable to voters had Obama been white. Obama is, in this respect, America's first "affirmative action" president. Some (though by no means all) of the important standards used for selecting candidates for holding the office of the president were lowered or ignored to permit this particular black man to win.

2) Obama's identity as a black man should be understood mostly in terms of the politics of protest, an adversarial posture toward the political mainstream grounded in the belief that the original moral

Introduction

flaws of slavery and racism have been seared permanently onto American life.

3) Obama believes these fundamental flaws are manifest in America's domestic policy, which gives too much autonomy to individuals with unfair advantages, as well as its foreign policy, which reflects America's contempt for less powerful countries and serves mostly to preserve an unjust social hierarchy at home and abroad.

4) These flaws render America rather unexceptional, similar to other powerful but flawed countries of the past and present.

5) America must atone for this basic corruption through a massive restructuring of both domestic and foreign policy. Specifically:

    a.   members of formerly marginalized groups (blacks, Hispanics, gays, non-whites, the poor) need to be given legal status as members of protected classes in order to live dignified lives;

    b.   private property rights need to be significantly modified to allow for more collective (governmental) control over the production and distribution of resources and opportunities;

    c.   The rewards accruing to individuals for excellence and achievement, productivity and risk taking must be reduced to ensure universal security.

    d.   The U.S. must lead the way in recognizing nationalism and pride in country for what it is: a harmful and artificial obstacle to world peace and the ideal of human brotherhood or, at the very least, solidarity based on more "authentic" modes of identity like race, religion, and ethnicity. Therefore,

e. America must cede significant amounts of sovereignty to international institutions (e.g. the United Nations).

6) That as its first black president, Obama believes he is the perfect instrument for purifying the country, for liberating it from its false pride, and for navigating it to its proper, more modest place among nations.

7) As a result, Obama's agenda -- including large doses of national self-denigration and government intervention -- stands as a direct challenge to the belief held by a large majority of Americans that they are part of an "exceptional" nation, a unique and noble experiment in human history.

Electing the first black president of the United States could have been an occasion for true racial reconciliation. If the same standards used in electing a white president were in place when electing a black president this would have been a distinct probability. If that black candidate for president were expected, as all previous modern presidents were, to have demonstrated a love of country through public service or personal achievement, to have expressed through compromise or leadership a sincere appreciation for the complexity of American life, for the distinctiveness of the institutions designed to draw strength rather than conflict from that complexity, this could no doubt have transpired. Instead, electing a black man whose personal identity and professional status was forged on the pyres of racial grievance, whose political ambitions were effectuated by a belief in the necessity of recompense, has guaranteed a period of unusual social bitterness and resentment, and the reemergence of race as the primary conduit through which the vast and growing political chasm in America is expressed.

Chapter 1

OBAMA'S PROBLEM WITH AMERICA

Despite his amazing rise to power and the overwhelming political endorsement he has received from voters across many of the most powerful sectors of society, Obama clings to beliefs that most Americans reject: namely, that America's mistakes are at least as important in defining the country as its triumphs; that America's influence on the world has been at least as harmful as it has been helpful; and that America therefore lacks the moral authority to wield disproportionate global influence. These convictions have, of course, become a central tenet of the political left throughout the world in the post-Soviet era. They also play a role in the worldview of Islamic extremists and many of the world's aggressive nationalisms. Electing for the first time in U.S. history, then, a president who holds these views presents challenges of a very significant magnitude.

America, after all, has been the country under whose leadership Nazism and Soviet style communism were defeated, which did the most to create and sustain the postwar economic system under which billions have thrived, and which has become the only military power capable of stamping out tyrants, terrorists and other threats to world peace. While Obama and others may see something better in the offing, at this moment in time it is American power that underwrites European security against an increasingly autocratic and aggressive Russia. It is American power that insures against Iranian dominance of the Middle East, and against the nuclear ambitions of that country's radical mullahs. It is American power that brings the likes of Milosevic, Hussein, Al Zarqawi, and Osama bin Laden to justice and, if need be, the likes of Ahmidinejad, Chavez, and Kim Jong Il as well. As the only superpower capable of protecting both parties from lethal diplomatic error, it is American power that holds out the only hope for Israeli security and Palestinian democratization. And it is American power that, to the degree possible, sees that the most egregious violations of international norms are punished, that trade routes remain open, that airways and seaways remain safe, and that international responses to natural disasters are sufficiently funded and competently manned. As the world stands now, in other words, there is no close, desirable successor to the *Pax Americana,* the preponderance of American power that has provided the world the relative peace, affluence, stability, and the chance for a redress of grievances it has enjoyed during the post-World War II era. But that fact has not prevented Obama from believing, in the words of columnist Charles Krauthammer, "that America is so intrinsically flawed, so inherently and congenitally sinful that it cannot be trusted with, and does not merit, the possession of overarching world power."[1]

Obama's conviction that American power must be harnessed to the predilections of a world parts of which are eager to see it weakened has been repeatedly on display. Before the United Nations in September of 2009 Obama exhibited a clear discomfort talking about national self-interest, beginning his remarks with the apologetic comment "Like all of you, my responsibility is to act in the interest of my nation and my people" before negating this unnecessary declaration of presidential responsibility with his next clause: "But it is my deeply held belief that in the year 2009 . . . the interests of nations and peoples are shared." Obama didn't specify how, except in the vaguest possible sense, the interests of Zimbabwe, Iran, China, Russia, and the U.S., for example, are shared. But his willingness to allow narrowly defined American interests to be subsumed by broad international ones has been a common theme in his speeches. While in Oslo to accept the first Nobel Peace Prize to be awarded a head of state with less than a year on the job, Obama elated some conservatives by appearing to back the unilateral use of armed force. "There will be times when nations -- acting individually or in concert -- will find the use of force not only necessary but morally justified," Obama said. But he quickly nullified that statement by insisting "[I]n a world in which threats are more diffuse, and missions more complex, America cannot act alone."[2]

Even when Obama recognizes American power it is with great reluctance, apologetics, and even regret that he does so. This was apparent nowhere so much as it was in the midst of the massive uprisings against autocratic regimes in the Arab world in 2011. The President's refusal to take the lead in the overthrow of the chronically anti-American regime of Col. Moammar Gadhafi in Libya caused his own Secretary of State, Hillary Clinton, to declare that she would not serve under him beyond the 2012 election, even if Obama won. Clinton was said to be especially disappointed with Obama's initial refusal to back the NATO enforced no-fly zone over Libya. European leaders and diplomats expressed bewilderment with Obama's reticence over removing the notorious sponsor of the 1988 terrorist attack on Pan Am flight 103 over Lockerbie, Scotland, which killed 179 Americans. After French President Nicolas Sarkozy and British Prime Minister David Cameron took the lead in establishing a no-fly zone over the North African country in March, 2011, *Foreign Policy* magazine quoted a European diplomat: "Frankly we are just completely puzzled. We are wondering if this is a priority for the United States." Another European insider described Obama's foreign policy thusly: "It's amateur night." When allied forces finally decided to strike Gadhafi by air, Obama gave his reluctant approval from Rio de Janeiro, Brazil at the start of an ill-timed five day Latin American tour. He also authorized his top commander on the ground, Admiral Mike Mullen, to release an anemic statement about U.S. goals for military action against this sworn and erratic enemy of the nation: the goals of the international campaign "are limited and it isn't about seeing him [Gadhafi] go."[3]

It is true that Obama has shown an admirable determination to use the full resources of the U.S. military in Afghanistan and in the forbidding Afghan-Pakistan border region. But the particular provenance of those policies suggests they are unrepresentative of Obama's foreign policy in general. On May 24, 2007, Obama voted as a U.S. senator to cut off funding for military operations in Iraq and Afghanistan, something Republican presidential candidate John McCain seized upon as a symbol of Obama's weakness in foreign affairs. To reduce his vulnerability to such charges, Obama quickly became a vocal supporter of expanding the Afghanistan war, defining that particular conflict as the "right" and "just" war, as opposed to the war in Iraq, which in Obama's view was the critically mistaken "war of choice" started by President George W. Bush. This position provided Obama with a foundation for criticizing Bush as a warmonger who "took his eye of the ball," while presenting himself as a tough on terrorism centrist. As a consequence of this clear campaign position, and perhaps a belated but strong personal conviction, in this particular theater of war Obama continued and even expanded the policies of the Bush administration once in office. These policies included the unilateral use of force, the aggressive use of pilotless drones to bomb terrorist hide outs, and the use of special forces operations inside Pakistan. Ironically, Obama's pursuit of these policies, combined also perhaps with his failure to successfully close the Guantanamo Bay terrorist detention center, ultimately contributed to the greatest achievement of his term as president: the May 20011 killing of 9/11 mastermind and al Qaeda leader, Osama bin Laden.

But outside of this narrow theater, Obama's discomfort with exercising U.S. power has been obvious. At the beginning of allied military action against Libyan targets, Obama refused to acknowledge the very specific national interest the U.S. had in seeing Gadhafi removed from power. Gadhafi had been the most outspoken Muslim enemy of the U.S. before the rise of Saddam Hussein in Iraq and al Qaeda in the 1990s. He was also, for a time, the primary sponsor of terrorism and terrorist attacks against the U.S. Before the Lockerbie attack, Libyan operatives bombed a Berlin disco, killing two U.S. servicemen and injuring 200 others. Despite a thorough retaliatory bombing of Gadhafi's compound in Tripoli, the Muslim gadfly managed to cling to power. And indeed, the U.S. had been successful in isolating and neutering Gadhafi on the world stage, an effort that culminated with the 2003 invasion of Iraq. Fearful that President George W. Bush might have him directly in his crosshairs, a chastened Gadhafi publicly renounced his nuclear program.

But it wasn't until March of 2011 that the opportunity to finally remove the Libyan tyrant presented itself. It was not known at the time of the U.N. sponsored, NATO enforced no-fly zone whether rebel forces fighting Gadhafi were Muslim extremists, anti-American, al

Qaeda, or even politically representative of the Libyan people. It was not known, either, whether they would govern more humanely than Gadhafi should they eventually take power, or whether they would be less of a threat to world stability. In terms of America's national interest, the issue that presented itself to Obama was whether the U.S. should use military force to overthrow a decades old enemy of the United States who carried the blood of American innocents on his hands, and who seemed to be teetering on the edge of power. Obama answered this call by subordinating this narrow but paramount national interest behind the veneer of human rights, and by shackling American power with self-imposed international restraints, stating from Brazil that the goal of NATO intervention was not to ensure the ouster of a sworn enemy; it was "about supporting the United Nations resolution, which talked to limiting or eliminating his [Gadhafi's] ability to kill his own people, as well as support [of] the humanitarian effort." Always mindful, if not outright solicitous, of the international left's view of America as an aggressive, imperial power, Obama abashedly told a press conference that "Our mission right now is to shape the battle space in such a way that our partners may take the lead in . . . execution."[4]

Obama's lack of enthusiasm for the exercise of American power is rooted in his ambivalence toward America's superpower status, and his sensitivity to accusations of American imperialism. This was apparent at the close of a two day summit on nuclear security in April 2010, where the President suggested that being a superpower is, in fact, an unfortunate burden to the United States. Responding to a question concerning efforts to achieve peace in the Middle East, Obama said "It is a vital national security interest of the United States to reduce these conflicts because whether we like it or not, we remain a dominant military superpower, and when conflicts break out, one way or another we get pulled into them." Obama was not specific in detailing who might "like it" or who "might not" that the U.S. is a military superpower. But given that the vast majority of Americans are likely pleased that the U.S. maintains its superpower status, the use of such wording suggests the President has a global, not a national sensibility when he considers foreign policy.[5]

It is telling that in his statement at the summit Obama reduced the nation to only "a dominant superpower," presumably just one of a number of nations roughly equal in strength and influence. That may have been the case prior to World War I, and possibly even during the Cold War. It may even be the vision that Obama holds for America's future. But it is not the case at this point in time. The U.S. today is, in fact, the world's only military "hyperpower," the one country that alone possesses a global, multi-war capability. It is also the only country that possesses a leader who is publicly ambivalent about his nation's military superiority, a leader who is apparently aloof to the dynamism, sacrifice, and sense of purpose that went into making that achievement possible.

So despite the standard, boilerplate odes to America's greatness Obama is careful to include in his public utterances, it is clear that what Obama believes in most fervently is America's imperfection. Obama almost never provides a defense of America without subordinating it to a larger criticism, as when he told CNN's Fareed Zakaria that he believes America is right to wage war on Islamic extremists, but that more importantly, America has been guilty of slandering Islam. "We should be going after al Qaeda and those networks fiercely and effectively . . . But what we also want to do is to shrink the pool of potential recruits. And that involves engaging the Islamic world rather than vilifying it." Once again, Obama preferred to beat up on a lazily erected straw man -- a caricature, really -- of American foreign policy rather than spell out exactly how America has vilified Islam. It is difficult to know whether Obama is so bitterly alienated by his own country's dominant position in the world that he can't unqualifiedly acknowledge its positive actions, or whether he is simply ignorant of his country's efforts on behalf of Muslims. America has, after all, been the only country that has consistently, and often at great cost, defended large Muslim populations throughout the world. Since the end of World War II the U.S. has made a friend and ally of Turkey, defending this frontline nation against the Soviets through military and financial support. Not surprisingly, Turkey is the only Muslim nation (recently and tentatively joined by Iraq) that, despite problems, has drawn an acceptable balance between religion and governance, and that feels comfortable enough with the west to seek membership in the European Union and to run military exercises with Israel.

In the late 1970s, when the Soviets invaded neighboring Afghanistan and the communist jackboot was pressing on the Muslim throat, it was America that armed the *mujahedeen* in defense of their country in what many military strategists consider the most successful guerilla campaign of the modern era. Then, in the early 1990s, when Kuwait lay prostrate before Saddam Hussein's invading forces, America's 101st Airborne led the international coalition that liberated the oil-rich city state. By the middle of that decade the world stood idle as 250,000 Bosnian Muslims were killed by Serbian nationalists. The U.S. finally bombed the Serbs into submission. In 2001, the American military, with boots on the ground and "daisy cutters" in the air, liberated Afghanistan from the Taliban's lethal grip in three weeks, sending the Islamic fascists running for the hills, something Soviet forces couldn't do in fifteen years of trying. Two years later American forces toppled the most brutal dictatorship in the Arab world, freeing the people of Iraq (Sunnis, Shia, Kurds -- Muslims all) to fight for that region's first Arab democracy. To date, America has lost more than 4,000 men and women in that fight and has suffered 25,000 serious injuries, spending hundreds of billions of dollars in the effort. Before Obama's presidency -- before the relaxed standards for tolerating presidential self-denigration set in, that is -- it would have been considered, at the very least, a demonstration of gross incompetence for a president to begin a discussion of policy toward a particular part of the world without the noble sacrifices made by his own country first to fly from his tongue.[6]

Obama's failure to express national pride at levels typical for American presidents could reflect the absence of direct foreign policy experience in his background, or discomfort on the world stage, explanations that will not convince those able to recall his virtuoso performance at the bewildering (and still rather mysterious) mass rally in Berlin in front of a Prussian victory column during the 2008 presidential campaign. It may also reflect a personal aversion to bluster, though his speeches from the campaign -- "this was the moment when the rise of the oceans began to slow and our planet began to heal" and "I am absolutely certain that generations from now, we will be able to look back and tell our children that this was the moment when we began to provide care for the sick" -- offer strong evidence to the contrary.[7]

Whatever the case may be, Obama has left little doubt about the depths of his distaste for what America has been up until his presidency. Even when it comes to the U.S. Constitution, an area in which Obama claims great expertise, he is equivocal. "I think we can say that the Constitution reflected an enormous blind spot in this culture that carries on until this day and that the Framers had that same blind spot," Obama once told an interviewer. "I don't think the two views are contradictory, to say that it was a remarkable political document that paved the way for where we are now, and to say that it also reflected the fundamental flaw of this country that continues to this day."[8]

For Obama, the "blind spot" that he sees in American life has convinced him that America's power must be scaled back for the sake of world peace, a view point that has dominated his approach to America's nuclear defense. Obama believes -- again unlike any previous president, Democrat or Republican -- that the primary obstacle to stemming nuclear proliferation is America's stubborn refusal to weaken its nuclear deterrent. So on September 17th, 2009, precisely seventy years to the day that the Soviets invaded Poland, Obama cancelled the long planned deployment of nuclear missile interceptors to Poland, as well as the deployment of a radar system to another ally, the Czech Republic. Obama followed this with the signing of the "START II," or "New START," agreement in March of 2010 with Russian President Dmitri Medvedev. The treaty proposed to cut the number of strategic warheads each of the two countries possess from 2,200 to 1,550. In practice, though, the treaty would require only the United States to dismantle up to 1,000 nuclear warheads and delivery vehicles: the Russian arsenal is so badly decayed and obsolete that they possess only 700 operational nuclear weapons to begin with. More worryingly, the treaty completely ignores tactical nuclear weapons, which are developed for use on the battlefield. Russia's stockpile of tactical nuclear weapons, which can be affixed to rockets, submarines, and bomber planes, outnumbers that of the United States by a ratio of

10 to 1. When the lame duck, Democrat controlled U.S. senate ratified New START in December of 2010, it insured Russia's tactical nuclear advantage, as well as its ability to produce more of these weapons at will, at least until 2021.[9]

Most troubling of all about New START was Medvedev's insertion of a clause reserving for Russia the right to walk away from the treaty if the United States pursues the development of missile defense systems. The Russians have long feared U.S. superiority in the area of missile defense. Documents that came to light after the Soviet Union's collapse indicate that Ronald Reagan's effort to exploit America's technological superiority with his proposal to build a "star wars" missile shield (officially "strategic defense initiative") was helpful in bringing on the communist empire's demise. In December of 2009, in the midst of New START's negotiations, Russian Prime Minister Vladimir Putin explained the Russian position: "By building such an umbrella over themselves, our partners [the U.S.] could feel themselves fully secure and will do whatever they want, which upsets the balance and the aggressiveness immediately increases in real politics and economics."[10]

In the simplest terms, the view that an America "fully secure" from nuclear attack is a danger to world peace requires a belief that America's actions are as morally corrupt as that of autocracies like Putin's Russia, and must therefore be held in check by the deterrent capability of other powerful nations. That is the view of Russian leaders, who project onto the United States and other democracies their own motivation to maintain their hold on power through international *realpolitik*. It is, by all appearances, the view of President Obama, who voluntarily slowed the U.S. missile defense program even before signing the treaty with Russia, and who failed to ask Medvedev why Russia would oppose the United States protecting itself and its allies from, say, an Iranian nuclear attack. But it is not the view of the more than thirty nations -- including some in the former Soviet bloc -- that depend on the U.S. for anti-missile defense. Many of these allies, especially those in the Middle East, are anxious for the U.S. to make progress with missile defense technology, as they are in striking distance of an Iranian nuclear warhead. Some of these countries have implicitly agreed not to pursue a nuclear deterrent for themselves because the U.S. has guaranteed them safety under the U.S. nuclear defense umbrella. Despite these concerns, Obama pressed on with his headlong effort to put America's adversaries at ease over U.S. nuclear policy. After the treaty was signed, the Russians effectively declared victory on the matter, issuing a statement that the treaty "can operate and be viable only if the United States refrains from developing its missile defense capabilities quantitatively or qualitatively."[11]

In the same week that he signed the New START treaty, the Obama administration issued a "Nuclear Posture Review" (NPR) which pledged the United States not to respond with nuclear weapons to a biological or chemical attack as long as the attacking nation is "in compliance with the Non-Proliferation Treaty (NPT)." The NPR also reduced the number of nuclear warheads on most U.S. long range missiles, dropped the term "rogue" to describe states like North Korea and Iran in favor of the much more vague "outliers," and committed the U.S. to a much slower, "phased" program of missile defense development. While Obama might believe that America has been the principal source of nuclear danger in the world, many less powerful nations -- Qatar, Poland, Czech Republic, Taiwan, Japan, Kuwait, Saudi Arabia, Jordan, Turkey -- don't agree. These countries have not sought nuclear capability precisely because they have enjoyed the security provided by the now weakened U.S. arsenal. As Charles Krauthammer, Obama's most salient critic, has explained, "Since World War II, smaller countries have agreed to forgo the acquisition of deterrent forces -- nuclear, biological and chemical -- precisely because they placed their trust in the firmness, power, and reliability of the American deterrent . . . There is no greater spur to hyper-proliferation than the furling of the American nuclear umbrella."[12]

Obama seeks the diminution of American power relative to other nations. He believes this will recalibrate a global imbalance of power with deep roots in the military aggression, racism, greed, and avarice of the western world. This alone would be a difficult problem for an electorate that generally looks with favor upon American power and influence in the world. But the challenge for America of having elected a president eager to preside over a neutered great power is complicated by its racial pedigree. That is, the President arrives at his worldview from his personal struggle, as he writes in his autobiography, to find "a workable meaning" for his "life as a black American."[13] Obama discovered rather soon that "a workable meaning" for being black in America most often means possessing a certain set of political beliefs deemed essential to black identity. It means subscribing to a point of view, a set of attitudes originating from both the external and internal pressures of the black experience in America. Those who stray from the core attitudes of "blackness," regardless of skin tone, are said to lack racial "authenticity," or even to be non-black, by the guardians of racial purity. Historian Roger Wilkins, one of the self-appointed custodians of black legitimacy, explained it best when he wrote that "In arguing about how best to struggle, there is some political and intellectual behavior in which you engage that keeps you from being a black person."[14]

The existence of cultural traits or attitudes that demarcate the boundary between a majority and an ethnic or racial minority group are common. Immigrants to New York from southern Italy at the turn of the twentieth century, for example, brought with them such a high level of distrust of governmental authority -- a vestige of corruption in their native land -- that Italian children had the highest rates of public school truancy among all ethnic groups. Soon, though, like other immigrant groups, especially those from Europe, Italians "melted" and adopted standard, middle class expectations for their progeny.[15]

The black "adversarial culture" developed differently. The color line in American history was too powerful to allow for melting. Even when blacks were legally enfranchised in the early 1960s, it was never expected that their distinctiveness would disappear or that Americans would be able to erase the memories and scars resulting from the nation's past. Historian Eugene Genovese has explained that in the south, where the vast majority of blacks lived in America until the middle of the twentieth century, and then even in the large northern and mid-western metros after the "great migration," "there was hardly any room at the top or in the middle for blacks who tried to play by the rules of bourgeois society." Accordingly, blacks developed a unique set of values, attitudes, habits, styles, and forms of expression.[16] Some of these black cultural deviations have greatly enriched American life. Black expression in music, literature, worship, linguistic style, athletics, dance, humor, and cuisine come to mind. So too does the black style in politics. American life is freer politically because of the black model of civil rights protest, with its stirring religiosity, its patient but assuredly righteous indignation, its fierce courage and painstaking forbearance, and its particular mode of charismatic leadership, all hallmarks of black American life.

The success of the civil rights protest model of racial advance was by no means guaranteed, of course. In the early part of the twentieth century there was a great battle between protest advocates like W.E.B. Du Bois and economic integrationists like Booker T. Washington. It was Washington's hope that after slavery blacks would give priority to making themselves economically indispensable through vocational expertise, rather than seeking equality via governmental fiat. But after the "great migration" of blacks from south to north, from farms to cities, and after the long struggle for legal equality was finally won, white elites realized the political benefits of granting racial protesters special treatment -- "riot insurance," as one urban scholar has called it. Before the twentieth century was more than two-thirds over, avenues of black advance that did not look to politics and governmental intervention lost their appeal. Even the initial goals of the protesters were eclipsed. Where DuBois, Martin Luther King Jr. and others argued powerfully for equality under the law and political enfranchisement as the necessary first steps for black mobility, their goal – considered far too modest today -- was to furnish blacks only with the opportunities afforded to other Americans, to have the general principles upon which the republic was built applied to them, too. Instead, politicians of all races -- as well as the institutions they controlled -- discovered that there was too much to gain from earmarking special benefits for blacks. The immediate gratification generated by race conscious programs, and the emergence of a black professional class guaranteed by protective laws, was too enticing, leaving blacks mired in what urban historian Fred Siegel calls the "dependency model" of social mobility: the belief that racism remains so determinative of black success that only a full cadre of special programs, legal exceptions, governmental assistance, and racial preferences could even partially compensate for it. The panoply of government supported, grievance based programs -- including affirmative action, race conscious college aid programs and job training, welfare and housing assistance, "Afrocentric" school curricula, minority contract set asides, and lenient criminal justice policies, along with the jobs generated in the vast bureaucracies associated with race based university departments, centers, museums, think tanks, and non-profits -- have made it almost impossible for blacks to dispense with the notion that they face a prohibitive level of discrimination, that the proverbial American playing field can never be made even, and that these special dispensations and protections are therefore integral to their well-being.

Permanent victimization has provided the key to maintaining strong political solidarity among blacks, despite vast and growing differences between the black middle and lower classes, and despite the existence of regional, linguistic, religious, and ancestral differences. The psychologist Ellis Cose has used the term "black rage" to describe the anger that many in the black middle class share with their poorer brethren, and it is not difficult to see where such frustration might come from.[17] The large black middle class is sustained today in large measure by government jobs, programs, policies, and laws, thus depriving many black professionals of the assurance one gains from the "earned success" of the market place, via the only objective measure of productive behavior: profitability. It is no surprise that the nation's wealthiest majority-black suburb, Prince George's County in Maryland, is a "bedroom" community of Washington D.C., where 41 percent of employed blacks work for the state, local, or federal government and another 10 percent work in the non-profit sector. The government programs and equal opportunity laws that have sustained the black middle class are in existence due to politics, not markets, and black gains are seen as fragile and politicized, with the consequence that individual blacks see their own fate as tied to the political success of blacks as an organized interest. Even as white racism has receded, then, racial protest has served as the central organizing principle for black Americans.[18]

This has had enormous political implications. Believing that the fate of the race depends on the helping hand of government keeps blacks firmly entrenched in the left/liberal/Democratic political camp (the "Democratic wing of the Democratic party," according to former National Democratic Party Chairman Howard Dean), despite the relatively conservative social views of many blacks. Blacks have managed to become a powerful political force in America through the sheer intensity of their opposition to what has historically been thought of as the "American creed," a set of beliefs and attitudes born from a revolution against state authority and centered on the ability of individuals to determine their own destiny. In the last fifty years black political activism has been the leading force in transforming American political culture from one that understands equality in terms of opportunity to one that sees it in terms of outcomes; from one with an axiomatic belief in the moral efficacy of individual initiative, to one that sees risk taking and entrepreneurship as manifestations of greed and rapaciousness; from one that defines liberty as protection from government encroachment to one that measures liberty by increasing levels of governmental support; from one that sees America's forays in the world as basically generous and noble to one that sees them as serving to worsen existing social stratification.

Simply put, black Americans tend to be more suspicious of American power than white Americans, are more ambivalent about the trajectory of American history than whites, are more likely to see tragedy in the nation's founding documents, institutions, and values than whites, are more likely than whites to prefer a more activist government, and are more likely to look skeptically upon free market competition, entrepreneurship, and individualism. In their seminal work *America in Black and White,* race scholars Abigail and Stephan Thernstrom note that "A high degree of commitment to an expansive, protective federal government clearly separates blacks from whites." Their book discusses a multitude of survey data, with one poll showing that on the issue of government assistance to blacks, 74 percent of blacks but only 16 percent of whites said too little was being spent. There is as well a marked racial divide on questions such as: "Would you rather have the federal government provide more services, even if it means more taxes?," "Do you think that the federal government can do something to help those African Americans with severe problems?," "Is it the responsibility of government to reduce the differences in income between people?," And, "do you agree that the government has an obligation to help people when they're in trouble?" These differences stem from the historic sense of vulnerability that continues to impact black political attitudes, a sense of defenselessness shared by even the educated black middle class, which also believes its fate is tied to an activist government. As Gerald David Jaynes and Robin Williams write in their book *A Common Destiny*, "the long history of discrimination and segregation have produced among blacks a heightened sense of group consciousness and a stronger orientation toward collective values and behavior than exists generally among Americans."[19]

As much as blacks remain, in other words, residentially segregated and the one race still least likely to intermarry with whites, so too they remain the most politically segregated group: blacks are more densely clustered than other voting blocs along the spectrum of political opinion, typically on the far left, but because of their generally conservative social views not exclusively so. Even in the deep south, where blacks make up more than one-third of the population and are far more integrated economically and socially with whites, this political isolation remains. A befuddled Thomas F. Schaller of the University of Maryland, a leading scholar of voting behavior, has asked "How is it that working class whites -- especially those in the rural parts of the south who sit side by side with similarly situated working class southern blacks at high school sporting events on Friday nights, shop at the same businesses on Saturday afternoon, attend similar (if different denominational) Christian churches on Sunday morning, and send their kids to the same public schools the following Monday -- troop to the ballot box on the first Tuesday every other November and pull the lever for the Republicans while their black neighbors are voting overwhelmingly Democratic?"[20]

There is indeed, in America, no greater predictor of voting patterns than being black -- not income, not education level, not marriage status, not age, not religiosity, not religion, not profession. The first thing an investigator wants to know about a voter in order to predict how they will vote in a presidential election is whether or not they are black. Once the voter is known to be black, it can be estimated with roughly 90 percent confidence -- the standard in social science research -- that the voter will pull the lever for a Democrat. When the voter is of any other race, human complexity takes hold and other variables come into play.

And this is perhaps the most troubling point: the politicization of black racial identity is dehumanizing. A greater violation of the principle of free will and individual conscience could hardly be imagined. To think that skin color (or hair color, or height, or weight) should determine how a person thinks is to deny blacks their individuality, their ability to react as sentient beings to the full range of human experience. One should not be imprisoned, a famous literary critic once explained, by the belief that all blacks "had identical experiences, bore the same psychic wounds, suffered the same slights and irritations."[21] Some black critics have spoken out against this kind of black "essentialism." The novelist Ralph Ellison spent a good part of his career rebuking those who would define blacks solely by the experience of white racism. "American Negro life," Ellison wrote, "is also a discipline . . . There is a fullness, even a richness here; and here despite the realities of politics, perhaps, but nevertheless here and real. Because it is a human life."[22]

Most Americans -- white, black, and other -- have been largely unaware of the important differences in political and social viewpoints between blacks and whites stemming from the black experience in America, and carried forward by the enfranchisement of blacks through a regime of racial recompense. Certainly some Americans have vague notions or intuitions about these racially distinct political attitudes. There are pockets of people in America for whom these differences provide the basis for deep seated prejudice. But by and large the American public has been willing to let blacks preside over matters of political concern to them, content to refrain from commenting publicly about race, or from openly discussing any aspect of black American life, mostly for fear of appearing racially insensitive.

Many white elites, in fact, go so far as to embrace and celebrate expressions of black difference, or ignore "black rage" or wrongdoing, in order to prove their compassion. Not surprisingly, the *New York Times* offers the best examples of both tendencies. In the 1990s, black *New York Times* editorial writer Brent Staples recalled in his memoir the white editor who screened him for his "racial *bona fides,*" i.e. his credentials as the legitimate voice of black anger, before being hired. And in 2003, when black reporter Jayson Blair of the *Times* was discovered fabricating events he wrote about for the paper, *Times* editor-in-chief Howell Raines wrote to *Times* readers, "I believe in aggressively providing hiring and career opportunities for minorities . . . Does that mean I personally favored Jayson . . . When I look into my heart for the truth of that, the answer is yes."[23]

Embracing black rage or ignoring black incompetence in order to demonstrate racial compassion, in the words of Stephan and Abigail Thernstrom, has enabled "whites to distance themselves while simultaneously experiencing a certain fascination with the seemingly exotic and thrillingly dangerous stranger in their midst." And indeed, many self-appointed black spokespersons look increasingly strange to whites. One suspects most white viewers turned quietly, but incredulously, from their television sets when Jesse Jackson told an interviewer from CNN, in the wake of the destruction of black New Orleans by Hurricane Katrina, that Americans "have an amazing tolerance for black pain."[24]

Whites have preferred to remain supplicants in a game in which blacks angrily accuse whites of racism and whites retreat, desperate to show understanding. Even the supposedly irreverent, white dominated talk radio medium, in the end, respects this seemingly universal pattern: committing an act perceived by blacks (or white liberals) to be racially insensitive followed by a show of public repentance. After serving a year long suspension from radio for his on air slur against an all-black women's college basketball team, talk radio icon Don Imus returned to broadcasting, but only after genuflecting with controversial race hustler Al Sharpton, and hiring two black sidekicks (Tony Powell and Karith Foster). Imus also committed to regular on air racial therapy sessions with far left black comedian Dick Gregory and appropriately radical "black studies" scholars, evidence, in Imus's own words, that in America "you can't make fun of everybody."[25]

The pattern of black rage and white retreat has had significant social costs. While racism itself has been a source of national division since the start of the republic, today it is black grievance and white acquiescence that presents the most sizable obstacle to forging a common national identity. This is reflected most ominously in the lack of agreement over what children should learn about American history. There are complicated reasons for the history curriculum mess. But its origins are rooted in the attempt to meet (mostly) black demands for "inclusion," to revise U.S. history curricula to reflect positive contributions by non-white groups, and the acquiescence of the (mostly) white educational establishment in this demand. The education theorist E.D. Hirsch has noted that in the view of the Founding Fathers,

"The school would be the institution that would transform future citizens into loyal Americans. It would teach common knowledge, virtues, ideals, language, and commitments."[26] But surveys show that high school and college students are grossly ill informed about basic U.S. history, the result of attempting to cram into the curriculum esteem building information for non-white (and, perhaps, non-Christian) students. More high school students are aware of who Harriet Tubman is than who President and Civil War general Ulysses S. Grant is. Students have been introduced to escaped slave and first Revolutionary War casualty Crispus Attucks, but not Alexander Hamilton. Rather than a great victory over fascism through heroic battles like the Bulge or Okinawa, most students are taught about World War II as the story of Japanese internment and America's "unnecessary" use of atomic bombs against people of a different race. In a 2008 survey by the conservative think tank American Enterprise Institute, fewer than half of all high school seniors could identify within a half century when the Civil War took place (43 percent), but 77 percent could identify Harriet Beecher Stowe's abolitionist novel *Uncle Tom's Cabin* as a major reason why slavery was defeated. Ninety-seven percent of students could identify Martin Luther King Jr. as the author of the "I Have a Dream" speech. But without knowledge of the (mostly) British origins of America's fealty to liberty and tolerance, and the heroic experiment with democracy of America's first European settlers, there can be little shared meaning for our national identity. The opening in 2007 of the Khalil Gibran International Academy in New York City, the first English-Arabic public school in the country, emphasizing the study of Arabic language and culture, is testimony to the difficulty of establishing a unified national identity going forward.[27]

Another harmful misunderstanding resulting from the one way racial dialogue is the infamous "income gap" between white and black households. According to census statistics, average black family income was only 51 percent of average white family income in 1947, rose to 56 percent in 1964, the year that the federal law forbidding employment discrimination (Title VII of the Civil Rights Act of 1964) was enacted, and by 2004 was still only 58 percent that of white families ($35,000 for blacks compared to $60,000 for whites). All manner of explanation for this are routinely offered by the media, public officials, scholars, and civil rights leaders: persistent employment discrimination, changing job markets, poor educational opportunities, bad housing, high incarceration rates for black males, to name a few. But the bulk of the gap is explained by one factor: the average black family has fewer workers than other American families on average, since a higher proportion of black families lack fathers. While 31 percent of black children were born to unmarried women in the early 1930s, that proportion rose to 71 percent by 2009. When comparing married couple families, on the other hand, there has been great progress. Blacks earned 88 percent of the national average for married couples in 2000 -- $50,690, compared to a national average of

$57,345. Since 1994, the poverty rate among black husband-wife families has been below 10 percent, compared with a 25 percent poverty rate overall for blacks.[28] Many other social pathologies typically believed to be caused by the white-black "income gap" -- high crime rates, residential segregation, high dropout rates, high rates of joblessness -- are in fact largely attributable to low marriage rates among black women. As sociologist Kay Hymowitz has written, "read through the megazillion words on class, income mobility, and poverty . . . and you still won't grasp two of the most basic truths on the subject: 1) entrenched, multigenerational poverty is largely black; and 2) it is intricately intertwined with the collapse of the nuclear family in the inner city."[29]

Still, as harmful as the racial accommodation has been in some respects, it hasn't been disruptive enough to prevent a large number of blacks, indeed a majority of them, from availing themselves of the great American opportunity machine. The black middle class has expanded. The decline in the poverty rate among blacks from 36 percent to 22 percent between 1980 and 2002 has been accompanied by an increase in the proportion of black Americans over the age of 25 with high school diplomas from 49 percent to 80 percent. For blacks in the 25-29 age group the figure is 86 percent, the same as for whites. In less than twenty years, the number of black college graduates has doubled. And while median household incomes for blacks hover around $35,000, 51 percent of black married couple families had incomes of $50,000 or more. College educated, black married-couple households make roughly the same as their white counterparts. In America today, education and marriage status has become a far better indicator of socioeconomic position than race.[30]

Up until Obama's election, Americans of all races seemed content to let the black elite continue their domination of racial matters, and to divorce their own political inclinations from their attitudes toward race. The drop in welfare rolls and crime, areas in which blacks are disproportionately represented, beginning in the 1990s mollified the most obvious white racial concerns. And until 2008, America's almost incessant economic growth, combined with restrictive public referenda in many of the largest states, had quelled white anxiety over affirmative action. For most white Americans the black grievance campaign had become a sideshow. The nation seemed to have moved on, concerned more about terrorism and the relationship of Arabs or Muslims to the rest of the nation, the question of Hispanic immigration, and perhaps even the question of gay marriage.

But electing a president steeped in the politics of racial identity has illuminated for many Americans the vast gulf that separates black and white perceptions of American life, differences that have bubbled just beneath the surface of public events for decades, differences with which a livable accommodation had been made, but that now, with a racialized presidency, can no longer be ignored.[31]

Obama's presidency has made it impossible for whites to continue their game of retreat. Citizens of all races and political affiliation, but particularly white voters, have been stunned at the depth, the breadth, and the rapidity of the kind of "change" Obama has attempted to institute, change that has been roughly representative of a vision widely shared among blacks: more centralized decision making authority in Washington, a growing public sector in relation to the private sector, a reliance on government to spur economic growth, increased dependency, wealth redistribution, and expansive social services. In his first year in office President Obama rammed two massive bills through congress in a concerted and mostly successful effort to reorganize American life around these objectives. One bill, the "economic stimulus" act (formally the American Recovery and Reinvestment Act of 2009), added $862 billion to the federal budget, increased federal spending by 34 percent in a single year, and tripled the budget deficit to 10.2 percent of Gross Domestic Product (GDP). Even in the depths of the Great Depression, Franklin Delano Roosevelt raised federal spending by more than 34 percent only once in a failed attempt to quash a national unemployment rate of 21.7 percent. But when FDR raised spending by 42 percent in 1934, federal spending amounted to only 10.5 percent of GDP. By contrast, with less than half of FDR's unemployment problem, federal spending as a percentage of the economy surged to 24.4 percent in 2010 (from 21.1 in 2008). Spending for all governmental levels, largely a function of Obama's "stimulus" aid to state governments, came in at 42.7 percent of GDP in 2010, up from 36.4 percent only two years earlier. This massive expansion of government in such a short period of time brought the United States so close to the European social welfare model that Peter Bernholz, a member of the Academic Advisory Board of the German Minister of Economics, stated that the stimulus constituted "an experiment on a scale which has never been seen before in the history of fighting crises."[32]

While sold to a skeptical public as an emergency infrastructure and consumer spending "jolt" to a slumping economy, a peek at the details of where actual stimulus spending went reveals a raw ideological power grab on the part of Obama and the Democrats in congress. The Obama administration's January 9th, 2009 report *The Job Impact of the American Recovery and Reinvestment Plan* projected that the stimulus would create 3 to 4 million jobs by the end of 2010 and that without the stimulus the unemployment rate would hit 8.5 percent in 2009. With the stimulus the administration predicted the unemployment rate would peak at just below 8 percent.[33]

Needless to say, these projections missed the mark. The stimulus bill was signed into law in March of 2009, but the national unemployment rate reached 10.1 percent in October of that year. For the next eighteen months the unemployment rate would stabilize in the 9 percent range, a post-World War II record. After seven quarters (twenty-one months) of the Obama recovery, unemployment fell only 1.3 percentage points from its peak, with a postwar record 45 percent of the unemployed out of work for twenty-seven weeks or longer (the "long term unemployed"). In 2010, the U.S. Census Bureau reported that the total number of Americans in poverty was the highest in the fifty-one years that Census had been recording the data.[34]

While critics maligned Obama for shifting his measure of success for the stimulus from jobs "created" to jobs "saved," there was in one sense a valid reason for doing so. The largest portion of stimulus money spent by the first quarter of 2011 -- $173 billion -- was issued to state and local governments, which used half the money to finance employee salaries, wages, and benefits. As a result, the jobs of roughly 900,000 state and local government employees, a key Democratic constituency, were "saved," at a time when the private sector lost 5.7 million jobs. Government employment rose to 17.1 percent of all jobs in 2010, up from 16.6 percent in 2008, thus enlarging a crucial Obama voting bloc.[35]

The question of whether fiscal spending and borrowing of such magnitude is necessary or prudent during economic downturns remains open. What is not in doubt is that the stimulus bill that was signed into law by Obama was not the one that was needed. Of the $250 billion allocated in the bill for "infrastructure," at least $164 billion remained unspent two years later. The federal government did issue one time payments to households in the form of temporary tax cuts, but direct federal purchases for goods and services -- the intended economic "injection" -- increased by only $20 billion, or 3 percent of the $862 billion authorized. Of the $20 billion spent directly by the feds only $4 billion was devoted to infrastructure projects. Federal infrastructure spending due to the 2009 act, in other words, amounted to only .04 percent of GDP by the fourth quarter of 2010. Stimulus money committed to future "infrastructure projects" targeted two experiments in their embryonic design and planning stages -- "high speed" rail and "green energy" -- not the "shovel ready" projects Obama insisted were the only ones eligible before the bill's passage.[36]

In fact, a study by Timothy Conley of the University of Western Ontario and Bill Dupor of Ohio State University in May of 2011 found that despite the influx of federal money, highway construction jobs actually plunged by nearly 70,000 between 2008 and 2010. Conley and Dupor explained that many states simply took the free federal money and shifted their own highway funds to meet other needs. In some states highway spending dropped, even with the added federal money.[37]

The other half of the stimulus grants to states went for Medicaid and other transfer programs. These grants were designed to achieve the Obama administration's goal of increasing government subsidized health care, an admirable purpose in some people's estimate, but one that is far different from the stated goal of stimulating aggregate economic activity. The 2009 stimulus conditioned a state's receipt of Medicaid funds on its willingness not to reduce benefits nor restrict eligibility rules. In some instances, this has meant undoing cost saving measures and eligibility restrictions that had been enacted prior to the stimulus program.[38]

Like the effort to save the jobs of mostly unionized public sector employees, the second primary focus of federal stimulus spending on transfer payments also fulfilled a fundamental political goal of Obama's: reorganizing American institutions around liberal notions of "fairness" rather than around the imperative of economic growth. By August of 2010 government anti-poverty programs served a record one in six Americans. More than 50 million Americans were on Medicaid, an increase of 17 percent since the recession began in December 2007. Vernon Smith, a consultant for the Kaiser Family Foundation, told *USA Today* that "virtually every Medicaid director in the country would say that their current enrollment is the highest on record." The federal price tag for Medicaid jumped 36 percent in the two years 2009-2010, to $273 billion.[39]

Medicaid wasn't the only government anti-poverty program to receive stimulus money. Unemployment benefits, food stamps, and welfare cash assistance grew by over 50 percent between late 2008 and early 2011, as the stimulus also boosted those benefits. Jobless benefits soared from $43 billion to $160 billion. The food stamp program rose 80 percent, to $70 billion, while welfare cash assistance grew by 24 percent, to $22 billion. Taken together with Medicaid, these programs cost more than Medicare, the medical insurance program for the aged financed through the social security system. According to Obama's own 2009 budget proposal the combined two year, inflation adjusted increase in welfare spending from 2009 through 2010 was projected to reach $263 billion, more than any increase in welfare spending in history.[40]

Like the stimulus itself, the efficacy of welfare programs can be fairly debated, but the political implications of this growth in the dependent population cannot. In 2008, Obama won 60 percent of voters with household incomes under $30,000 and 73 percent of those under $15,000, households that qualify for most forms of public assistance. A Gallup poll from July of 2010 showed that voters with under $20,000 income approved of Obama's performance by 55 percent, his best showing among income groups. In short, like other voters, recipients of government benefits favor parties or candidates who promise to protect and increase their benefits. Not surprisingly, then, in 2010 Obama's Justice Department issued new guidelines strengthening mandates on states to offer voter registration services at welfare offices. The new guidelines for implementing the 1993 "motor voter" law (or the "National Voter Registration Act"), require state public assistance agencies to offer voter registration services with the same "degree of attentiveness" as other benefit programs. Project Vote, a voter advocacy group, estimates nationwide compliance with the new welfare agency voter registration rules could add two to three million more voters to official rolls per year.[41]

In sum, then, the Obama economic stimulus bill failed to keep the economy from deteriorating further, dangerously increased the debt burden of the United States for generations, threatened federal government solvency and the ability to pay for vital programs like national defense and social security, all but ignored the nation's crumbling infrastructure, and guaranteed slower economic growth accompanied by inflation for years to come. It succeeded, however, in sparing the jobs of almost one million tax supported government workers, vastly expanding the population dependent on government anti-poverty programs and ensuring an increase of as many as four to five million likely Obama voters for the 2012 election.

Sponsors of famous federal government boondoggles like the 1960s expansion of Aid to Families with Dependent Children ("welfare"), which contributed to decades of pathology in America's inner cities, or the Urban Renewal program of the postwar decades, which promised to clear "blighted" slums, but mostly crammed the poor into inhospitable ghettos, could at least claim the virtue of good intentions. About the failed stimulus, Obama can make no such claim. At a time when America was facing an historic economic crisis, and a desperate nation was being promised "hope," "change," bipartisanship, and transparency, Barack Obama used more public resources than any other president before him, and committed more of the nation's future resources than all presidents before him combined, primarily for crass partisan political purposes.

And all of this growth in the number of dependent people, it is important to note, has taken place before the second of Obama's two main legislative accomplishments adds an estimated sixteen million more to the rolls, beginning in 2014. The health care reform bill (formally the Patient Protection and Affordable Care Act) signed into law by Obama on March 23, 2010, seeks to put under the control of Washington D.C. almost 20 percent of the U.S. economy through a series of reforms, program expansions, mandates, fees, and taxes. Consisting of well over two thousand pages of boilerplate legalese and detailed fine print, the main provisions of the law require insurance companies to charge the same for premiums regardless of preexisting conditions, the expansion of Medicaid eligibility to include all those with incomes up to 133 percent of the income threshold, the subsidization of privately bought health insurance for those making up to 400 percent of the poverty level, fines -- or "shared responsibility payments" -- for firms not offering health insurance and for individuals who refuse to purchase health insurance, along with a slew of other provisions, fees, taxes, and changes, some of which have been challenged in court. The full impact of the bill will not be known for years. But Obama's own Medicare chief actuary says that "Obamacare" would raise overall U.S. health costs, while the Congressional Budget Office has estimated that repealing Obamacare would save $1.4 trillion in new spending over the next decade. "In other words," according to one analysis, "without repeal, Obamacare's costs would skyrocket --

from $66 billion in 2014 to $233 billion in 2021, and upward from there -- even under the CBO's rather conservative estimates."[42]

It is unlikely voters were aware of Obama's obsessive determination to use the nation's spiraling health care costs as an opportunity to sharply shift power in the direction of government, away from individuals and the free market, particularly in the midst of an historic financial crisis and in defiance of the most rudimentary principles of fiscal responsibility and national well being. National polling on the health care overhaul shows that the reform was never popular with a majority of voters. By May of 2011, more than eighteen months after the law was passed, a Rasmussen poll showed Americans supported the repeal of Obamacare by a margin of 17 percentage points (55 to 38 percent). President Obama has claimed that Obamacare would lower health costs, reduce deficits, and improve the quality of health care. Likely voters, however, disagree. By a margin of three to one (54 to 18 percent), the Rasmussen poll found they think Obamacare would raise, rather than lower, health costs. By a margin of better than three to one (53 to 17 percent), they think Obamacare would raise, rather than lower, deficits. And by a margin of better than two to one (48 to 20 percent), they think Obamacare would reduce, rather than improve, the quality of care. Other polls showed similar results. In January of 2011, the Kaiser Foundation/Harvard University School of Public Health tracking poll -- an "outlier" in health care polling, usually showing better numbers in support of reform -- found that 50 percent of respondents held an "unfavorable" opinion of the law and 41 percent held a "favorable" opinion of it.[43]

In addition to setting up a huge regulatory bureaucracy for both the health and financial sectors, Obama has also set about creating a new "green energy" economy funded and regulated by government. In December 2009 Obama's Environmental Protection Agency claimed jurisdiction over the regulation of carbon emissions by declaring them an "endangerment" to human health, confirming Czech President (and economist) Vaclav Klaus's assertion that environmentalism has become the new socialism. Every human activity -- everything consumed, made, produced, or purchased -- emits carbon. It is not possible to effectively control and regulate carbon without controlling and regulating every aspect of human existence. While some members of congress are fighting EPA's determination, as it stands in 2011, no institution that emits more than 250 tons of carbon dioxide a year will fall outside of its control. By one estimate, this means effective control over one million building complexes, hospitals, plants, schools, businesses and similar enterprises. As Charles Krauthammer has written: "His [Obama's] goal is to rewrite the American social compact, to recast the relationship between government and citizen. He wants government to narrow the nation's income and anxiety gaps. Soak the rich for reasons of revenue and justice . . . And fund this vast new social safety net through the cash cow of a disguised carbon tax."[44]

Some critics have even suggested that Obama's lunge away from American power in foreign affairs has everything to do with his program of social leveling at home. Charles Hill, a research fellow at the Hoover Institute and advisor to former Secretary of State George P. Schultz, has said that Obama's goal is to "Close out the wars, disengage, and distance ourselves in order to carry out the real objective: the achievement of a European style welfare state. Just as Reagan downsized government by starving it through budget cuts, Obama will downsize the military-industrial complex by directing so much money into health care, enviro-care, etc., that we, like the Europeans, will have no funds available to maintain world power."[45]

The political and social environment in the United States is today at a fever pitch largely because of the public's sense that the current debates over health care, carbon capping, and "stimulus" spending are really debates about whether America will remain, or even deserves to remain (or even ever was) a "light unto the nations." And if these three items weren't enough to convince voters that Obama is intent on centralizing decision making authority over crucial aspects of American life, the administration has also instituted the unusual policy of appointing "czars," officials who have enormous power over private industry but who don't require senate confirmation. Obama's "compensation czar" Kenneth Feinberg, for example, retains the power to arbitrarily determine pay for executives at some of the most important financial institutions. While Feinberg has focused mainly on banks that have received direct government bailouts, there is nothing to stop him from expanding his purview over any bank that benefits from Federal Deposit Insurance or borrows money from the Federal Reserve (meaning virtually all of them). Indeed, taking a cue from Feinberg's actions, the Federal Reserve, which oversees 7,000 banks, announced in 2009 that it will "evaluate" the salaries of bank officers of even non-bailed out banks based on how carefully they "manage risk," something many observers doubt the government is qualified to assess. But not Obama. He told an audience in Quincy, Illinois in April, 2010 that he doesn't begrudge success that's "fairly earned," but "at a certain point, you've made enough money."[46]

Another czar, Mark Lloyd, the Associate General Counsel and Chief "Diversity" Officer at the Federal Communications Commission, has floated plans to require radio stations to provide "political balance" in their programs, regardless of what the listening audience wants to hear or what advertisers are willing to pay for. The Orwellian sound of this proposal (the "fairness doctrine") should not surprise anyone, given that Lloyd has praised the Marxist regime in Venezuela, which has sought to eliminate private media companies. The administration has also floated the idea of providing federal subsidies to struggling newspapers, creating a situation in which newspaper editors would be fully aware that their survival depends on publishing content that doesn't irk government officials.

Other appointments, though less powerful, symbolize the troubling ease with which Obama associates with ideological extremists. Before public pressure forced him to resign, Van Jones was appointed to the position of "green jobs czar." Jones was an admitted communist who signed a petition backing the idea that the Bush White House was involved in the terrorist attacks of September 11th, 2009. Anita Dunn, Obama's first White House Director of Communications, once told a group of students that her favorite philosopher was Chinese Communist Party Chairman Mao Tse-Tung, a sworn enemy of the United States and the engineer of mass murder on an incomprehensible scale. Kevin Jennings is Obama's "safe school czar," the Deputy Director of Education for Safe and Drug Free Schools. He is also a founder of the Gay, Lesbian, Straight Education Network, which supports the provision of positive portrayals of homosexuality for children in public schools starting in kindergarten. Critics who have charged Obama with neglecting to vet these appointees adequately are, in the words of political economist Thomas Sowell, missing the point. "Why should we assume that Barack Obama didn't know what such people were like, when he has been associating with precisely these kinds of people for decades before he reached the White House?"[47]

One of Obama's most important appointments thus far has been that of Sonia Sotomayor to the U.S. Supreme Court. Sotomayor is a female jurist of Hispanic descent who is convinced that a judge's competence can, in part, be gauged by their race, gender, and nationality, having said at one point that Latina judges arrive at "better conclusions" than white male judges. Sotomayor apparently feels race can determine competence in firemen as well. In one case she presided over, Sotomayor gave her approval to the City of New Haven, Connecticut's decision not to promote a white fireman who finished first on a civil service test because no blacks scored high enough to qualify for promotion.[48]

Obama has stated that he plans to "change the United States of America." But it is far from clear that most voters understood this to mean the adoption of policies and appointments to powerful positions of people who, again in Sowell's words, "reject American values, resent Americans in general and successful Americans in particular, as well as resenting America's influence in the world"[49]

What has been true in domestic affairs has been true in foreign policy and national security. Obama had promised during his campaign to chart a different national security course than his predecessor George W. Bush. Among the changes Obama said he would implement were the closing of the Guantanamo Bay military prison for captured terrorists, the closing of CIA secret prisons in foreign countries ("black sites"), and the prohibition of "enhanced interrogation techniques," including "waterboarding." Obama presented these changes as reasonable and humane, and portrayed himself as a centrist for advocating them. Two months into his term as president he told Steve Kroft of *60 Minutes* "Now, do these folks [captured terrorists] deserve

Miranda rights? Do they deserve to be treated like a shoplifter down the block? Of course not."[50]

Yet in June of 2009 the Obama Justice Department quietly ordered FBI agents to read Miranda rights to high value detainees captured and held at U.S. detention facilities in Afghanistan. Then, in November of 2009, Obama's Attorney General Eric Holder announced that Khalid Sheik Mohammed, 9/11's self-proclaimed mastermind, would be given a civilian trial in New York federal court, the first "unprivileged enemy belligerent" to be captured overseas and tried in American civilian court.[51] Mohammed, who was captured in Pakistan shortly after the start of America's 2003 assault on the Taliban in Afghanistan, was ready to plead guilty and face the death penalty in a military commission. But he was rescued in the nick of time by Holder, who provided Mohammed the broad rights of cross examination and discovery, as well as access to crucial information about intelligence sources and methods.

It is not clear whether the Obama administration will be rethinking the policy of civilian trials for terrorist combatants in the aftermath of the stunning legal defeat it suffered on November 18, 2010 in the federal trial of another terrorist suspect. On that day a New York jury found Ahmed Ghailani, an al Qaeda terrorist who conspired to blow up American embassies in Kenya and Tanzania in 1998, not guilty of more than 280 charges, including one count of murder for each of the 224 people killed in the simultaneous attacks. The jury found Ghailani guilty of only one charge: conspiracy to destroy U.S. government buildings, for which he is expected to serve twenty-five years in jail.[52]

The Ghailani decision was only the most bitter repudiation of the administration's "global justice" initiative, which starts out with the premise that virtually all terrorist suspects will end up in a U.S. civilian court, with all or most of the rights of American civilians. The core strategy of the initiative has been to shift the approach to Islamic terrorism from fighting a war to fighting crime, an effort that elevates the FBI and other law enforcement agencies and diminishes the role of intelligence and military officials.[53]

Since his first day in office Obama has set out to eliminate any official indication that America is at war with Islamic jihadism. In March 2009 the Defense Department's Office of Security Review e-mailed a message to Pentagon staff members stating that "this administration prefers to avoid using the term 'Long War' or 'Global War on Terror' [GWOT.] Please use 'Overseas Contingency Operation.'" The memo was not a bureaucratic snafu. It was part of a programmatic effort to de-couple Islam and terrorism, beginning with Obama's initial trip to Cairo, Egypt, during which he promised a "new beginning" in the relationship between the United States and the Muslim world.[54]

In the spring of 2010 the Obama administration removed the term "Islamic extremism" from the central document outlining U.S. national security policy, the National Security Strategy. This document previously outlined the "Bush Doctrine" of preventive war and stated "The struggle against militant Islamic radicalism is the great ideological conflict of the early years of the twenty-first century." Obama's discomfort with the image of America deeply engaged in fighting Islamic radicalism was revealed by his National Security Council staffer Pradeep Ramamurthy, who asked a reporter "Do you want to think about the U.S. as the nation that fights terrorism or the nation you want to do business with?"[55]

The lengths to which the Obama administration has gone to dissociate Islam from religious extremism is itself fairly extreme, including a shocking rewrite of the mission of the one federal agency presumably bereft of any involvement in ideological warfare, the National Aeronautics and Space Administration. Charles Bolden, the Chief Administrator for NASA, said in an interview in July of 2010 that his "foremost" mission as the head of America's space exploration agency is to improve relations with the Muslim world. Bolden explained in his interview with *Al Jazeera*, the Arabic language news agency, that strengthening ties with Muslim countries was among the top tasks President Obama assigned him and that better interaction with the Muslim world would ultimately advance space travel. "When I became the NASA administrator -- or before I became the NASA administrator -- he [Obama] charged me with three things. One was he wanted me to help re-inspire children to want to get into science and math, he wanted me to expand our international relationships, and third, and perhaps foremost, he wanted me to find a way to reach out to the Muslim world and engage much more with dominantly Muslim nations to help them feel good about their historic contribution to science," Bolden said in the interview.[56]

When Obama announced in February 2010 that he would slash NASA's $100 billion plan to return astronauts to the moon, he didn't mention where the resources would be redirected. The President said only that the moon program (Constellation) is behind schedule, over budget and less important than other space investments. Few would have predicted that at least some of the money would go toward improving Muslim self-esteem. And NASA has not been the only federal agency to have its mission radically changed in pursuit of Obama's goal of diverting attention from the Muslim world's connection to terrorism. Obama's secretary of the Department of Homeland Security, Janet Napolitano became the first head of that agency since its creation in 2003 to drop the term "terror" and "vulnerability" altogether from remarks to the U.S. House of Representative's Homeland Security Committee. She did this despite the fact that the department's top priorities spelled out in the legislation that created it are "preventing a terrorist attack in the United States; reducing the vulnerability for such an attack; and helping with the recovery if the U.S. is attacked." Anyone who doubts the seriousness of these changes in language need look only to the moral confusion exhibited by Napolitano in an interview with the German news magazine *Der Spiegel,* where she defended her decision to drop the terms. "In my speech, although I did not use the word 'terrorism,' I referred to 'man-caused' disasters. That is perhaps only a nuance, but it demonstrates that we want to move away from the politics of fear toward a policy of being prepared for all risks that can occur." Thus, in the eyes of the Obama administration, does the purposeful murder of 3,000 civilians on 9/11 become the equivalent security threat of the Exxon Valdez oil spill. Even with the reemphasis of Homeland Security on "man-caused disasters" the agency failed to protect residents and businesses from the worst oil spill in the Gulf of Mexico's history, caused by the April 20th, 2010 explosion at the British Petroleum owned Deepwater Horizon rig off the Louisiana coast. By May of 2010, one month after the explosion, when the amount of oil spilled exceeded that of the Exxon Valdez twenty years earlier, Obama himself was forced to admit the government relied too long on BP to figure out the extent of the damage.[57]

The reason for these language and policy reversals from that of prior administrations may be complex, but at its core is an ideology driven by a belief that the U.S. is responsible -- maybe partially and maybe indirectly -- for the anti-American animus of the Islamic world. In an interview with *60 Minutes* Obama stated that the prior administration's policy of military action, intelligence gathering, harsh interrogation methods, and the Guantanamo Bay prison, have led to Muslim anger. "It hasn't made us safer. What it has been is a great advertisement for anti-American sentiment, which means that there is constant effective recruitment of Arab fighters and Muslim fighters against U.S. interests all around the world." Given that the Arab Muslim world doesn't contain any democracies where civil rights and liberties are given high regard, and that the terrorists themselves openly mock and exploit the U.S. system of justice, often asking to be put to death immediately, it is hard to see how Guantanamo Bay or harsh interrogation techniques could be the source of Muslim rage. More importantly, given that the attacks on the World Trade Center in 1993 and again on 9/11, along with the unending series of kidnappings, hijackings, airliner bombings, and beheadings going back to the Iranian hostage crisis in 1979 all occurred before the existence of Guantanamo Bay or the use of enhanced interrogation techniques against terrorist suspects, it is perplexing that Obama should ask about America's anti-terror policies "Are we going to just keep on going until, you know, the entire Muslim world and Arab world despises us?"[58]

Obama was so petulant in his opposition to aggressive interrogation methods that he not only signed an executive order aiming to close Guantanamo Bay two days after taking office, but he also pursued a preliminary investigation into whether some CIA operatives broke the law in coercively interrogating suspected terrorists in the years following 9/11. The Justice Department then reopened criminal investigations into the conduct of CIA interrogators -- inquiries that had been closed years before by career prosecutors who concluded that there were no crimes to prosecute. One particular target of the investigations was Jose Rodriguez, who ran the CIA's Counterterrorism Center from 2002-2005, the period when top al Qaeda leaders Khalid Sheikh Mohammad and Abu Faraj al-Libbi were taken into custody and subjected to waterboarding and other forms of interrogation at secret overseas prisons. In a speech at the National Archives Obama eviscerated the men and women of the CIA, accusing them of "torture" and declaring that their work "did not advance our war and counterterrorism efforts -- they undermined them."[59]

Ultimately, practical difficulties prevented Obama from closing Guantanamo Bay. After several setbacks extraditing Guantanamo prisoners to European allies and various Arab countries, on March 7, 2011 Obama signed an order authorizing Guantanamo Bay to stay open and the resumption of military tribunals for terrorist suspects being held there. It was an historically fortuitous and ironic reversal of a major campaign promise: on May 1, 2011 Obama announced to the world that 9/11 mastermind and al Qaeda head Osama bin Laden had been killed in Pakistan by U.S. special forces. Two days later CIA Director Leon Panetta told Brian Williams of NBC News that "enhanced interrogation techniques" were used to extract information that led to the mission's success. Panetta, an Obama appointee who told a congressional confirmation committee in 2009 that "waterboarding is torture and it's wrong," acknowledged that one of the successful techniques used to get bin Laden included waterboarding. Several news sources and intelligence officials confirmed Panetta's statements. The *New York Times* reported the day after bin Laden was killed that a courier for the terrorist king pin who led American intelligence to the terrorist leader was identified by Guantanamo Bay detainees, including Khalid Sheikh Mohammad. Another report, by investigative reporter Michael Isikoff of *Newsweek,* said that "The trail that led to the doorstep of Osama bin Laden in Pakistan began years earlier with aggressive interrogations of al Qaeda detainees at the U.S. detention facility at Guantanamo Bay and CIA 'black site' prisons overseas, according to U.S. officials."[60] Still, at the time of his signing of the order to continue operations at Guantanamo, Obama did his best not to publicly renounce his prior position on the issue. "The president does remain committed to closing the prison at Guantanamo Bay," said a senior administration official who briefed reporters.[61]

The actions of this administration in relation to Islamic terrorism belie Obama's belief in American complicity in many of the world's major problems. Obama is loath to talk about Islamic terrorism, to say that we are in a "war on terrorism," to choose sides in the Arab/Israeli conflict or, for another example, to call the November 2009 massacre by an Islamist of fourteen U.S. servicemen at the Fort Hood, Texas military base an act of terror because he believes that Muslim grievances against the United States have some validity. Obama is first and foremost a multiculturalist, an apostle of the idea that no culture is morally superior to another, and which therefore posits external or "structural" causes for the failures of a particular nation or people. In this view no civilization, or individual for that matter, is inherently flawed because there is no universal standard by which to make such a judgment. Islamic terrorism can't be simply a matter of a major religion succumbing to an ideology that is inhumane, undemocratic, and intolerant. Islamism must be a response to outside forces acting upon it. The United States, as the most powerful country in the world, obviously shares a measure of responsibility for creating those external conditions, for presiding over a world order that can produce that kind of hate.

It is for this reason that in addressing the radical regime in Iran from Egypt in June 2009, Obama spoke openly about America's role in a 1953 Iranian coup. Iran's descent into a virtual slave colony based on medieval moral codes, in Obama's narrative, is in some ways an understandable response to CIA intervention in the 1950s. On his first world tour, Obama repeatedly disowned American policies of prior eras -- those that in his dismissive words were implemented when he "was three months old" -- and apologized on three continents for America's "arrogance," its use of atomic bombs, its tendency to "dictate its own terms," it's "unwillingness to listen," and its refusal to embrace the Muslim world. As Dorothy Rabinowitz noted in the *Wall Street Journal* shortly after Obama's tour, "No sitting American president had ever delivered indictments of this kind while abroad, or for that matter at home, or been so ostentatiously modest about the character and accomplishment of the nation he led."[62]

In November of 2009, when world leaders gathered in Berlin to celebrate the twentieth anniversary of the fall of the Berlin Wall -- a symbol of America's and the west's historic victory over Soviet communism -- Obama declined to go, choosing instead to address the gathering by video conference. In his two and a half minute address Obama managed to avoid mentioning the names of any past western leaders central to its Cold War victory (Harry Truman, John Kennedy, Henry "Scoop" Jackson, Ronald Reagan, British Prime Minister Margaret Thatcher, and Pope John Paul II come to mind). But he did find time to conflate his own more recent election with the events of twenty years ago. "Few would have foreseen on that day that a united Germany would be led by a woman from Brandenburg or that their American ally would be led by a man of African descent," Obama said, straining credulity by implying a direct connection between the struggle against communism and his own rise to power. Obama's attempt to mask his spectacular self-absorption by including German chancellor Angela Merkel in his self-congratulation is particularly odious. Merkel no doubt remembers Obama had been to the Brandenburg Gate in the summer of 2008 for a campaign speech at which delirious European leftists treated him like a rock star. At the time, the Chancellor found the reasoning for the speech "odd" and had "little sympathy for the Brandenburg Gate being used for electioneering."[63]

On a November 2009 trip to the Far East, it became clear why Obama omitted any mention of President Harry Truman at Brandenburg Gate. In Japan, Obama refused to defend Truman's decision in World War II to drop atomic bombs on two Japanese cities, which brought an end to history's bloodiest war and freed Japan from fascism. When asked by a reporter "what is your understanding of the historical meaning of the A-bombing in Hiroshima and Nagasaki? Do you think that it was the right decision?," a stumbling Obama dissembled for several minutes before deciding to ignore the question completely. "No, there were three sets of questions, right? You asked about North Korea?," Obama responded.[64]

Americans have become increasingly cognizant of Obama's political ideology over the first two and a half years of his term. Not only have Obama's approval ratings retreated from their sky high levels of his first few months in office, but they have done so along distinctively racial lines. Presidential job approval polls by the Gallup organization have tracked two consistent trends in President Obama's ratings: overall decline and a widening racial gap between black and white Americans. As early as the week of November 16-22 of 2009 Obama's approval among whites had dropped to 39 percent from 61 percent in the week of January 26th-February 1st, 2009, while it actually increased slightly to 91 percent among blacks from 90 percent. By October of 2010, Obama's approval had dropped to a new low for whites (36 percent), but remained at 91 percent for blacks, a 55 percentage point difference that has persisted, minus the first three months, throughout the first twenty-six months of his presidency.[65]

Democratic presidential candidate Barack Obama speaks to a crowd estimated at over 250,000 in Tiergarten Park in Berlin, Germany on Thursday, July 24, 2008. Photo by David Katz/Obama for America.

Under Obama, young blacks and whites have diverged in the way they view their own futures, with black students feeling empowered and white students growing more cynical. A nationwide poll released April 29th of 2010 by Hamilton College in New York found that 70 percent of black students aged 15 to 18 thought their standard of living would be better than their parents, compared with just 36 percent of white students. At the time the survey was taken, the black teen unemployment rate had spiked to roughly 50 percent, but the level of optimism among black students was clearly tied to their enthusiasm for President Obama.[66] Undoubtedly, and conversely, the pessimism of some white students at least in part reflected a sense of alienation among whites at all age levels. Asked about Obama's performance, more than two-thirds of black students rated it "good" or "very good," compared with 23 percent of white students.[67]

These findings were virtually duplicated in May of 2010 in an exhaustive study conducted by the Pew Research Center designed to gauge the impact of the recession that began in 2008. The study found that among the population at large, blacks were nearly twice as likely as whites to call U.S. economic conditions "excellent" or "good" (25 percent to 13 percent). They were also significantly less likely than whites to say that the American economy was still in recession (45 percent to 57 percent). Looking ahead, blacks were significantly more likely than whites to say that their personal financial situation would improve over the coming year (81 percent to 57 percent), and to agree with the statement that "although there may be bad times every now and then, America will always continue to be prosperous and make economic progress" (81 percent to 59 percent). This "optimism gap," as one analyst labeled it, occurred despite the fact that the same month of the Pew survey the U.S. Bureau of Labor Statistics reported that the seasonally adjusted unemployment rate among blacks stood at 15.5 percent -- 17.1 percent among black men aged 20 and over -- while the rate among whites was 8.8 percent. Additionally, a much larger proportion of blacks than whites told Pew that the economic slump had forced them to accept reduced work hours, to take unpaid leave, or to switch from full-time to part-time employment. While the study took note of the partisan divide in outlook, with Democrats far more optimistic than Republicans, it is unlikely that partisanship alone could account for such a disparity among blacks and whites: despite the fact that the black unemployment rate climbed from 9 percent in December 2007, when the "Great Recession" began, to 15.5 percent in May 2010, roughly one-third (32 percent) of blacks told Pew that their household finances were in better shape than they had been prior to the recession, compared with only 18 percent of whites. A similar report conducted by Pew in the fall of 2009 acknowledged the racial dimension of the "optimism gap." "Barack Obama's election as the nation's first black president appears to be the spur for this sharp rise in optimism among African Americans," Pew concluded.[68]

The "Obama Effect" was also visible in the Gallup organization's Standard of Living Index, which measures how Americans rate their standard of living and whether they believe it is getting better or worse.

Black scores in the index "continue to exceed those for whites," Gallup reported in July, 2010, "a pattern that has persisted since early 2009 . . . blacks began to be more optimistic around the same time that Barack Obama was inaugurated as president." By March of 2011 Obama's approval rating in an *All State/National Journal/Heartland Monitor* poll among whites remained at just 39 percent, while it hovered in the high 80s among blacks. That same month, the U.S. Bureau of Labor Statistics reported that unemployment remained at 15.5 percent among blacks and 8.3 percent among whites.[69]

Presidential approval ratings wax and wane, and Obama is not the first contemporary president to experience a noticeable racial approval gap. Black animosity toward Presidents Reagan and Bush (Sr.), who were generally liked by whites, was a salient feature of the 1980s. But it is different when the president is the first black president and the low approvals are coming from whites. This has stirred deep resentment among blacks. In October of 2009, Gallup reported that post-election racial optimism had waned among all Americans, and particularly among black people. Responses to the question "Do you think that relations between blacks and whites will always be a problem for the United States or that a solution will eventually be worked out?" reflected patterns similar to those in 1963, with 40 percent of Americans expecting race always to be a problem. In November of 2008, the day after Obama's election, 67 percent of Americans said that a solution to America's race problems would be worked out. That dipped to 56 percent by October of 2009, pre-election levels. And though black Americans had become more optimistic immediately after Obama's election, they were, only twelve months later, significantly more pessimistic about race relations in America. Immediately after the election 50 percent of blacks told Gallup they expected a solution to America's race problems to be worked out. By October of the following year, that number was 42 percent. In 1964 it was 70 percent. By April of 2011, black commentators and white liberals, including radio show hosts Tavis Smiley, Ed Schultz, Whoopi Goldberg, and Bob Schieffer were declaring that opposition to Obama derived mostly from white racism, and that 2012 would be the "most racist" election in American history. Not quite the "bipartisan racial success story" that some pundits had trumpeted immediately after Obama's election.[70]

Whites will no longer be able to retreat from race as they had done previously now that the demands of racial politics are embodied in the presidency. Policies that are formulated upon the belief that what tens of millions of Americans have achieved was actually usurped through corruption, violence, dishonesty, and white skin privilege, rather than through hard work and sacrifice, has met fierce resistance. A diplomacy of apologetics with a world that America has protected from predators and for which they have generously opened their purses, borders, and markets could stoke ferocious bitterness.

The most ominous possibility is the "re-racialization" of the white vote. Unlike blacks who are staunchly Democrat in their voting habits, whites are far more evenly distributed between parties in their national voting preference and make up the vast majority of "swing" or "independent" voters who lend the country it's tone of moderation, centrism, and support for checks and balances. Indeed, Obama carried almost half of them. But a racialized presidency steeped in identity politics could send many more whites fleeing the Democratic Party.

"White flight" from the Democrats may already be evident. In the 2009 off year elections, Virginia voters went Republican in the Governor's race by an overwhelming margin after having voted for Obama, a Democrat, in 2008 for the first time in 44 years. The Republican gubernatorial candidate Bob McDonnell beat his Democratic opponent Creigh Deeds by 17 points, amounting to a 23 point swing in one year. New Jersey went from a 15 point Democratic victory in 2008 to a 4 percent Republican victory in that state's gubernatorial race, a 19 point swing. In Virginia in 2009, the black vote was off 20 percentage points from 2008. Independents in Virginia, most of who are white, went Republican by a staggering 33 points and by an equally shocking 30 points in New Jersey.

This trend continued in the mid-term elections of 2010, in which Republicans won whites by a 23-percentage point margin (60 to 37 percent) and had their best showing ever, winning large majorities in the House of Representatives, the state houses, and the Governorships. Democrats performed worse with whites in the 2010 midterms than in any other congressional election since the Second World War. And the

2010 midterms were all about Obama. Exit polls showed that more voters said Obama was a factor in their vote than said Bush was a factor four years prior. Of course economic conditions and high unemployment were and always will be the dominant factor in a year like 2010. "But," political reporter David Paul Kuhn wrote after the election, "the recession cannot be separated from Obama's agenda . . . Obama's priorities were not the majority's priorities, especially not whites. Most whites have favored a smaller government over a bigger government for decades. Obama's election, his first year agenda, heralded the return of active-state liberalism."[71]

A re-racialized white vote could have a devastating impact on America's civic life. It would likely result in greater alienation among blacks who would see the white turn against Obama as cruel, racial rejection. The Democratic party could become even more dependent on blacks and other minorities. Democratic candidates who are white might continue to have trouble exciting minority voters. Arrayed against the party of minorities will be the predominantly white Republican Party, completely bereft of blacks and heedless of their concerns. It is conceivable that the country could atrophy into race based political partisanship the likes of which has not been seen in the modern era.

Obama could, of course, embark on a significant change of direction. In December of 2009, before the end of his first year in office, Obama made an acceptance speech for the Nobel Peace Prize that sounded in some spots strangely similar to those of his predecessor George W. Bush. For the first time Obama acknowledged that "Those who seek peace cannot stand idly by as nations arm themselves for nuclear war"; that "Evil does exist in the world"; that "A nonviolent movement could not have halted Hitler's armies"; that "Negotiations cannot convince al-Qaeda's leaders to lay down their arms"; and that "The United States of America has helped underwrite global security for more than six decades with the blood of our citizens and the strength of our arms." This came on the heels of another speech at West Point two weeks earlier where Obama announced his decision, months long in the making, to send more troops and expand the U.S. war effort in Afghanistan, a decision that stoked talk of a major shift in Obama's foreign policy approach. Some conservatives even praised Obama's first Oval Office speech in August of 2010 for sounding positively "neoconservative." In that speech, ostensibly given to announce the end of U.S. combat operations in Iraq, the President praised Iraq's elections, said that the new Iraqi government "will have a strong partner in the United States," and that this is a "message to the world that the United States of America intends to sustain and strengthen our leadership in this young century."[72]

This may reflect a genuine shift in policy, brought on by a year in which Obama gained a greater appreciation for the exceptional role of the United States in the world and a greater awareness of the U.S. military as a force for good. Stranger occurrences have been known to happen after having direct dealings with adversaries like China, Russia, and Iran, and after spending some time commanding a military force as dominant and humane as the U.S. armed forces are. Perhaps Obama has become less enamored of the idea that the Nobel committee attributed to him, that "those who are to lead the world must do so on the basis of values and attitudes that are shared by the majority of the world's population." Since making this speech, Obama enjoyed his single most important achievement -- the killing of Osama bin Laden -- the result of quick and immediate unilateral action taken without the help of international public opinion or United Nations approval.[73]

It is also possible that Obama was motivated to toughen his stance in Oslo because of the embarrassment of having been awarded the Peace Prize in the first place, being only "at the beginning, and not the end, of my labors on the world stage." Perhaps the contrast between Obama's Nobel image as a global leader willing to yield American power to popular international approval and the political and military realities that have left Obama waging three wars were just too obvious not to address.

Perhaps. But Obama's discomfort, uncertainty, and obfuscation when espousing a muscular foreign policy and defending America's role in world affairs is still his predominant set of presidential traits. They emerged in full force when he abdicated global leadership to France and Britain during anti-Gadhafi uprisings in Libya. Obama still reverted to form even in his Oslo Nobel speech, managing to imply that torture and human rights violations were regular practice for the United States before he became president. When he unveiled his Afghanistan war expansion at West Point, one critic noted, Obama managed to talk for thirty-three minutes without "either truly setting expectations for the difficult year ahead in Afghanistan or explaining why his policy would work." During the same speech Obama also announced a withdrawal date for American troops of July 2011, something critics have said greatly undermined the military mission and revealed Obama's true lack of commitment to the effort.[74]

It is also true that during the Oval Office speech on the withdrawal of troops from Iraq, Obama implied that a trillion dollars had been squandered to no good purpose in both Iraq and Afghanistan over the last decade, and that only by withdrawing militarily from these parts of the world can a president "jump-start industries," reform education, and make "tough decisions" about issues at home. He also said "It is time to turn the page," a phrase that, when combined with his failure to announce another troop surge, and his decision in April, 2011 to relieve General David Petraeus of his central role in the Afghan theater, could be taken by America's allies and enemies alike as a signal of Obama's intention to meet America's military obligations through other channels.[75]

Domestically, by the summer of 2010, Obama appeared to have dropped all measure of subtlety in expressing his own belief in a voting public organized along sharp lines of racial solidarity. Gone were code words like "empathy," which he used when nominating Sonia Sotomayor for the Supreme Court to indicate his approval of building into legal decisions an assumption of victimhood for non-white plaintiffs. In an unprecedented appeal to the Democrat voter base months prior to the 2010 congressional elections, Obama taped a video address for the Democratic National Committee urging "young people, African Americans, Latinos, and women who powered our victory in 2008 to stand together once again" in order to "to keep building a fairer, stronger, and more just America." Obama was careful to identify these groups as having a lot of "first time voters" in 2008, but the video made clear the type of voters Obama (and the DNC) did not want "standing together" for a fairer and more just America: namely, older white males. Other presidents of the modern era have used their office to campaign for off year partisan victories. But never has a president done so in such a racially divisive and exclusionary way. By the summer of 2010, even the black former head of the U.S. Civil Rights Commission and Obama supporter Mary Frances Berry acknowledged that the Obama administration has taken to polarizing America for the purpose of crass partisan advantage. "The charge of racism is proving to be an effective strategy for Democrats. . . . Having one's opponent rebut charges of racism is far better than discussing joblessness," Berry said.[76]

Be all of this as it may, if Obama does not embark on a significant change of course, or if the American political system does not work to sufficiently modify his policies, Obama's America is destined to be one that looks quite a bit different from the one most voters grew up in, or envisioned for their children: a United States in which a wealthy governing class rules a dependent, discouraged majority with little hope for a better life through enterprise, excellence, or hard work. It will be an America that is looked at askance by most whites and, because of the politicized nature of black racial identity and the peculiar vulnerability blacks have experienced in America, received favorably by most blacks. And race will again become the primary social cleavage in American life.

Chapter 2

OBAMA AND THE POLITICS OF RACE

Far from proving that America has moved beyond race, the election of Barack Obama in 2008 proved America remains obsessed with race. Bromides about the post-racial future and the use of Obama's election to declare an end to identity politics ignore the enormous emotional investment black supporters have in Obama not only as a black man, but as a black man with a "black" or "Afrocentric" world view.

Though estimates on total numbers differ, data extrapolated from the National Election Pool exit poll showed that Obama pulled 3.6 million additional black voters into the voting booth over 2004, 27 percent more black voters than had ever voted before in a presidential election. This increase occurred over a period in which the eligible black voting population grew by only 20,000.[1] There has always been a sense of racial solidarity among black voters when a black candidate faces a white one. But there is only a sense of racial purpose when the black candidate possesses the "right" ideology, best reflected in a strict adherence to left wing politics and symbolized at the national level by membership in the Democratic party. It is unlikely that blacks would turn out in such large numbers for a viable black Republican presidential candidate (such as Colin Powell). Indeed, Ebonya Washington, a Yale University economist, has found that a black Democrat on the ballot increases black voter turnout in congressional races by 3 percentage points. Black Republican candidates, on the other hand, are associated with no increase in black voter turnout. As a consequence, only fifty-nine black Republicans hold an office requiring a partisan election in the United States out of a total of over 9,000 black elected officials.[2]

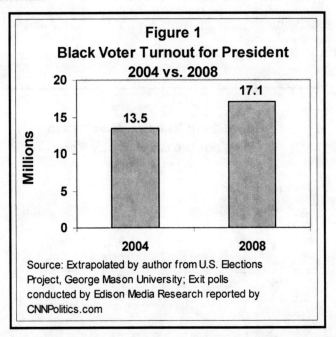

Figure 1
Black Voter Turnout for President
2004 vs. 2008

Source: Extrapolated by author from U.S. Elections Project, George Mason University; Exit polls conducted by Edison Media Research reported by CNNPolitics.com

The most convincing evidence that black voters overwhelmingly support only black candidates of the "correct" ideology surfaced in 2006. During that year's election season the *Washington Post* speculated that the candidacies of then Lieutenant Governor of Maryland and eventual GOP national chairman Michael Steele (for U.S. Senate), Ken Blackwell (for Ohio Governor), and former football great Lynn Swann (for Pennsylvania Governor) might make 2006 the "year of the black Republican." All three black GOPers lost their elections, with Steele winning just 25 percent of the black vote, Blackwell winning 20 percent, and Swann winning 13 percent. In the 2010 mid-term elections, the Republican party nominated fourteen black congressional candidates. The only two black Republican candidates to win, Tim Scott from South Carolina, and Allen West from Florida, represented majority white districts.[3]

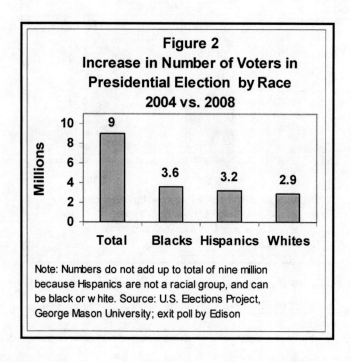

The fact that there is little or no turnout response to black Republicans on an electoral ticket suggests that ideology, at least as much as black skin, is the predominant factor dictating black voting patterns, a strong indication that blacks voted for Obama with very different purposes than did whites. While other Americans are roughly split between political parties, the black vote, reflected in the tidal wave of support for Obama and unbroken loyalty to the Democratic party, is driven by deeply held convictions that non-black Americans view with great ambivalence.

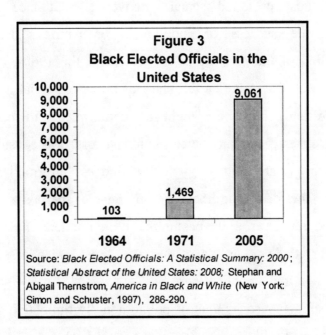

For many blacks, being black means absorbing an ideology based on opposition to "white" standards and the received understanding of

American ideals. Of course, this is a highly illiberal approach to race and culture. It ties the inherited racial characteristics of an individual to a rigid set of ideas, denying him the essential human rights to freedom of thought, expression, and association commonly understood to be the foundation of liberal societies everywhere. It is also antithetical to America's core idea: that nothing should be assumed about a person's character from an "accident of birth." For that reason, such thinking about race was rejected in the twentieth century, discarded after a hefty battle with "scientific racism," in favor of one of the twentieth century's most profound social discoveries: that race does not determine the success of individuals or nations.[4] Before the radicalization of the civil rights movement of the 1960s, the liberal consensus was that America fell short of providing equal opportunity for all and that it must be brought into conformity with that national ideal. "Blackness," like any other ethnic category, was considered fine as a basis for private identity, but "color blindness" in America's public square was the ideal. The liberal compromise of the postwar decades represented a break from the past in that it did not deny the importance of racial or ethnic pride, but at the same time demanded strict non-discrimination in the public sphere.

Liberalism achieved its goal of public non-discrimination and black enfranchisement with the passage of the Civil Rights Act of 1964 and the Voting Rights Act of 1965. But with the demise of laws that held blacks down for so long, the stigma of black inequality became, in some respects, even more troubling than it had been when its cause was more obvious. Black leaders changed the focus of their mission from achieving equality under the law to equality of outcomes. In practice, this meant a demand for proportional representation in all fields of employment, academic and cultural institutions, and government, a tectonic shift in America's social contract between the government and its citizens.

Over the course of the previous century, American citizens came to expect that if they followed the rule of law, fulfilled their responsibilities as parents and spouses, worked hard, and saved money they, or at least their children, would realize a certain amount of economic mobility. The government's role was to provide legal protections and basic essential services, such as police, public schools, infrastructure, and a social safety net.

But the unique history of racial discrimination convinced many blacks that gaining mobility through the same means by which the white majority moved into the middle class was not viable. More would be required from government and from the law. Civil rights leader Bayard Rustin gave voice to the new approach to black mobility when he wrote in 1965 that he is now "concerned not merely with removing the barriers to full opportunity *but with achieving the fact of equality.*"[5] Often, this new approach meant rebellion against most things associated with the white middle class -- most importantly, it turns out, the implicit agreement to play by the established rules of citizenship.

"Earlier assumptions about the close connection between work and well-being, the need for a common culture, and the importance of public order were redefined as racist and obsolete," Fred Siegel has written about the changing social order in the 1960s. "Urban America," Siegel explains, "began to renounce its role as the proud center of commerce and innovation, increasingly presenting itself as the hopeless victim of racism and economic dislocation, in need of ever more government handouts."[6]

The nation's leadership class met this challenge to the traditional expectations of citizenship with the meekness born of centuries of pride and arrogance. With barely audible opposition they committed American institutions to a regime of racial preferences, race based government programs and patronage, and an expansive deference to black grievance, thus ensuring civil rights protest as a way of life and wedding blacks to an identity based on the permanence of white racism. In what turned out to be his most fortuitous speech, president Lyndon Baines Johnson secured black votes for the Democrats for decades by acknowledging the transformation of racial politics. Speaking to Howard University's graduating class of 1965 Johnson said that we seek "equality not just as a right or a theory, but equality as a fact and equality as a result."[7]

Political protest proved a remarkably cohesive foundation for black identity. Along with shared ways of speaking, of style, of worship, and cuisine came a political ideology reflected in voting patterns far more uniform than that of any other ethnic voting bloc. The "adversarial" or "oppositional" culture of black America embraced most of the leftist critique of the United States, insisting, in the words of Dr. Alvin Poussaint, that "for blacks to mindlessly strive to be like the white middle class in a white racist, capitalist, exploitative society is without question detrimental to the cause of black people."[8] Black dissidents -- those who touted assimilation and the value of middle class habits -- were derided as "oreos", lawn jockeys, Uncle Toms, and even "non-black." To this day, few high status blacks who fail the strict ideological litmus test for blackness escape with their reputations intact. Political scientist Manning Marable has said of conservative black Supreme Court Justice Clarence Thomas that "ethnically, Thomas has ceased to be an African American." When Alabama Congressman Artur Davis became the only black congressman to vote against the health care reform bill that passed the House of Representatives in November of 2009, he drew a rebuke from the Reverend Jesse Jackson, who told a Congressional Black Caucus reception "We even have blacks voting against the health care bill. You can't vote against health care and call yourself a black man."[9]

The thoroughness with which black identity is immersed in radical politics is not often a matter openly or easily discussed. So absent has it been from public debate that few are even aware of it. But Barack Obama is. The son of a Kenyan father and a white mother from Kansas, Obama spent most of his formative years growing up in Indonesia and

Hawaii, experiences far removed from that of most blacks in the continental United States. Yet Obama made a conscious decision to *be* "black," a crusade spelled out in his identity obsessed first memoir, which he aptly subtitled *A Story of Race and Inheritance*. The book reveals, in Shelby Steele's phrase, "a man nothing less than driven by a determination to be black." At one point in *Dreams from My Father*, upon leaving Indonesia to live with his white grandparents in Hawaii, Obama writes "I was engaged in a fitful interior struggle. I was trying to raise myself to be a black man in America." Obama claims to have rejected an identity based on his white mother, his white grandparents, or even his "brown" Indonesian stepfather, Lolo Soetoro. "It was into my father's image, the black man, son of Africa, that I'd packed all the attributes I sought in myself, the attributes of Martin and Malcolm, Du Bois and Mandela."[10]

It is of some importance that Obama chose his father as the font for his personal identity, a man who left his home when he was two years old and who didn't reappear (briefly) until Obama was ten. The writer Dinesh D'Souza has observed that besides being a polygamist and a raging alcoholic (he ultimately died in a drunken automobile accident in 1982), Obama's father was a fierce "anti-colonialist." A Luo tribesman who grew up in Kenya and studied at Harvard, Obama Sr. believed African governments must confiscate private property in order to throw off the shackles of European rule. In one article, appearing in 1965 in the *East Africa Journal,* the senior Obama suggested the state confiscation of land and taxes on wealth with no upper limit. "Theoretically," he insisted, "there is nothing that can stop the government from taxing 100 percent of income so long as the people get benefits from the government commensurate with their income which is taxed."[11]

There is no way to know how deeply Obama imbibed of his father's beliefs. Despite being a rigorous student of his father's life, Obama has never publicly discussed this or any other article, and the media has shown no interest in asking him about it. But Obama describes his own memoir as "a record of a personal, interior journey -- a boy's search for his father, and through that search a workable meaning for his life as a black American."[12]

Having spent seventeen years of his own life overseas, mostly in Hawaii and Indonesia, but with several visits to Pakistan and Africa (in all likelihood to connect with his father's side of the family), it is a safe bet that Obama's path to an identification with other black Americans through radical politics was at least partially lubricated by knowledge of his father's own anti-western, socialistic beliefs. When Obama discovered that the "workable meaning for his life as a black American" he sought required adopting a political ideology based on the suspicion of free enterprise and the espousal of collectivist economic policies, knowledge of his father's anti-western, socialistic beliefs smoothed the way. As James Hund has written in *Black Entrepreneurship,* "Capitalism and its institutions are basically individualistic. But the ethos of the black community is collectivistic."[13] Or, as John McWhorter explains in his book *Losing the Race,* "One factor has helped recruit blacks to collectivist ideas faster and more thoroughly than any other racial group in America: the idea that blacks are held back by pervasive, inescapable white racism. Told repeatedly that they have little chance to succeed in a racist world, blacks were and are ripe for collectivist ideas that promise them a better future." This orientation has manifested itself culturally in a number of ways, one of them being the 1966 advent of the holiday of Kwanzaa by Afrocentric activist Maulana Karenga and modeled on African harvest celebrations. Kwanzaa, born in America and practiced almost exclusively in the U.S., is based upon seven guiding principles with Swahili names, most stressing collectivist ideas, from unity (umoja) and collective responsibility (ujima) to cooperative economics (ujamaa).[14]

Obama acted early in his adulthood to affirm his blackness through protest politics, and through association with black nationalists, community leaders who take race as the fundamental dividing line in the United States and the basis for making political judgments. Obama moved to Chicago, the "capital" of black America, from New York City in the 1980s with the stated intention of "organizing black folks." In a 2004 interview with *Chicago Sun-Times* reporter Cathleen Falsani, Obama explained "The way I came to Chicago in 1985 was that I was interested in community organizing and I was inspired by the Civil

Rights movement." Upon his return to Chicago in 1991 after finishing law school at Harvard, Obama practiced civil rights law and taught a seminar on racism and law at the University of Chicago. He also joined a stridently Afrocentrist church where he was so influenced by the "black liberation theology" of its preachers that he would tell the *Chicago Reader* in 1995 "We have some wonderful preachers in town -- preachers who continue to inspire me -- preachers who are magnificent at articulating a vision of the world as it should be." When Obama joined this Afrocentric church -- the Trinity United Church of Christ in Chicago, home to the now infamous radical preacher Reverend Jeremiah A. Wright -- he pledged allegiance to something called the "Black Values System," a code of non-Biblical ethics written by blacks, for blacks. The Black Values System encourages blacks to group together and separate from the larger American society by pooling their money, patronizing black only businesses and backing black leaders. The code also warns blacks to disavow the "Pursuit of 'Middleclassness,'" to avoid the white "entrapment of black 'middleclassness,'" and suggests that settling for that kind of "competitive" success will rob blacks of their African identity and keep them captive to white culture.[15]

Despite Obama's insistence throughout the 2008 presidential campaign that he was only a passive congregant at Trinity, evidence indicates he was rather enthusiastic about the church, which calls itself "Unashamedly Black" and which gave a "Lifetime Achievement" award to Nation of Islam leader Louis Farrakhan. In his 2004 *Chicago Sun-Times* interview Obama explained that in the late 1980s a group of churches on the South Side of Chicago was "where I think what had been more of an intellectual view of religion deepened." Specifically, Obama continued, "one of the churches that I became involved in was Trinity United Church of Christ. And the pastor there, Jeremiah Wright, became a good friend. So I joined that church and committed myself to Christ in that church." When Falsani asked "Did you actually go up for an altar call?," Obama answered "Yes. Absolutely . . . And it was a powerful moment."[16]

Obama has revealed a strong sympathy for radical black nationalists in his memoir and in real life. In *Dreams* Obama writes that his disagreement with the black nationalist Rafiq, widely believed to be based on the real life Chicago figure Salim al Nurridin, stemmed mostly from "questions of effectiveness, and not sentiment." Rafiq was, Obama explains in the book, a Black Muslim in Chicago who blamed the city's white power structure for the struggles of public housing residents. If black leaders like Rafiq failed to achieve some of their most important goals, Obama also "learned to respect these men for the struggles they went through, recognizing them as my own." Obama imagined his own father espousing his brand of black nationalism, "inspiring, rebuking, granting or withholding approval. You do not work hard enough, Barry. You must help in your people's struggle. Wake up, black man!"[17]

It is not surprising, therefore, that when the *Chicago-Sun Times* asked Obama "Do you have people in your life you look to for guidance?" Obama named three political radicals, two of them strong black nationalists and one a sympathetic white priest. "Well, my pastor [Jeremiah Wright] is certainly someone who I have an enormous amount of respect for . . . Reverend Meeks is a close friend and colleague of mine in the state Senate. Father Michael Pfleger is a dear friend, and somebody I interact with closely." All three of these individuals hold extreme views. Reverend Jeremiah Wright famously created problems for Obama during the 2008 primary campaign when his sermons were found to contain comments like "The government gives them [blacks] the drugs, builds bigger prisons, passes a three strike law and then wants us to sing 'God Bless America.' No, no, no, God damn America, that's in the Bible for killing innocent people." The Reverend James T. Meeks of the Salem Baptist Church in Chicago has also been the subject of controversy, uniting with white Christian evangelicals in an anti-homosexual crusade and making a comment that blamed "Hollywood Jews for bringing us *Brokeback Mountain*." Father Michael Pfleger, a radical white priest, worked with Wright at Trinity United, giving sermons in which he affects a black vocal style to denounce "white entitlement and supremacy wherever it raises its head." In one instance Pfleger accused former presidential candidate Hillary Rodham Clinton of being deluded by white skin privilege. "I'm white and this is mine!" Pfleger described Clinton's alleged attitude toward the Democratic nomination for the presidency. "I just gotta get up and step into the plate' and then out of nowhere came, 'Hey, I'm Barack Obama,' and she said, 'Oh, damn. Where did you come from? I'm white! I'm entitled! There's a black man stealing my show!'"[18]

Obama's empathy for and connection with the views of radical black preacher's may be even stronger than some of his critics have suggested. Despite reluctantly denouncing Wright during the 2008 campaign, and despite a long period of churchlessness while living in the White House, Obama spent his 2011 Easter in the pews of the Shiloh Baptist Church of Pastor Wallace Charles Smith in Washington, D.C. During that sermon Smith was reported to have said he hears the sounds of racism in the gurgling of his four week old grandchild. "I am here . . . they tried to write me off as three-fifths of a person in the Constitution, but I am here right now." Videos on Youtube.com show Smith previously equating Rush Limbaugh and Fox News to the Klu Klux Klan and southern segregationists. "Now Jim Crow wears blue pin stripes . . . because now he can wear the protective cover of talk radio, or can get a regular news program on Fox." Smith continued: "Even such venerable saints as Rush Limbaugh know the lines they are not to cross. But any of their constituency can hear clear the same vile filth spewing forth in their statements that was once the purview of Robert Shelton and members of the Ku Klux Klan and the White Citizen's Council."[19]

Obama's friendship with the white Father Pfleger indicates that even when Obama's friends were white, left wing extremists, he came to the relationship through racial politics. This is true of Obama's most famous radical white associate, William Ayers, a member of the terrorist Weather Underground in the 1960s. Ayers once described himself as "a radical, leftist, small 'c' communist" and summed up the philosophy of the Weather Underground in 1970 as: "Kill all the rich people. Break up their cars and apartments. Bring the revolution home; kill your parents, that's where it's really at." In 1969, a profile of Ayers in *Chicago Magazine* included a picture of him stomping on the American flag and predicting "there will be another mass political movement because I believe that the kind of injustice that is built into our world will not go quietly into the night." In his book *Fugitive Days*, Ayers writes that he participated in the bombings of New York City Police headquarters in 1970, the Capitol building in 1971, and the Pentagon in 1972. Ayers has never expressed regret for his actions, telling the *New York Times* in a profile appearing on none other than September 11th, 2001, the day of the worst terrorist attack on U.S. soil in history, "I don't regret setting bombs. I feel we didn't do enough." Today, not surprisingly, Ayers is "distinguished professor of education" at the University of Illinois at Chicago living in the upscale Hyde Park district, where he held a gathering to launch Obama's first run for the Illinois State Senate in 1995.[20]

William Ayers at Georgetown University Law School, November 17th, 2008. Photo by Joshua Landau.

In the mid-1990s Obama was hired to be the chairman of Ayers' brainchild, the politically charged "educational" program named the Chicago Annenberg Challenge (CAC). The CAC blamed poor academic achievement among racial minorities on capitalism and the "dominant white" educational establishment. Documents at the Richard J. Daly archives at the University of Illinois at Chicago make clear that Mr. Ayers and Mr. Obama were partners in the CAC, which called for infusing students and their parents with a radical political commitment, and which downplayed achievement tests in favor of activism. Little money from the CAC program went to schools, but rather to the "external partners" with which schools were required to affiliate. Proposals from groups focusing on math and science achievement were denied funding. Instead, CAC disbursed money through various far left community organizing outfits, such as the Association of Community Organizations for Reform Now. ACORN, with which Obama had a deep and lasting relationship through the 2008 presidential campaign, is the largest radical political organization in America, the successor to the 1960s National Welfare Rights Organization (NWRO). NWRO's main claim to fame was its role in winning the expansion of welfare benefits to single mothers, which ultimately resulted in a vicious political backlash, giving Republicans control of congress and leading to the "end of welfare as we know it" in 1996. As its successor, ACORN played a similarly large and destructive role in another national disaster, the financial crisis of 2008-2009. ACORN was a major force pushing for loosened standards for mortgage lending to the poor, including the Community Reinvestment Act of 1977. This act forced lending institutions to make a significant percentage of loans available to minorities in run down neighborhoods, even if property values were in decline and qualified applicants scarce, a primary reason for the wave of housing foreclosures that led to real estate plunge of 2008. ACORN, which also advocates for raising the minimum wage, affirmative action, bilingual education, and the rights of illegal immigrants was convicted in several states of voter registration fraud on a massive scale and, in 2009, was defunded by a Democratic controlled congress. Several weeks later ACORN ceased operations, but has reemerged since under several guises.[21]

In the 1990s Obama conducted "leadership training" seminars for ACORN, and ACORN members served as volunteers in Mr. Obama's early state senate campaigns. Obama provided legal services for ACORN in the mid-1990s, succeeding in winning a law suit liberalizing voter registration requirements and, later, paid ACORN $800,000 for "get out the vote" efforts during his 2008 presidential campaign.[22] Given this history, it was a natural transition for Obama to head CAC and to partner with ACORN, the South Shore African Village Collaborative, the Dual Language Exchange, and other radical groups focused more on indoctrinating young minority students into Afrocentricity, bilingualism, victimization, and grievance activism than in teaching them to read, write, and do arithmetic.

During his campaign for president, Obama did his best to downplay his collectivist leanings and its roots in the racial politics of Chicago. In his 2004 speech to the Democratic National Convention, the speech that brought him to national attention, Obama laid out the centrist theme of color blind unity: "There is not a Black America and a White America and Latino America and Asian America -- there's the United States of America." During the Democratic primary campaign, after the revelations about Reverend Wright, Obama gave a speech on race in which he claimed "we may have different stories, but we hold common hopes . . . we may not look the same and we may not have come from the same place, but we all want to move in the same direction." It was effective. In many white minds Obama was, to use one critic's phrase, "absolutely indifferent to the whole business of race, identity, and protest politics."[23]

But the view of Obama as a color blind centrist is at variance with his record, however thin that record has been. Obama demonstrated his race centered views as early as his senior year at Harvard Law School in 1990, when he complained to a campus newspaper that law firms were not seriously recruiting minorities from average law schools. "The issue you confront is: What kind of minorities are the firms looking for?," Obama explained. Firms are "reluctant to take a chance on students who do not have the top credentials. It has been said that it may be time to ask if minorities are getting the same right to be 'mediocre' as white males."[24] As an Illinois state legislator from 1996 to 2004 Obama supported race based quotas and government contract minority set asides, fought to keep legislative districts majority black, opposed stop and search practices by Chicago police because he thought they were racist, and accused other black officials of not voting together as a unified block. Indeed, Obama wrote publicly in support of the U.S. Supreme Court's 2003 acceptance of racial preferences at the University of Michigan (*Grutter v Bollinger*). As Obama expert and Ethics and Public Policy Center fellow Stanley Kurtz has written, "the question of race plays so large a role in Obama's own thought and action that it is all but impossible to discuss his political trajectory without acknowledging the extent to which it engrosses him."[25] The Reverend Jeremiah Wright, Father Michael Pfleger, Reverend James

Meeks, Nation of Islam leader Louis Farrakhan, and Pastor Wallace Charles Smith, in other words, are not just radical black activists who happened to be at the same place at the same time as Barack Obama. They are people whose political and theological outlook Obama sought to associate himself with closely.[26]

Chapter 3

THE RACIALIZED BLACK VOTE

Most of the available evidence thus far runs in direct opposition to the claims of the Obama campaign and its supporters that its electoral victory symbolized a new post-racial America. To borrow from university admissions nomenclature, the evidence that Obama's race was given "substantial weight" by voters is overwhelming.

Table 1
Presidential Voter Breakdown by Race
2004 vs. 2008

	2004	2004 Percent of Total	2008	2008 Percent of Total	2004-2008 Difference
Total Voter Turnout For President	122,294,978		131,302,732		9,007,754
Total Non-White Voter Turnout	28,127,845	23	35,451,738	27	7,323,893
Kerry/Obama Non-White Vote	20,533,327	73	28,113,228	79	7,579,901
Total Black Voter Turnout	13,452,448	11	17,069,355	13	3,616,908
Kerry/Obama Black Vote	11,838,154	88	16,215,887	95	4,377,734
Total Hispanic Voter Turnout	8,560,648	7	11,817,246	9	3,256,597
Kerry/Obama Hispanic Vote	5,136,389	60	7,917,555	67	2,781,166
Total Vote Bush	62,040,000	51			
Total Vote Kerry	59,028,109	48			
Bush/Kerry Difference	3,011,891	2			
Total Vote Obama			66,882,230	53	
Total Vote McCain			58,343,671	47	
Obama/McCain Difference			8,538,559	7	
Total White Voter Turnout	94,167,133	77	97,164,022	74	2,996,889
Obama/Kerry White Vote	38,608,525	41	42,752,170	44	4,143,645
Total Bush White Vote	55,558,609	59			
Total Bush Non-White Vote	7,594,518	27			

Source: U.S. Elections Project, George Mason University; Exit polls conducted by Edison Media Research reported by CNNPolitics.com

As early as March of 2008, in the heat of the Democratic primary, Hillary Clinton campaign operative and former vice presidential candidate Geraldine Ferraro told the *Daily Breeze* of Torrance, California, that "If Obama was a white man, he would not be in this position. And if he was a woman (of any color) he would not be in this position. He happens to be very lucky to be who he is. And the country is caught up in the concept." While Ferraro's comments garnered serious opprobrium, there's little doubt that a top heavy black vote pumped up for a promising black contender powered Obama's crushing wins over Clinton in the south from where she originates -- and helped him stay competitive in Ohio and Indiana, states he lost. Exit polls in North Carolina showed that nearly a quarter of black voters admitted that race was a big factor in motivating them to vote for Obama. Political scientist Michael Dawson has noted that blacks rallied to Obama at the polls by margins the Rev. Jesse Jackson didn't achieve until his second run for president in 1988. As author Earl Ofari Hutchinson wrote in a May 22, 2008 post to the New America Media web site, "Obama could not have come as far and as fast as he has without the votes and cheers of African American voters."[1]

Black solidarity around Obama was most evident when Obama attempted to distance himself from black militancy. Prodded by Hillary Clinton and Tim Russert in a February 26th primary debate, Obama was pressured to say he would "reject and denounce" Minister Louis Farrakhan of the Nation of Islam (NOI). Farrakhan responded with understanding, telling readers of the NOI's newspaper *The Final Call,* "Those who have been supporting Senator Barack Obama should not allow what was said during the presidential debate to lessen their support for his campaign. This is simply mischief making intended to hurt Mr. Obama politically." For most black voters, criticism of Obama coming from other blacks was simply unacceptable. Radio personality and activist Tavis Smiley quit his long running spot on radio's popular "Tom Joyner Morning Show" because of the relentless attacks on him for criticizing Obama. As Joyner explained it, Smiley couldn't endure "the hate he's taking over this whole Barack Obama thing. People are really upset with him. He's always busting Barack Obama's chops. They call. They e-mail. They joke. They threaten." In an essay on *TheRoot.com* in February of 2008, political scientist Michael Dawson wrote, "It is supremely ironic that Barack Obama, the candidate who seeks to bury race as an issue in this campaign season, owes his overwhelming support among blacks to the continued power of black nationalism."[2]

Also crucial to Obama's primary victory over Hillary Clinton was the speed and uniformity with which black elected officials withdrew their endorsement of Clinton and gave it to Obama. The torrent began with Obama's January 26th victory in South Carolina, when the candidate first displayed his tremendous popularity among blacks by winning 78 percent of their vote. In the weeks following, black elected officials ranging from Virginia state senator Louise Lucas to New Jersey state senator Dana Redd to Georgia Congressman David Scott switched from Clinton to Obama. The list grew to include former Cleveland Mayor Michael White and New Jersey super delegate Christine "Roz" Samuels. Then came the defection of Georgia Congressman John Lewis, a long time "friend" of the Clintons and bloodied civil rights icon. Lewis backed Clinton in Georgia's February 5th, 2008 Democratic primary, but announced he was switching to Barack Obama before the month was out. The eleven term congressman said in a statement that he had "a deep and abiding love" for the Clintons, but that "the candidacy of Senator Obama represents the beginning of a new movement in American political history that began in the hearts and minds of the people of this nation. And I want to be on the side of the people, on the side of the spirit of history."[3]

In terms of the general election, racial solidarity may have been even more decisive than in the primary. Chris Cillizza of the *Washington Post* writing immediately after the election insisted it was a "myth" that "a wave of black voters and young people was the key to Obama's victory."[4] He was wrong, at least with regard to the black vote. Final vote tallies released in December of 2008 show that the total number of voters grew by 8.9 million between 2004 and 2008, with the black component of that increase accounting for 3.6 million. By increasing the Democrat share of the black vote from 88 percent to 95 percent, Obama attracted 4.4 million more black votes than John Kerry did in 2004. The National Election Pool exit poll confirms that the increase of

4.4 million new black votes for Obama had in large measure to do with their enthusiasm for voting for a black candidate. The poll found, despite the obvious social stigma of admitting racial prejudice to a pollster, that race was a factor for twenty-five million voters (roughly 19 percent of the total). Obama won 13.5 million of those voters, roughly 54 percent. Of the almost three million who admitted that race was the "most important" factor, Obama won 58 percent to McCain's 42 percent. After perusing the exit polls, U.S. Civil Rights Commission Vice Chair Abigail Thernstrom concluded that "the number of white voters who saw Obama's race as a plus outnumbered those who harbored racial doubts."[5]

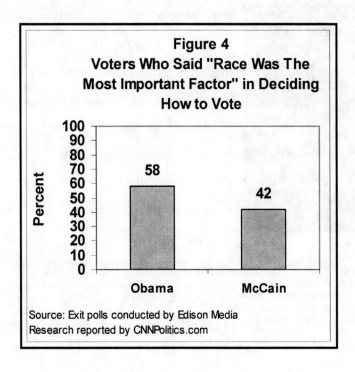

The racial aspect of the campaign was also apparent in enthusiasm levels among Obama's supporters. Polling by the Pew Center for the People and the Press reported a 15 percentage point "enthusiasm advantage" for Obama among his supporters in the waning days of the election. Popular t-shirts linking Barack Obama's presidential run to Rev. Martin Luther King Jr.'s dream of racial equality read "We had a dream. Now it's a reality." Another t-shirt popular with blacks read "Barack is my homeboy." Polling after the election by CNN/Opinion Research Corporation found that 80 percent of blacks believed Obama's election was a "dream come true." Overall, 19 percent of black voters were first time voters compared with 8 percent of white voters, a clear indication of Obama's drawing power among blacks, even those who never voted previously.[6]

Enthusiasm for Obama flowed freely at black media outlets. Obama conducted frequent interviews with black radio personalities during the primary season, appearing on programs like "The Tom Joyner Morning Show" and the "Michael Baisden Show." In July of 2008 *Ebony* magazine listed Obama first among the "25 Coolest Brothers of All Time," alongside

Senator Barack Obama and Senator Hillary Clinton pose for photographers prior to the CNN/Los Angeles Times Democratic presidential debate in Hollywood, California January 31, 2008. © Copyright 2008 by Jonathan Alcorn.

Muhammad Ali and Malcolm X. Caribbean stations played songs about him, including "Barack Obama" by Cocoa Tea and "Barack the Magnificent" by the calypso star Mighty Sparrow. Attendees of the black oriented television network BET's (Black Entertainment Television) annual awards program in 2008, including the musicians Alicia Keys and P. Diddy, turned the event into an impromptu rally for the candidate. "Obama, y'all!" Keys shouted upon receiving an award before a television audience of nearly six million people. BET showed Obama's acceptance speech at the Democratic convention live, but not John McCain's. BET's smaller rival, TV One, said it would not cover the Republican convention at all. As Jim Rutenberg of the *New York Times* reported, "there is generally little pretense of balance in major black media outlets. More often than not, the Obama campaign is discussed as the home team."[7]

Historical gravitas. Artist Ben Heine juxtaposed images of Barack Obama with that of Martin Luther King, Jr. during the 2008 campaign.

Even the most powerful black media voice, Oprah Winfrey, dropped her career long pretense of non-partisanship to support Obama. Oprah, the actress and talk show host, built the biggest franchise in show business during the 1990s by providing electronic therapy sessions for millions of daytime viewers and espousing decency, hard work, and self-improvement. At her peak she reached eight million viewers daily while transcending the issues of race and partisan politics. Then, on December 8th, 2007 Winfrey took the stage at a massive Iowa rally to introduce and personally endorse Senator Barack Obama. "When you strip us all down, we are American at our core. We are America. We are America with our hopes and our dreams," Winfrey told the cheering crowd. Explaining Winfrey's enormously important and potentially alienating shift, Johns Hopkins University political science professor Lester K. Spence told the *New York Times*, "She literally talked about stepping out of her pew to endorse him. When she steps into the world of politics, a world she has always been above, and anoints someone, it is coming from someone that millions of people, especially women, trust and revere."[8]

Just as it was in the primaries, solidarity among black officials and celebrities ostensibly in the opposing camp of John McCain played a significant role in electing Obama. Black conservatives who considered throwing their support to Obama included radio talk show host Armstrong Williams, former Oklahoma Congressman J.C. Watts, writer and actor Joseph C. Phillips, senior fellow at the Manhattan Institute John McWhorter, and former Massachusetts Senator Edward Brooke.[9]

But the most significant instance of black Republican defection was that of Colin Powell. A former army general who served in cabinet level posts for both Bush administrations, Powell seemed a natural match for Senator McCain. Both men had exceptional military careers, both men fought in Vietnam, supported the Gulf War in 1991 and the Iraq war in 2003, and were considered centrist stalwarts in the Republican party. In fact, Powell campaigned for McCain in the Republican primary of 2000 against George W. Bush, who he later served as Secretary of State. Before Obama won the Democratic nomination in the summer of 2008, Powell donated the maximum amount to McCain's campaign.[10] But on October 19th, 2008 Powell appeared on NBC's *Meet the Press* to announce his support for Barack Obama. "I think he is a transformational figure," Powell said. "He is a new generation coming . . . onto the world stage and on the American stage. And for that reason, I'll be voting for Senator Barack Obama." Powell denied that race was the dominant factor in his decision, and he offered the obligatory regrets over McCain's choice of Alaska Governor Sarah Palin for Vice President and, without offering specifics, the "negative tone" of McCain's campaign. But he went on to say "I think we need a transformational figure. I think we need a president who is a generational change and that's why I'm supporting Barack Obama, not out of any lack of respect or admiration for Senator John McCain." The endorsement by Powell was a stunning rejection of McCain, a twenty-six year veteran of congress and a former Vietnam prisoner of war who had campaigned as the "foreign policy" candidate, a weakness for the inexperienced Obama.[11]

Obama rally at Victory Landing Park, Newport News, October 4th, 2008. Photo by James Currie.

It is worth mentioning that Hispanic voters, too, turned out heavily for Obama, many of them no doubt motivated by the prospect of voting for a non-white candidate. The increase in the Hispanic vote between 2004 and 2008 is difficult to estimate. Some analysts have suggested that the 2004 exit polls were inaccurate in measuring Hispanic turnout, and therefore misleading for purposes of comparison. The 2004 National Exit Poll indicated 44 percent of Hispanics voted for George W. Bush and that Hispanics counted for 8 percent of the electorate. Researchers from the Pew Hispanic Center have disputed the 2004 National Exit Poll estimate of the number of Hispanic voters, noting that it was higher than the U.S. Census Bureau's November voting supplement to the Current Population Survey (CPS).[12] But the Edison Media Research exit poll published by CNN found that in 2008 Hispanics voted for Obama over McCain by 67 percent to 31 percent, and that they made up 9 percent of the electorate. Assuming that the 2004 numbers for Hispanics are somewhere in the middle of the range of estimates (say 40 percent voted for Bush in 2004 and they constituted 7 percent of the electorate that year), the Hispanic electorate grew by approximately 3.3 million voters, and Obama appears to have received 85 percent of these new votes: Obama polled 2.8 million more Hispanic votes than John Kerry, despite the fact that McCain had been an outspoken liberal on immigration and had served over twenty years in the senate on behalf of a border state with a large Hispanic population, a background similar in some ways to that of George W. Bush. In total, Obama's electoral margin of 8.5 million over John McCain included 7.6 million more votes from non-whites (including Asians and "others") than John Kerry received in 2004. In short, if Obama received the same number of non-white votes as John Kerry did in 2004, almost 90 percent of his 8.5 million vote margin over John McCain would have been erased, reducing his popular vote victory from 7 percentage points to around 2 percentage points. This 2 percent advantage would have taken place in an election year that saw the generic ballot for congress favoring Democrats by 9 percentage points.[13]

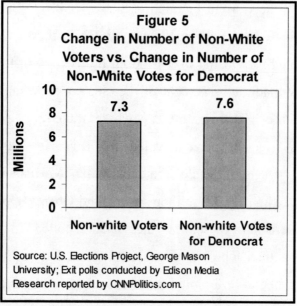

Figure 5
Change in Number of Non-White Voters vs. Change in Number of Non-White Votes for Democrat

Source: U.S. Elections Project, George Mason University; Exit polls conducted by Edison Media Research reported by CNNPolitics.com.

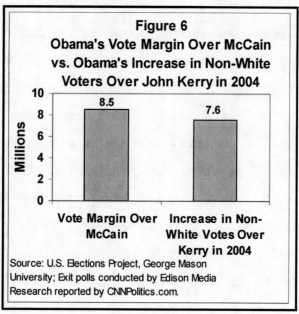

Figure 6
Obama's Vote Margin Over McCain vs. Obama's Increase in Non-White Voters Over John Kerry in 2004

Source: U.S. Elections Project, George Mason University; Exit polls conducted by Edison Media Research reported by CNNPolitics.com.

The importance of Obama's non-white vote was revealed most starkly after the presidential election, once in 2008's U.S. senate race in Georgia, and again in the 2010 midterm elections. Most of the Democratic base in Georgia is black, and largely because of black turnout for Obama, Republican incumbent Saxby Chambliss failed by about 9,000 votes to gain a 50 percent majority against his Democratic opponent Jim Martin on election day. But a month later, on December 1st, Chambliss won the runoff against Martin 58 to 42 percent. Needless to say, black turnout for the runoff was down sharply throughout the state, and was worth 8 percentage points for Chambliss.[14]

Obama playfully indulged his most enthusiastic supporters in this photo taken in front of the Superman Statue in downtown Metropolis IL, known as the home of the DC Comics super hero.

The Racialized Black Vote

Two years of the Obama presidency has only exacerbated the racial polarization of American politics. Democrats performed worse with whites in the 2010 midterms than in any other congressional election since the Second World War. Still, despite 60 percent of the white vote going to Republicans (and a drop in the Hispanic vote of 9 percentage points for the Democrats), the black vote for Democrats remained steady between the midterms of 2006 and 2010 at 89 percent. As David Paul Kuhn wrote after the 2010 midterms, "Presidents are the ghost candidates of midterms," and the vast racial difference in the perception of the Obama presidency was clearly on display.[15]

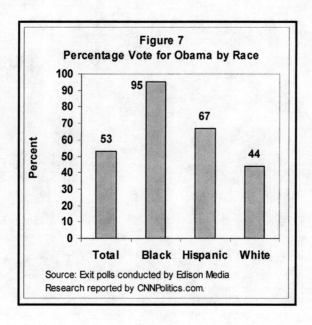

Chapter 4

THE DERACIALIZED WHITE VOTE

A child of a white American born mother and a black father from Kenya, Obama convinced many voters that his presence in the presidential race as a serious major party candidate would usher in a new era of racial acceptance. "I was raised with the help of a white grandfather . . . and a white grandmother . . . I am married to a black American who carries within her the blood of slaves and slave owners . . . I have brothers, sisters, nieces, nephews, uncles and cousins, of every race and every hue, scattered across three continents," Obama told a worldwide audience in a speech delivered after the discovery of Reverend Jeremiah Wright's bigoted sermons.[1] This was apparently enough to convince *New York Times* columnist Paul Krugman, who wrote in June, 2008 that Obama's candidacy was both a symbol of and a step toward greater racial tolerance. "Mr. Obama's nomination wouldn't have been possible twenty years ago . . . Racial polarization used to be a dominating force in our politics, but we're now a different, and better, country."[2]

It may be true that Obama's election symbolized a more accepting and tolerant America. But any notion that his presidency would ultimately result in less racial polarization now seems quaint. Approval ratings have diverged sharply along racial lines. There was broad white flight from the Democratic party in the 2010 midterm elections. White support sunk below the symbolic 40 percent threshold, while black support for Democrats stood fast at 89 percent. Krugman himself has taken to equating Obama's main opposition group, the Tea Party, to the Ku Klux Klan.[3] But a more important point to make about the meaning of Obama's candidacy is that he was the beneficiary, not the midwife, of an era of racial acceptance that began more than just twenty years ago and which Obama had nothing to do with. There have, after all, been black Supreme Court justices, congressmen, senators, governors, CEOs of fortune 500 corporations, secretaries of state, leading journalists, editors, intellectuals, cultural figures, armed forces generals and joint chiefs of staff chairs, and college and university presidents. Detailed data are not available, but when the historic Civil Rights Act was passed in 1964, there were not more than 103 black elected officials at any level of government -- national, state, or local -- while the black population was twenty million. When the first edition of *Black Elected Officials: A National Roster* was published in 1971 -- after the Civil Rights Act's "sister" law, the Voting Rights Act of 1965 was passed as well -- there were 1,469 black elected officials in the United States. The 2000 edition of that report states that there were

9,040 black elected officials, a more than 600 percent increase. In 2002 there were 9,061 black elected officials nationwide. Growth over this period has been especially impressive at the state level. In five southern states -- Georgia, Louisiana, Mississippi, South Carolina, and Texas -- the total increase between 1970 and 2000 was more than tenfold. In 2000, Mississippi and Alabama together had more black elected officials (1,628) than the entire nation had in 1970. There were nine black members of the U.S. House of Representatives in 1970. In 2008 there were forty-one members, not including the two black members from the non-voting District of Columbia and the Virgin Islands. In 1970 the only black mayors of big cities were Carl Stokes in Cleveland and Richard Hatcher in Gary, Indiana. By 1996 there were 405 black mayors. Black mayors have even governed in cities where blacks are a minority of the voting population, including New York City (David Dinkins), Los Angeles (Tom Bradley), and Philadelphia (Wilson Goode). Blacks have been mayors of Augusta and Lewiston in Maine, a state with a 0.5 percent black population.[4]

While the major civil rights legislation and the groundbreaking campaigns of Jesse Jackson (for president), Douglas Wilder (for Virginia Governor), and Harold Washington (for Chicago Mayor) have increased black voter participation, there is another reason blacks have won so many prominent and not so prominent electoral offices: whites started to vote in increasingly large numbers for them. This has provided many black candidates for office with a distinct advantage.

According to Stephan and Abigail Thernstrom, "In a contest that pits a black against a white, blacks will generally vote for one of their own, but whites won't necessarily support the candidate who is white. That is, while black candidates can usually count on almost every black vote, whites who run in a racially diverse setting have no such advantage."[5]

Crowds like this one at the Key Arena in Seattle, Washington greeted Obama throughout the 2008 campaign. Photo by Ethan Jewett.

No one, of course, has reaped the benefits of this "de-racialization" of the white vote and the persistently racialized black vote more than Obama. Obama did better with white voters than Al Gore in 2000 and John Kerry in 2004, both of whom managed to get only 41 percent of the white vote. In 2008, by contrast, Obama won 44 percent of the white vote and received 4.1 million more white votes than Kerry. The much feared white racists failed to show up at the polls (at least in significant numbers). Voter participation rates among non-Hispanic whites in historically red states Alaska (with Sarah Palin on the ticket!), Arizona, Colorado, Arkansas, Idaho, Kansas, Kentucky, Missouri, Montana, South Dakota, North Dakota, New Mexico, Ohio, Oklahoma, South Carolina, Texas, Utah, West Virginia, and Wyoming declined. And although white, non-Hispanic voters increased nationally by roughly one million, the turnout percentage among eligible voters declined from 65.8 percent in 2004 to 64.8 percent in 2008. White, non-Hispanic voter turnout was up in only fourteen states, seven of them blue or battleground states (Connecticut, District of Columbia, Nevada, New Hampshire, Rhode Island, Virginia, Washington). McCain polled only 51.8 million white, non-Hispanic voters, compared with Bush's 54.6 million in 2004.[6]

Still, that more whites voted for Barack Obama than for John Kerry does not mean that the vote for president was not polarized along racial and class lines. Obama gained a larger number and percentage of white votes than any Democrat since Jimmy Carter. But a three percentage point increase in the white vote since the prior presidential election at a time when the incumbent president of the opposite party carried a 30 percent approval rating, the nation was in a financial meltdown, and gas prices had risen by 250 percent the summer before the election, suggests that a majority of whites were inured to Obama's charm.

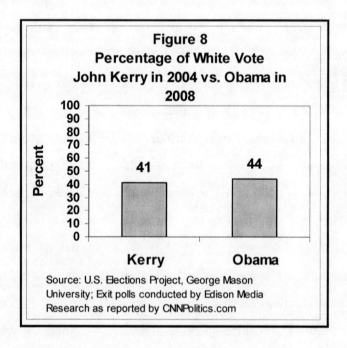

Barack Obama's candidacy had obvious appeal to black and other non-white voters, who saw in his election the ultimate refutation of black subjugation. But his appeal to white supporters is more complicated. Writing in *National Review*, John O'Sullivan attributes Obama's appeal to his being "a charming sphinx-like enigma" with personal qualities that appeal to many different types of Americans. "His Ivy League law background excites educated voters. His stance of 'ironic cool' in interviews wows the young. His gentlemanly manners and lithe elegance . . . charm suburban whites generally and white women in particular," O'Sullivan wrote. Obama seems to agree, writing in the prologue to his second autobiography *Audacity of Hope*, that "I serve as a blank screen on which people of vastly different political stripes project their own views."[7]

Shelby Steele sees race as central to Obama's appeal to white Americans. Obama effectively played the role of "bargainer," he writes, a black figure who says implicitly that he will assume whites are free of racism if they show him "gratitude" for doing so. In contrast to black "challengers" like Jesse Jackson, Al Sharpton, and Louis Farrakhan, who seek white retreat in the face of black anger, Obama skillfully gave whites a chance to jettison themselves from this interminable racial gamesmanship. O'Sullivan concurs, writing speculatively that "most whites have long wanted to vote for a black president -- Colin Powell would have won handily twelve years ago if he had thrown his helmet into the ring."[8]

Both these theories have much to recommend them, but white attraction to Obama needs further unpacking. Obama did not win the white vote outright. Indeed, lower income, white voters in Republican leaning states in the south and south-central states appeared even less supportive of Obama than they were of white Democrats Bill Clinton,

Al Gore, and John Kerry. As Jay Cost and Sean Trende have written at *Realclearpolitics.com*, "Democrats like Clinton and to a lesser extent Carter were able to carry these states by forming bi-racial voting coalitions of lower income whites and African Americans . . . Obama was unable to do that."[9]

In fact, despite the massive surge in voter turnout among racial minorities, the number of voters in households making below $75,000 annually declined between 2004 and 2008. Since 82 percent of black households made less than $75,000 in 2007, and since there was record breaking turnout among blacks at all income levels, the falloff in voter turnout at this moderate to low household income level most likely represents a precipitous decline in voter turnout among white, rural residents in states where incomes tend to be low. The support that Obama received among whites, in other words, came from demographic groups other than poor and working class white voters.

Obama and White Evangelicals

Those whites who did vote for Obama were concentrated in voting blocs enamored of racial idealism. In fact, it is difficult not to conclude that Obama's race played a large role in one of the most shocking outcomes of the election: his increase over John Kerry of two million white Christian "Evangelical/Born Again" votes, a 3 percentage point increase among this conservative leaning group. Some critics have suggested this gain was a result of Obama's strong showing at an

August 2008 forum at Rick Warren's Saddleback Church in California. "Evangelicals and other Christians listened as Rick Warren called Obama and McCain 'friends' and 'patriots' and watched as Warren winced no more than would have Larry King when Senator Obama said it was above his 'pay grade' to consider if and when an unborn child has human rights," fumed conservative columnist Star Parker.[10]

Obama with Rick Warren at Warren's Saddleback Church in Lake Forest, California, August 2008. Photo by Jonathan Alcorn.

It is possible that Warren, founder and senior pastor of Saddleback, an evangelical megachurch located in Lake Forest, California, could have had this kind of effect on evangelical voters. Warren holds traditional evangelical views on social issues such as abortion, same sex marriage, and stem cell research. But he has also called on churches worldwide to focus their efforts on fighting poverty and disease, expanding educational opportunities for the marginalized, and caring for the environment, viewpoints that might be perceived as more in line with Obama's.[11]

But it is difficult not to conclude that something else attracted white evangelicals to Obama at a level higher than previous Democrats. Warren, who went on to give a sermon at Obama's inauguration in January of 2009, hosted the "Civil Forum on the Presidency" with both presidential candidates at his church in August of 2008. By most accounts, John McCain performed exceedingly well. The Arizona Senator delivered crisp, fluid answers with compelling anecdotes compared with Obama's more stoic and non-committal responses. A comparison of the candidates' responses to Warren's question on the rights of the unborn is demonstrative.

WARREN: Forty million abortions -- at what point does a baby get human rights, in your view?

SEN. OBAMA: Well, I think that whether you're looking at it from a theological perspective or a scientific perspective, answering that question with specificity, you know, is above my pay grade. But let me just speak more generally about the issue of abortion because this is something obviously the country wrestles with.

One thing that I'm absolutely convinced of is that there is a moral and ethical element to this issue. And so I think anybody who tries to deny the moral difficulties and gravity of the abortion issue I think is not paying attention. So that would be point number one.

Republican presidential candidate John McCain looks on at a McCain-Palin rally in Virginia Beach, October 13, 2008. Photo by James Currie.

But point number two, I am pro-choice. I believe in Roe versus Wade. And I come to that conclusion not because I'm pro-abortion but because ultimately I don't think women make these decisions casually. I think they wrestle with these things in profound ways, in consultation with their pastors or their spouses or their doctors and their family members.

vs.

WARREN: (At) what point is a baby entitled to human rights?

SEN. MCCAIN: At the moment of conception. (Cheers, applause.) I have a twenty-five year pro-life record in the congress, in the senate. And as president of the United States, I will be a pro-life president and this presidency will have pro-life policies. (Cheers, applause.) That's my commitment. That's my commitment to you.[12]

Even the Obama camp felt their candidate did not perform as well as McCain at Saddleback. Soon after the event Obama operatives circulated the idea that McCain, who took the stage after Obama by virtue of a coin toss, might have heard the questions Warren posed to Obama, giving him time to prepare his responses. No evidence was ever cited to back up the claim, but it didn't stop NBC's Andrea Mitchell from dutifully reporting that some "Obama people" were suggesting "that McCain may not have been in the cone of silence and may have had some ability to overhear what the questions were to Obama. He seemed so well prepared."[13]

Table 2					
Presidential Voter Breakdown by Church Attendance					
2004 vs. 2008					
		2004		2008	
		Percent		Percent	2004-2008
Frequency Attending Church	2004	of Total	2008	of Total	Difference
Weekly	50,140,941	41	52,521,093	40	2,380,152
Kerry/Obama	19,554,967	39	22,584,070	43	3,029,103
Occassionally	48,917,991	40	55,147,147	42	6,229,156
Kerry/Obama	25,926,535	53	31,433,874	57	5,507,339
Never	17,121,297	14	21,008,437	16	3,887,140
Kerry/Obama	10,615,204	62	14,075,653	67	3,460,449
White Evangelical/Born Again	28,127,845	23	34,138,710	26	6,010,865
Kerry/Obama	5,906,847	21	8,193,290	24	2,286,443
Bush/McCain	21,939,719	78	25,262,646	74	3,322,927

Source: U.S. Elections Project, George Mason University; Exit polls conducted by Edison Media Research reported by CNNPolitics.com

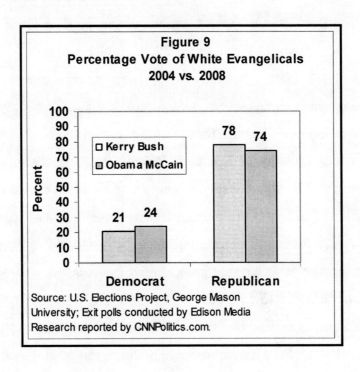

Figure 9
Percentage Vote of White Evangelicals
2004 vs. 2008

Source: U.S. Elections Project, George Mason University; Exit polls conducted by Edison Media Research reported by CNNPolitics.com.

All other things being equal, Obama's assertion that determining when life begins was "above my pay grade" at Saddleback should have sounded the alarm for evangelicals. It certainly drew attention to Obama's less widely reported comment during the Democratic primary that he supports abortion because he wouldn't want his daughters to be "punished with a baby."[14] It also led to more scrutiny of his opposition as an Illinois legislator in 2002 to three bills that would have outlawed "live birth" abortions -- a procedure which allows for an infant who survives an abortion to die without medical treatment, and a decision that put Obama way to the left of any previous presidential candidate on that issue. This may have been why self-described "White Evangelical/Born Again" voters surged at the polls in 2008. Their numbers went from 28.1 million in 2004 to 34.1 million in 2008, an increase of six million voters, or 21.4 percent, the largest increase among any religious denomination, and, ironically, second only to the percentage increase among those who reported "never" going to church, which grew by 22.7 percent. It was because of the increase in the size of this block that despite winning a smaller percentage of them than Bush in 2004, McCain managed to increase the total Republican take of evangelicals by 3.1 million votes. Still, Obama increased the Democratic take of this voting group by 38.7 percent from 2004, even more than McCain's 15.1 percent.

It is difficult to believe that racial sympathy did not play a role in the evangelical vote for Obama, especially since much of the increase seems to have come from young evangelicals aged 18-29. A Pew Research Center survey of young evangelicals found that 18-29 year-olds are even more conservative than the older generations of evangelicals on the issue of abortion.[15] This is not surprising, given the movement of America as a whole toward a more conservative stance on abortion since the 1990s. A Gallup poll in May 2009 found that, for the first time since Gallup polled on this issue in 1995, more than half (51 percent) of Americans called themselves "pro-life," compared with 42 percent who called themselves "pro-choice."[16] Obama's votes against the live birth abortion bills in Illinois put him to the left of every single member of the U.S. House of Representatives, which passed a similar bill in 2002 and which includes such leftist luminaries as John Conyers, Nancy Pelosi, Barney Frank, and Henry Waxman.[17] Yet Obama faced none of the repercussions among evangelical voters that Al Gore, John Kerry, and Hillary Clinton faced due to their support of abortion. These candidates furiously distanced themselves from the controversial practice of "late term" or "partial birth" abortion. All three candidates "triangulated" the issue, arguing, as John Kerry did in a 2004 presidential debate, that he opposed partial birth abortion, but would not vote for a bill to ban it because it did not allow "for the exception for situations where the health of the woman is at risk."[18] For his trouble, Kerry received 16 percent of the vote of white evangelicals aged 18-29. Obama received 32 percent.[19]

The Deracialized White Vote

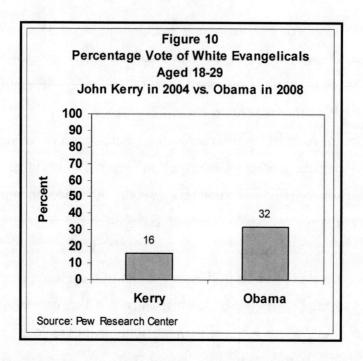

It is not clear whether Obama can maintain the support of young evangelicals. Despite being black, a member of perhaps the most religiously devout racial group in America, and despite his insistence on a high degree of fealty to Christianity, Obama has quickly become the most secular of all modern U.S. presidents. Obama refused to let the Air Force fly over the "God and Country Festival" in Idaho in July 2009, a favor the Pentagon has provided to fair organizers for forty years. Obama also did not attend any events on the National Day of Prayer that year. When Obama spoke at Georgetown University, a Catholic institution, he requested that a religious symbol behind him be covered. On a Friday evening in September of 2010, when Obama addressed the Congressional Hispanic Caucus Institute, he quoted the most famous passage in the Declaration of Independence while omitting its most consequential clause: "We hold these truths to be self-evident, that all men are created equal [pause], endowed with certain unalienable rights: life and liberty, and the pursuit of happiness." In Obama's version, there is no "Creator" endowing these unalienable rights. As pro-Obama radio host Warrant Ballentine has said "This president is purposely taking the position that he's not going to be connected with any religion." Obama's reported difficulty in finding a suitable church in Washington D.C. more than a year after he left Chicago's Trinity United Church under political pressure to do so elicited the following remark from conservative radio talker Laura Ingraham: "If the Obamas aren't careful serious Christians are going to start believing that for them religion is not a personal relationship with Christ, it's not about salvation, but it's about managing and manipulating the political process." Obama's concerted effort to reach out to the Muslim world, along with his determination to appear religiously neutral and his unexplained reticence about his past have all no doubt contributed to the finding that almost one-fifth of Americans believe he is a Muslim, according to an August, 2010 survey by the Pew Forum on Religion and Public Life.[20]

Obama and White Liberals

Not surprisingly, the largest white voting bloc to turn out heavily for Obama was high income urban liberals, a population that had doubled in its proportion of the electorate between 1999 and 2005 and is now 40 percent of the Democratic base. It was expected that Obama would need the youth vote to carry him to victory, a vote that typically favors the Democratic ticket. But turnout for Obama among these voters underperformed expectations, and gave him only 560,000 additional white votes compared with Kerry in 2004. The most significant and racially motivated shift among white voters was the tidal wave of support for Obama of voters from households with over $200,000 in annual income. Obama captured 52 percent of these voters, compared to 35 percent for John Kerry, an increase of 2.8 million votes and a jaw dropping shift of 17 percentage points away from the Republican Party since 2004. McCain, in fact, fared worse among high income households than George W. Bush did in 2004, despite running a campaign that focused on the dangers of Obama's "spreading the wealth around," socialist style redistribution plans.

It was expected that wealthy whites, a group that Obama explicitly targeted for a tax increase, would finally end up in the Democrat column. In 1995 a Pew Research Center survey found that among households with annual incomes greater than $135,000 -- the top ten percent -- there were nearly twice as many Republicans (46 percent) as Democrats (25 percent). In 2007, there were as many Democrats (31 percent) as Republicans (32 percent). Another Pew Research Center survey on American political typology offers insight into why this shift has taken place. This study found that for the 83 percent of liberals who are white, taxes and the economy remain low on the list of concerns, and few things are more important than a well articulated commitment to social justice. Authors such as Joel Kotkin, Nicholas Lemann, David Brooks, and Ruy Texeira have written extensively about the liberal transformation of America's idealistic, meritocratic, information age upper class, which is summed up nicely by Reihan Salam of *Forbes* magazine: "it is certainly true that more affluent voters tend to be more ideological. You might say that a wealthy liberal can 'afford' to indulge in a vote for higher taxes because social liberalism matters more to him than a few thousand dollars here or there."[21]

A mostly secular group living in or around urban centers, liberals are more likely than other voting blocs to believe that governmental power is the greatest force for social change, and to support programs specifically aimed at accelerating black progress -- school "bussing," affirmative action, racial gerrymandering, and "Afrocentric" public school curricula. For many liberals, Obama's candidacy -- that is, simply voting for America's first black president -- amounted to another demonstration of idealism aimed at black uplift and a testament to their benevolent racial stewardship. As Shelby Steele has written, "Obama's special charisma always came much more from the racial idealism he embodied than from his political ideas. In fact, this was his only true political originality." Another critic put it this way: "Mr. Obama inspires not because of anything he says, but because of who he is."[22]

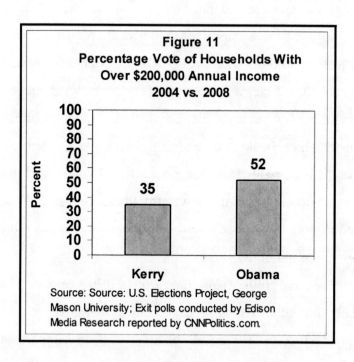

Figure 11
Percentage Vote of Households With Over $200,000 Annual Income
2004 vs. 2008

Source: Source: U.S. Elections Project, George Mason University; Exit polls conducted by Edison Media Research reported by CNNPolitics.com.

The enthusiasm for Obama of white, wealthy, big metro area liberals is affirmed by the very wide margins he enjoyed in the cities. According to Jay Cost and Sean Trende, Obama did worst in the rural and small town areas across the country than Bill Clinton, who won a similar percentage of the two party vote in 1996 (54 percent), but Obama did better in the larger urban areas. Even in the so called "mega cities" of the southwest, like metro Dallas and Houston, Obama did better than Bill Clinton, actually winning in Dallas and Harris Counties -- a feat Clinton could not pull off in 1996. In total, according to Nathan Silver of the political prediction web site FiveThirtyEight.com, Obama accumulated a margin of victory of approximately 10.5 million votes in urban areas, roughly seven million more than John Kerry's 3.6 million in 2004. Obama's candidacy appealed to the extremes of rich and poor in increasingly stratified central cities. "Obama improved his performance not only among black and Hispanic voters but also among urban whites, with whom he performed nine points better than Kerry . . . With the votes that he banked in the cities, Obama did not really need to prevail in the suburbs," Silver wrote.[23]

Many observers attribute Obama's victory to the collapse in the financial markets in the middle of September before the election. Indeed, the *Realclearpolitics.com* average of polls showed an increasingly wide gap for Obama after mid-September.[24] But this does not explain Obama's gain of seven million votes over John Kerry's take among urban voters. The suburbs bared the brunt of the economic downturn, especially the mortgage crisis and the collapse of the housing market, as residents in these areas are 50 percent more likely to be homeowners than those in urban areas. Suburbanites are also more dependent on their cars and are disproportionately hurt by soaring gas prices. But the suburbs gave Obama only three million more votes than they gave John Kerry in 2004.[25]

The Deracialized White Vote

There is no more compelling indicator that a massive number of upper income whites voted for Obama because of his candidacy's history making potential (i.e. his race) than the fact that this group of voters grew from 3 percent to 6 percent of the entire electorate, an increase of 4.1 million voters over 2004. It may be comforting for some conservatives to consider that the absolute number of upper income households increased during the "Bush Boom" of 2002-2007. And indeed, between 2004 and 2007, the number of households earning above $200,000 increased by 1.3 million. But this is nowhere near enough growth to obviate the clumsy yet inescapable conclusion that wealthy professionals from dense coastal cities and large, media soaked metro areas flocked to the polls in record numbers primarily to become part of history, to demonstrate their commitment to "racial justice," and to stake their claim to a prideful place in the world of fashionable opinion.[26]

In sum, because he is black, Barack Obama was able to attract enough wealthy white elites to offset the loss of working class whites, while increasing his support among poor minorities, a feat that had escaped other "Ivy League" Democrats like John Kerry, Bill Bradley, and Paul Tsongas. As CBS Chief Political writer David Paul Kuhn explained, Obama's "exceptionalism" -- his ability to attract wealthy whites and poor minorities -- stemmed directly from his race: "Obama's race broke this Democratic law . . . his color proved to be not a weakness but a strength."[27]

Wealthy White Liberals: Money and the Media

The influence of upper income white liberals in 2008 extended far beyond the voting booth. Drawing heavily on these "gentry liberals" of Wall Street, Hollywood, Silicon Valley, and academia (employees at the University of California at Berkeley constituted Obama's largest single institutional contributor with almost $1.4 million) Obama was able to raise a record $750 million, roughly equal to the combined amounts raised by George W. Bush and John Kerry in 2004. Obama declined public financing and the spending limits that came with it, making him the first major party candidate since the system was created to reject public money for the general election.[28]

Obama's fundraising efforts reflected the deep investment in his campaign of this wealthy professional class. According to the Campaign Finance Institute, Obama received about 26 percent of his cash from "small donors" (under $200), about the same as George W. Bush four years earlier. The rest was raised by large contributors making numerous contributions along the way to the legal limit of $4,600, as well as big money "bundlers." By the end of the election, Obama had 13,800 donors who contributed the maximum amount of $4,600, compared to McCain, who had 6,700 of them. "After a more thorough analysis of data from the Federal Election Commission (FEC)," a CFI study found, "it has become clear that repeaters and large donors were even more important for Obama than we or other analysts had fully appreciated."[29]

Table 3
Presidential Voter Breakdown by Household Income
2004 vs. 2008

Income	2004	2004 Percent of Total	2008	2008 Percent of Total	2004-2008 Difference
Under $15,000	9,783,598	8	7,878,164	6	-1,905,434
Kerry/Obama Under $15,000	6,163,667	63	5,751,060	73	-412,607
$15-$30K	18,344,247	15	15,756,328	12	-2,587,919
Kerry/Obama $15-$30K	10,456,221	57	9,453,797	60	-1,002,424
$30-$50K	26,904,895	22	24,947,519	19	-1,957,376
Kerry/Obama $30-$50K	13,452,448	50	13,721,135	55	268,688
$50K-$75K	28,127,845	23	27,573,574	21	-554,271
Kerry/Obama $50K-$75K	12,094,973	43	13,235,315	48	1,140,342
$75K-100K	17,121,297	14	19,695,410	15	2,574,113
Kerry/Obama $75K-$100K	7,704,584	45	10,044,659	51	2,340,075
$100K-$150K	13,452,448	11	18,382,382	14	4,929,935
Kerry/Obama $100K-$150K	5,650,028	42	8,823,544	48	3,173,516
$150K-200K	4,891,799	4	7,878,164	6	2,986,365
Kerry/Obama $150K-$200K	2,054,556	42	3,781,519	48	1,726,963
$200K+	3,668,849	3	7,878,164	6	4,209,315
Kerry/Obama $200K+	1,284,097	35	4,096,645	52	2,812,548
Bush/McCain $200K+	2,384,752	65	3,781,519	48	1,396,767

Source: U.S. Elections Project, George Mason University; Exit polls conducted by Edison Media Research reported by CNNPolitics.com

But if the votes and money of wealthy white liberals were crucial to Obama's victory, the most significant source of power and influence exercised by this group was the mainstream press, which draws mostly on highly educated, high income urban liberals for the production, editing, writing, selling and consuming of its product. Since the "new journalism" of the 1960s, an academic movement which encouraged journalists to become active players in political conflicts, socially committed young people have flocked to journalism. Even more than government work or non-profit volunteerism, journalism has become perceived as a way to affect social reform and, in the process, achieve individual celebrity. Most of the recruits to the new journalism came from affluent backgrounds and were better educated, more culturally sophisticated, and more politically liberal than the journalists they succeeded.[30] One media watch dog group summed up these developments as they relate to journalists in a 2004 study: "Surveys over the past twenty-five years have consistently found journalists are much more liberal than the rest of America. Their voting habits are disproportionately Democratic, their views on issues such as abortion and gay rights are well to the left of most Americans and they are less likely to attend church or synagogue."[31]

This development dealt a heavy blow to the old ideal of neutrality in the news business. The new journalists looked disparagingly at media "objectivity," many even dismissing it as a vestige of the media's corrupt past. The change toward an activist media has been reflected in the coverage of presidential elections. Large scale content analyses of network news since 1980 have been suggestive if not conclusive: coverage of the 1984, 1992, 1996, and 2004 elections favored the Democratic nominee, while coverage of the 1980, 1988, and 2000 elections produced about equally negative portraits of both major party candidates. As S. Robert Lichter, the "dean" of media studies in the United States, sums it up: "the mainstream media do not always favor one presidential candidate over another, but the candidates they do favor are usually Democrats."[32]

By the 2004 presidential election media bias was pervasive and generally acknowledged. One of the most notorious misdeeds of presidential media coverage took place that year. CBS's *60 Minutes* aired a report in the heat of the campaign claiming to have discovered a new document proving that incumbent President George W. Bush had received preferential treatment during his service with the Texas Air National Guard in the 1970s. The story was retracted after internet "bloggers" noticed that some of the fonts used in the document were not available on commercial typewriters of the early 1970s, when the documents were purportedly drafted. The event resulted in the resignation of long time *CBS Evening News* anchor Dan Rather. An investigative report released on January 10, 2005 faulted CBS's rush to put the flawed story on the air and their "stubborn" defense of it in the days that followed. S. Robert Lichter reported that post-election polling showed record numbers of both Democrat and Republican voters described the campaign coverage as biased.[33]

In the post-1960s news business neutrality and objectivity have been superseded by the far more subjective standard of "fairness." But even the outward appearance of fairness was discarded in the presidential campaign of 2008, replaced by something more closely resembling electioneering on Obama's behalf. This has been widely acknowledged. Ombudsmen employed by the *New York Times* and the *Washington*

Post have questioned the coverage of their own newspapers. In mid-November, safely after the election, *Time* magazine's political news editor Mark Halperin called the media's performance during the campaign simply "disgusting." Halperin, a former ABC News political director, told a panel of media analysts at the *Politico*/University of Southern California conference on the 2008 election, "It was extreme bias, extreme pro-Obama coverage." Following the money, an analysis of federal records by *Investor's Business Daily* showed journalists contributed fifteen times more money to Democrats than Republicans during the 2008 election cycle. Journalists who gave to Obama outnumbered those who contributed to John McCain by a 20-to-1 margin. Overall, according to the Pew Research Center's Project for Excellence in Journalism, media coverage of Senator McCain was three times more negative than positive following the conventions.[34]

If some journalists and editors were willing to concede pro-Obama bias, others defended the bias, explaining that the greater coverage of Obama was justified given that, as the first major party black presidential candidate, he was more news worthy than McCain.[35] But a brief review of some of the more egregious examples of pro-Obama bias makes the studied and purposeful nature of the reporting obvious. In one instance, on October 2nd before the election, ABC's *Good Morning America* skipped reporting the results of its own poll, which showed a tight race between Obama and McCain in Florida and Ohio. Instead, it reported a Quinnipiac University poll far more favorable for

Obama. In another instance, the *New York Times* refused to publish an op-ed by Senator McCain about the Iraq war just days after publishing an op-ed on the same subject by Senator Obama. The *Times* did not ignore McCain altogether, though. On February 21st, 2008, just as McCain was wrapping up the Republican nomination, the paper ran a 3,000 word "hit piece" written by no fewer than four reporters, implying that McCain had an affair with a lobbyist, Vicki Iseman, thirty years his younger. McCain and Iseman both denied the charge, and after a severe public backlash against the paper, its public editor Clark Hoyt admitted that while the article "raised one of the most toxic subjects in politics -- sex -- it offered readers no proof that McCain and Iseman had a romance."[36]

In yet another instance, in late October before the election, when it could have had real impact, the *Los Angeles Times* refused to release a videotape that it said showed Barack Obama praising University of Chicago professor Rashid Khalidi, a former spokesman for the Palestine Liberation Organization while it was a designated terrorist group in the 1970s and '80s. In response to complaints from the McCain camp, the paper said it was protecting a confidential source, and endorsed Obama for president.[37]

These are not the kinds of actions that can be written off as mistakes or lapses in judgement. They are well considered, strategic decisions designed to affect a specific end. And it did not go unnoticed by the public. On October 22, 2008 the Pew Research Center released a survey showing that by a margin of 70 percent to 9 percent Americans believed most journalists wanted to see Obama, not McCain, win the presidential election. This margin was an historic high. At this stage of the 2004 campaign, 50 percent of voters said most journalists wanted to see John Kerry win the election, while 22 percent said most journalists favored George W. Bush. In October 2000, 47 percent of voters said journalists wanted to see Al Gore win and 23 percent said most journalists wanted Bush to win. In 1996, 59 percent said journalists were pulling for Bill Clinton.[38]

Data supporting the notion that the press was biased in favor of Obama accumulated in the year after the election. An analysis of the 2008 campaign coverage of network evening news conducted by the non-partisan Center for Media and Public Affairs at George Mason University (CMPA) found that on the three broadcast networks combined (ABC, NBC, CBS) evaluations of Obama were 68 percent positive and 32 percent negative, compared to the 36 percent positive and 64 percent negative for his Republican opponent. CMPA Director S. Robert Lichter added that, in fact, "Obama received the most favorable coverage CMPA has ever recorded for any presidential candidate since we began tracking election news coverage in 1988."[39]

By most accounts the media continued its "slobbering love affair" with Obama after his election.[40] A study by the Pew Research Center's Project for Excellence in Journalism conducted in late April 2009 concluded: "President Barack Obama has enjoyed substantially more positive media coverage than either Bill Clinton or George W. Bush during their first months in the White House." The study examined 1,261 stories by *The Washington Post*, the *New York Times*, ABC, CBS and NBC, *Newsweek* magazine and the "NewsHour" on PBS. Favorable stories (42 percent) were double the unfavorable (20 percent), while the rest were "neutral" or "mixed." Obama's treatment contrasts sharply with coverage in the first two months of the presidencies of George W. Bush (22 percent of stories favorable) and Bill Clinton (27 percent). Unlike Bush and Clinton, Obama received favorable coverage in both news columns and opinion pages. The nature of the coverage also changed. "Roughly twice as much of the coverage of Obama (44 percent) has concerned his personal and leadership qualities than was the case for Bush (22 percent) or Clinton (26 percent)," the report said. The Pew study found similar treatment of Obama in its analysis of cable channels, news web sites, morning news shows, and National Public Radio, as did the study released by the Center for Media and Public Affairs at George Mason University. These findings have not been lost on the American public. A national poll conducted by Sacred Heart University's Polling Institute in September of 2009 found that 70 percent of Americans agreed the national news media are intent on promoting the Obama presidency while 26.5 percent disagreed. The most probable reason for this continuing infatuation with Obama, according to *Washington Post* columnist Robert Samuelson, is that "most journalists like Obama; they admire his command of language; he's a relief after Bush; they agree with his agenda (so it never occurs to them to question basic premises); and they don't want to see the first African American president fail."[41]

Impact of Pro-Obama Coverage on the Election

Determining the influence of media bias on voting behavior is not a simple task. One study by University of California researchers suggests that media bias can influence the vote of anywhere from 4 to 8 percent of voters who are exposed to it.[42] But even if the impact on public attitudes were negligible, it appears likely the overwhelmingly positive coverage of Obama helped neutralize several contentious positions and past actions of the candidate. Several minor issues raised during the campaign never received a full airing in public, including Obama's decision to break his very first campaign promise by forgoing public financing, which seemed to contradict the signature purpose of his campaign of "change" and of ending "politics as usual." Also little discussed is the impossibility of giving 95 percent of households a tax cut as Obama had promised (40 percent of households don't pay income taxes), his votes against laws prohibiting the practice of live birth abortions, and his condescending comments to a San Francisco fundraiser in the spring of 2008 that low income rural Americans are "bitter" and "cling to their guns and their bibles." In three nationally televised debates with John McCain not one moderator, all of whom were drawn from the mainstream media, asked Obama about any of these issues. (In the third and final debate at Hofstra University, it was McCain, not moderator Bob Schieffer, who brought up the issue of Obama's vote against the "infant born alive" bill, and Obama replied.)[43]

The Media and Reverend Wright

Perhaps no pro-Obama bias compares with the impenetrable coat of armor the media placed over Obama to shield him from the revelation of his twenty year relationship with the fiery Reverend Jeremiah A. Wright of the Trinity United Church of Christ in Chicago. Wright was the Obama family pastor for twenty years, he married Obama to his wife Michelle, and baptized their two daughters. He also sold videos of sermons from the church's web site in which he made inflammatory remarks about the United States, Italians, Jews, Christians, and whites, and accused the country of bringing on itself the September 11th, 2001 terrorist attacks on New York's World Trade Center and the Pentagon. Indeed, Wright delivered a speech in the 1980s in which he stated "white people's greed runs a world in need," a speech that so impressed Obama that he made it the title of his own autobiography, *Audacity of Hope*. Wright's speech, Obama explained in June 2007, began his "religious conversion." "One Sunday, I put on one of the few clean jackets I had, and went over to Trinity United Church of Christ on 95th Street on the South Side of Chicago. And I heard Reverend Jeremiah A. Wright deliver a sermon called 'The Audacity of Hope.' And during the course of that sermon, he introduced me to someone named Jesus Christ. I learned that my sins could be redeemed."[44]

After Hillary Clinton's campaign for the Democratic presidential nomination brought Wright's sermons into public view in March 2008, Obama reluctantly acceded to making a speech for the sake of damage control. Calling it "A More Perfect Union" after Abraham Lincoln's speech of the same title, Obama drafted a complex statement aimed not so much at condemning the bigotry of his pastor as at blaming it on the black community. "Like other black churches, Trinity's services are full of raucous laughter and sometimes bawdy humor . . . The church contains in full the kindness and cruelty, the fierce intelligence and the shocking ignorance, the struggles and successes, the love and yes, the bitterness and bias that make up the black experience in America . . . I can no more disown him than I can disown the black community." Many critics found the speech confusing, at once both conciliatory and defiant. Did Obama mean by this, asked columnist Mark Steyn after the speech, "that the paranoid racist ravings of Jeremiah Wright are now part of the established cultural discourse in African American life and thus must command our respect?"[45]

The famous photo of Obama with his mentor Reverend Jeremiah Wright.

Obama seems to have answered Steyn's question in the affirmative, having more than once demonstrated a troubling passivity when confronted with black bigotry. In his autobiography *Dreams from My Father*, Obama marginalizes Malcolm X's hostility toward whites and, especially, Jews. A powerful and feared orator of black nationalism, Malcolm X was well known for giving speeches sprinkled with anti-white and anti-Semitic sentiment. Before breaking with the Nation of Islam over personal differences with its leader, Elijah Muhammad, Malcolm preached black supremacy, racial segregation, social uplift, and economic self-reliance. According to the NOI, where Malcolm was second in command, blacks were God's original creation and "out of the weak of the Black Nation, the present Caucasian race was created." While Jews were thought to be devils like all other whites, they were singled out for special opprobrium. At Temple Number Seven in Harlem in 1964, Malcolm explained that the Jews "know how to rob you, they know how to be your landlord, they know how to be your grocer, they know how to be your lawyer, they know how to join the NAACP and become the president . . . They know how to control everything you got." Malcolm continued "Goldberg always catches ya'. If Goldberg can't catch ya', Goldstein'll catch ya'. And if Goldstein don't catch ya', Greenberg will catch ya'." Malcolm also ridiculed the Nazi Holocaust against the Jews. "Everybody talks about the six million Jews . . . Now everybody's wet-eyed over a handful of Jews who brought it on themselves. What about our one hundred million?"[46]

But Obama described Malcolm's prejudice as not only incidental to the larger message of Black Power, but also as harmless and even necessary. "Only Malcolm X's autobiography seemed to offer something different," Obama wrote of the literature he familiarized himself with in college. "The blunt poetry of his words, his unadorned insistence on respect, promised a new and uncompromising order, martial in its discipline, forged through sheer force of will. All the other stuff, the talk of blue-eyed devils and apocalypse, was incidental to that program, I decided." Obama wrote in his memoir that black nationalism's messages of solidarity, self-reliance, discipline and communal responsibility "need not depend on hatred of whites any more than it depended on white munificence." But he also "came to see how the blanket indictment of everything white served a central function in their message of uplift; how, psychologically, at least, one depended on the other." Obama never bothered to explain how succumbing to bigotry and hatred served to "uplift" black people. Nor did he explain why he would be attracted to Malcolm but not to other purveyors of black uplift like Booker T. Washington or Malcolm's own rival, Martin Luther King Jr., who demanded that blacks not debase themselves by adopting the racial prejudice of their white oppressors. But ultimately Obama decided that the bigotry inherent in black nationalism was a necessary and, most likely, harmless evil. And in doing so, he debased black humanity by suggesting blacks cannot be held responsible for their own bigotry. "If nationalism could create a strong and effective insularity, deliver on its promise of self-respect, then the hurt it might cause well meaning whites, or the inner turmoil it caused people like me, would be of little consequence." After reviewing his life and his writing, including his praise of Malcolm and Reverend Wright, the *Los Angeles Times* noted that a "recurring character type has played a role in the life of Obama: a friend or associate who is quick to blame white America for the troubles of the black community."[47]

None of this -- Obama's worshipful relationship with Reverend Wright, his high regard for black nationalism and its leaders, his abiding of racism and anti-Semitism in black social thought, his breezy dismissal of black bigotry -- interested the mainstream media. After Obama's "More Perfect Union" speech the media swooped in to declare it a masterpiece in the annals of the spoken word, a classic in the lexicon of great things written about liberty and justice, calling it both "Lincolnesque" and a "landmark." The *New York Times, National Public Radio, MSNBC,* and *CNN* posted the video of the speech on their web sites, with commentary and public forums. Cable television news personality Chris Matthews of *MSNBC's Hardball* insisted that the speech be required reading in America's classrooms and the *New York Times* called it "Obama's Profile in Courage." As far as these sources were concerned, Obama had met the challenge of race head on. The issue of Obama's relationship with Reverend Wright was never a serious subject of discussion again in the media. This is true despite Obama's troubling remark in that speech that he could "no more disown him [Reverend Wright] than I can my white grandmother," a statement he had to contradict two months later in response to even more incendiary remarks by Wright at an April 2008 journalism conference. The speech was particularly rough on Obama's white grandmother, who raised Obama for a good portion of his childhood. Not only had Obama compared his loyalty to Reverend Wright with his loyalty to his grandmother, but he also compared her fear -- expressed to Obama privately when he was living with her as a teenager -- of a black man who accosted her at a bus station with Reverend Wright's very public and malicious bigotry. When some critics suggested that it seemed craven to take public aim at a family member who raised him in order to justify a disturbing relationship with a racist pastor, Obama went on to accuse all whites of racism. "The point I was making was not that my grandmother harbors any racial animosity. She doesn't," Obama said, unaccountably, after his speech. "But she is a typical white person, who, if she sees somebody on the street that she doesn't know there's a reaction that's been bred into our experiences that don't go away and that sometimes come out in the wrong way and that's just the nature of race in our society."[48]

Instead of probing further into this strained explanation, the media was content to let the matter drop. The prevailing mood was on display at CNN's *"360°"* show hosted by Anderson Cooper. Shortly after the Wright scandal broke Cooper lambasted Hillary Clinton supporter Lanny Davis for bringing up Reverend Wright. "Lanny," Cooper bellowed, "it is amazing. Lanny, it is amazing. I'm not taking sides here, but we all know what the [Wright's] comments were. It's funny that you feel the need to repeat them over and over again." But it was not in any way clear that most people knew of Wright's comments, and if they did, it is not likely that they learned of them through the major media outlets like CNN, which felt no compunction to "repeat them over and over again." On March 13, 2008 ABC news broke the Wright story, including Wright's notorious sermon in which he instructed parishioners not to say "God bless America" but rather "God damned America." The *New York Times* didn't run Wright's comments for months after the scandal broke. It was not until September 24, 2008 -- six months later -- that an article in the *Times* actually reported Wright's words, albeit in an article concerning alleged falsehoods in anti-Obama ads. For half a year, the paper's editors ignored the most damning aspect of one of the biggest stories of the presidential campaign. The *Times* was not alone in the boycott of the Wright story. Obama was not asked by any moderator in three nationally televised presidential debates about Reverend Wright. Apparently, the presidential debate organizers had gotten the message. Records obtained by *The Daily Caller* news web site in 2010 revealed that when ABC News anchors Charles Gibson and George Stephanopoulos asked Obama during a mid-April 2008 primary debate why it had taken him so long to dissociate himself from Reverend Wright, it touched off a firestorm of reaction from some of the most powerful journalists in America. An analysis of e-mails from "Journolist," a list service for liberal journalists of news organizations including *Time*, *Politico*, the *Huffington Post*, the *Baltimore Sun*, the *Guardian*, *Salon* and the *New Republic*, reveals that several hundred journalists went to extreme lengths to discourage coverage of Reverend Wright. In one instance, Spencer Ackerman of the *Washington Independent* urged his colleagues to "pick one of Obama's conservative critics. Fred Barnes, Karl Rove, who cares -- and call them racists." Michael Tomasky, a writer for the *Guardian*, implored Journolist members to "kill ABC and this idiocy in whatever venues we have . . . We need to throw chairs now, try as hard as we can to get the call next time. Otherwise the questions in October will be exactly like this. This is just a disease." Thomas Schaller, a columnist for the *Baltimore Sun* as well as a "political science professor" asked "why don't we use the power of this list to do something about the debate?" Schaller proposed coordinating a "smart statement expressing disgust" at the questions Gibson and Stephanopoulos had posed to Obama.[49]

In all likelihood, the frantic activity of the Journolist members wasn't necessary. By any and all accounts, ABC News, along with the other television networks, were very much in Obama's corner. A *Washington Examiner* analysis of data compiled by the Center for Responsive Politics showed that senior executives, on air personalities, producers, reporters, editors, writers and other self-identifying employees of ABC, CBS and NBC -- 1,160 employees in all -- contributed more than one million dollars to Democratic candidates and campaign committees in

2008. By contrast, only 193 of the employees contributed to Republican candidates and campaign committees, for a total of $142,863. Not surprisingly, Charles Krauthammer opined about the media after Obama's "More Perfect Union" speech, "they have reverted to form as protectors of the myth of Obama."[50]

It seems unlikely that a white presidential candidate could, in a similar fashion, quell a controversy stemming from the discovery of an intimate relationship with a racist pastor or other bigoted associate as thoroughly as Obama was able to do. Since the segregationist George Wallace ran for president as a regional candidate in four elections from 1964 through 1972 (and was shot and paralyzed during the 1972 campaign), nothing remotely close to the Obama/Wright relationship has surfaced in presidential races. But there are two instances where a contrast could be drawn between the kind of treatment white presidential candidates received when bigotry or racism turned up among people they associated with and the relatively benign treatment Obama received after Wright became public knowledge.

At the 1992 Republican convention, when President George H.W. Bush was running for re-election, perennial presidential contender and Washington commentator Patrick J. Buchanan made a speech declaring a "culture war" that was so caustic in its criticism of homosexuality, women's rights, environmentalists, and the urban poor it is thought to have alienated moderates from the party. At one point in his speech Buchanan stated that "the agenda Clinton and Clinton would impose on

America -- abortion on demand, a litmus test for the Supreme Court, homosexual rights, discrimination against religious schools, women in combat . . . is not the kind of change we can tolerate in a nation that we still call God's country."[51] Bush Sr. lost his re-election effort, with many Republican leaning independents fleeing to the third party candidacy of Ross Perot, who captured 19 percent of the vote. According to Steven Sark of the *Atlantic Monthly,* Buchanan's "speech is widely regarded as having launched a tremendous backlash against the convention which discredited the Republican Party and helped to elect Clinton."[52]

The media's role in launching that backlash against the Republican presidential campaign in 1992 was substantial. A search of "major U.S. and world publications" on the Lexis-Nexis Academic news database on June 15th of 2009 -- seventeen years after the election -- returned 202 articles for the words "Patrick J. Buchanan Republican Convention Speech" between August 18th, 1992 when Buchanan made the speech and November 4th, 1992, the day of the election. A search for the words "Obama and Reverend Wright" for the same period leading up to the 2008 election returned seventy-two stories.

The element of religiosity in the Wright scandal provides another dimension that exposed the media's favorable treatment of Obama. There is no sector of society more vilified in the mainstream media than white Christian evangelicals, and the worst kind of invective is typically reserved for white evangelical preachers, especially when they say or do something controversial. When the scandals involving several high profile "televangelists" broke in the 1980s, explains Randall Ballmer, a scholar of evangelical Christianity, "the tone of the media wrongly treated all evangelicals as the moral equivalents of Jimmy Swaggart." Swaggart was perhaps the most well known evangelical preacher caught up in a series of sex scandals. The treatment of black preachers by the media, including those of Reverend Wright's brand of "black liberation theology," is far more deferential and, in effect, patronizing. Black parishioners, in the eyes of the media, simply can not be expected to stand up to bigotry coming from the pulpit, an example if ever there was one of what President George W. Bush and others have called the "soft bigotry of low expectations." "The unspoken agreement to concede the black community to the sway of the pulpit is itself a form of racist condescension," wrote the critic Christopher Hitchens.[53]

Unlike Obama, who initially refused to "disown" Wright, the Bush family helped engineer Buchanan's exit from the Republican party later in the 1990s, forcing Buchanan to run for president in 2000 on the Reform party ticket with the endorsement of left wing extremist and Reform party big wig Lenora Fulani.[54]

The second instance in which a white presidential candidate had to defend himself against charges of racial bigotry also involves a Bush, this time the younger. During his 2000 campaign for the Republican presidential nomination, George W. Bush visited the fundamentalist, anti-Catholic, and racially segregated Bob Jones University in South Carolina. Bush was hounded by primary opponent John McCain for visiting the school and lambasted by the media, despite the fact that Bush was never associated with the school and that the school had previously hosted political candidates of both parties, both black and white. Bush himself later expressed regret for not using the forum to brow beat the institution and its leaders. The difference here was the media. Coverage of Bush's visit was intense and, in this particular case, actually did some good. Not three months after Bush's election to the presidency, Bob Jones officially changed its interracial dating policy, in part because of the media light focused on it by the Bush visit. In an interview on CNN's *Larry King Live* in March 2000, the school's president Bob Jones III confirmed that the ban on interracial dating had been dropped as of March 3, 2000 and cited the national scrutiny the school had received since George W. Bush's campaign appearance there in 2000.[55]

Timid treatment of Obama's relationship with Jeremiah Wright by the press resulted in no such epiphany or change of heart for Wright. On June 10, 2009, five months into Obama's presidency, the *Daily Press of Newport News* reported that Wright told the paper in an interview that "them Jews aren't going to let him [Obama] talk to me. I told my baby daughter, that he'll talk to me in five years when he's a lame duck, or in eight years when he's out of office." Wright later insisted he shouldn't have used the term "Jews." He meant "Zionists."[56]

The media's proud crusade against racism and bigotry, which overturned a decades old segregation rule at a private university, came to a screeching halt at the doorstep of Reverend Wright's Trinity United Church of Christ in Chicago.

Driver's Licenses for Illegal Immigrants

The media also seems to have taken a hands off approach to Obama's support for driver's licenses for illegal immigrants, a wildly unpopular idea even in blue states, and an issue that had been at least partially responsible for the downfall of two very powerful (white) Governors. This topic came up in the presidential campaign during the Democratic primary. In a debate on November 15th of 2007, Wolfe Blitzer of CNN asked the candidates who shared the stage that night if they supported New York State Governor Eliot Spitzer's proposal to allow illegal immigrants to obtain driver's licenses. After dissembling at previous debates on the topic, Hillary Clinton gave a crisp "no" response to Blitzer's question. Obama, after dissembling a bit at this debate (Blitzer had to interject to insist on a "yes" or "no" answer) said "yes."

A day earlier Governor Spitzer had discarded his controversial plan to give driver's licenses to illegal immigrants, making it easier for Clinton, a U.S. Senator from New York, to run against this policy. But Governor Spitzer suffered irreparable damage from this affair. After issuing an executive order in September 2007 directing state offices to allow illegal immigrants to be issued driver's licenses effective in

December, Spitzer was criticized publicly by U.S. Homeland Security Chief Michael Chertoff. On October 21st, 2007, the New York State Senate voted to oppose the Spitzer plan by a 39 to 19 vote. Eight Democrats broke with Spitzer on the vote. After the vote the *New York Times* called this issue "Mr. Spitzer's single most unpopular decision since he took office." A Sienna College poll in November of 2007 showed 65 percent of New Yorkers opposed the policy and that it was endangering Spitzer's political future. The poll showed only 25 percent of New Yorkers would vote to elect him again. Spitzer had been elected by 69 percent of voters one year earlier. Nevertheless, after Spitzer announced he would withdraw the plan, he was still hammered by the press. The Associated Press termed this reversal a "surrender" and WCBS-TV labeled him "Governor Flip-Flop."[57] Four months after this fiasco, the scandal involving Spitzer's liaisons with a call girl ring broke. The weakened Governor resigned shortly afterward.

But Spitzer wasn't the first governor gravely damaged by his support for issuing driver's licenses to illegals. In what many believe was a desperate attempt to lock up the Hispanic vote in the heat of an election to recall him from office, former Democratic Governor of California Gray Davis signed such a provision into law in 2003. Needless to say, the measure was unpopular. According to a *Los Angeles Times* exit poll after the recall vote, even 38 percent of Hispanic Californians opposed it. Davis was removed from office and replaced by Arnold

Schwarzenegger, who had campaigned against giving illegal immigrants' driver's licenses.[58]

Barack Obama did not suffer the same fate as these two formidable politicians. It is possible that he didn't because Senator McCain chose not to make an issue of Obama's driver's license position, either out of an as yet unarticulated principle or out of fear of drawing the attention of his base to his own immigration liberalism. But during the general election there was a virtual blackout on this issue from the major media. Not a single reporter for a national newspaper or network or presidential debate moderator thought Obama's position on a subject that had been integral to the downfall of the Governors of the first and third largest states was worth informing the public about.

"Just air-raiding villages and killing civilians"

John Kerry suffered tremendous damage to his electoral prospects when it became widely believed, via the campaign of the "Swift Vets and POWs for the Truth," that he had slandered his fellow soldiers serving in Vietnam upon his return to the United States in 1971. At that time, Kerry joined a left wing group called the Vietnam Veterans Against the War and testified before the Senate Committee on Foreign Relations on April 22, 1971 that American troops "had personally raped, cut off ears, cut off heads, taped wires from portable telephones to human genitals and turned up the power, cut off limbs, blown up bodies, randomly shot at civilians, razed villages in a fashion reminiscent of Genghis Khan, shot cattle and dogs for fun, poisoned food stocks, and generally ravaged the countryside of South Vietnam." Kerry also accused the U.S. military of committing war crimes "on a day-to-day basis with the full awareness of officers at all levels of command."[59]

Kerry never provided documentation for these accusations, but he did campaign for president twenty-three years later in the company of a handful of Vietnam veterans to bolster his military credentials. Kerry also made his experience in the military a major theme in his speech at the Democratic convention that summer. In response, a group called the "Swift Vets" representing servicemen who, like Kerry, patrolled parts of Vietnam in small, agile gunboats, organized 250 veterans to go on the record questioning Kerry's fitness to serve as Commander-in-Chief. Members of the group taped commercials, raised money, and used direct mail to inform the public they believed that Kerry had behaved dishonorably in making unverified claims about the behavior of the American military in Vietnam. Many observers believe the "Swift Vets" campaign damaged Kerry badly. One of the lessons that the Obama campaign took from Kerry's defeat in the 2004 presidential race was that political attacks must be responded to quickly and thoroughly. "In the summer of 2004, John Kerry let a slowly building media campaign against his Vietnam War experience explode into a debacle," wrote political reporter Domenico Montenaro of MSNBC.

The Deracialized White Vote

"From that campaign came a new phrase to the political lexicon -- swift boating."[60]

But John McCain, himself a prisoner of war in Vietnam, could affect no such loss of confidence in candidate Obama, either with the media or with the public, for his unverified comments about the U.S. military, this time in Afghanistan. During an appearance before about 800 people in Nashua, New Hampshire on August 14th, 2007 Obama was asked -- in what was most likely a pre-arranged question -- whether he would move U.S. troops out of Iraq to "better fight terrorism elsewhere." Obama brought up Afghanistan, saying "We've got to get the job done there and that requires us to have enough troops so that we're not just air-raiding villages and killing civilians, which is causing enormous pressure over there."[61]

While not as severe, as detailed, or as graphic as the accusations made by John Kerry upon his return to the U.S. from Vietnam, Obama's remarks do represent something of a first for a modern major party presidential nominee. Even in the depths of the Vietnam war, left leaning anti-war candidates like Eugene McCarthy and George McGovern were careful not to make undocumented accusations of atrocities or civilian killings by the military they sought to lead. Obama showed no such discretion, and he paid no price for it. The McCain campaign ran ads featuring Obama's comments beginning in October before the election, and his Vice Presidential candidate Sarah Palin brought up Obama's comments during her nationally televised debate with Obama Vice President Joe Biden. But the issue had little traction with voters, and even less with the media. Of the approximately seventeen stories written in major national or world publications in all of 2008 on these comments, at least thirteen of them were efforts to discredit the McCain/Palin camp's representation of the comments. Article titles say it all: "McCain Spot Distorts Obama Comment about the Military" (*Washington Post*), "Beyond the Palin" (*New Yorker*), "Distortions of Obama's Votes and Comments on Wars" (*New York Times*).[62]

In the end, perhaps the greatest help the media provided Obama came simply in the volume of coverage they gave him, much of it even before he became a candidate for president. A study of network evening news coverage by the conservative Media Research Center found that on just the three major networks' evening news programs alone, there were a total of 1,365 stories on Obama beginning in May 2000 through the end of the Democratic primaries in June 2008. The study found that Obama received his best press as he debuted on the national scene, with all of the networks lavishing praise on him when he was keynote speaker at the 2004 Democratic convention. The network evening news shows "did not produce a single negative story about Obama (out of eighty-one total reports) prior to the start of his presidential campaign in early 2007," the report found. Moreover, the networks referred to Obama as a "rock star" more times (twenty-nine) than they referred to him as a liberal (fourteen).[63] With all of this coverage, most of it overwhelmingly positive when not adulatory, Obama was able to burnish an image of himself in the public mind as an intelligent, trustworthy, well spoken centrist with an even temperament, youthful good looks, and a serious but gentlemanly demeanor. This made it impossible for John McCain to convince the public of Obama's extreme positions and attitudes. By October 2008, the protective armor around Obama's image was impenetrable. McCain's television ads focusing on Obama's ill-considered comments about U.S. military operations in Afghanistan became the political equivalent of spitting into the wind.

Chapter 5

"OBAMA EUPHORIA" AND BLACK PARANOIA

The ramifications of what one writer has termed "Obama euphoria" among blacks, together with sensitivity over the treatment of black public figures, may involve serious racial strife. The power of racism in the black cultural narrative has resulted in almost impermeable lines of black solidarity with black public figures and elected officials, even when there are serious doubts about the performance or behavior of blacks in the public eye. The perceived racism that binds the black public to black celebrities has resulted in not only more uniform voting patterns among blacks than among other racial groups, but in a prickly defensiveness when black public figures are under attack.[1]

The potential for serious racial discord emanating from an Obama presidency given the importance for blacks of having black people in positions of power is obvious. Think of white incredulity at the re-election in 1999 of convicted, crack smoking mayor Marion Barry in mostly black Washington D.C. Think of the NAACP (and Bill Cosby) rallying to the side of race hoaxer Tawana Brawley in the 1980s. Think of whites looking on despondently while blacks leapt for joy at the acquittal of O.J. Simpson by a predominantly black jury.

Whites may very well be looking on despondently again. Immediately after the election, Juan Williams observed that there was fear among black people that criticism of Obama "or any of his failures might be twisted into evidence that people of color cannot effectively lead" and warned against "treating all criticism of Mr. Obama, whether legitimate, wrong headed or even mean spirited, as racist."[2]

It is too late for that admonition. Critics of President Obama's health care reform effort became among the first to be accused of attacking Obama's policies because of his race. Obama's incendiary former preacher, Reverend Jeremiah Wright, appeared on Fox News in September 2009 to remind Americans that opposition to health care reform is the product of the "racist right wing" upset that "poor people will be helped."[3] On August 31st of that year black congresswoman Diane Watson (D-CA) told a town hall meeting in Los Angeles that critics of Obama's health care reform proposal were essentially attacking the president because he is black. "So remember," representative Watson told her constituents before extolling the virtues of the Cuban health care system, "they are spreading fear and they're trying to see that the first president who looks like me, fails." Several days later Watson was joined by the powerful black chairman of the House Ways and Means committee, Congressman Charles Rangel of New York. At a health care forum in early September 2009, before having to step down from the Ways and Means committee over an ethics scandal, Rangel said "bias" and "prejudice" are fueling opposition to Obama's health care reform. "Some Americans have not gotten over the fact that Obama is president of the United States. They go to sleep wondering, 'how did this happen?'" Rangel also likened the fight to provide health care for the uninsured to the fight for civil rights. "Why do black people have to bargain for what is theirs? Why do we have to wait for the right to vote?" Rangel said. MSNBC's Carlos Watson wondered whether "socialism" is really about the nationalization of industry and hyper-regulation of the private market or whether it's just "becoming the new N-word."[4]

The suggestion by some blacks that racism is the motivation for criticism of the Obama administration is one of the more portentous developments of the Obama era. Blacks and whites already disagree on the extent and reach of racism in the United States. A Gallup poll from 2008 found that while 64 percent of blacks see racism as a "major factor" in low black education levels, only 32 percent of whites agree. Seventy-one percent of blacks see racism as a "major factor" impacting black income levels, while only 35 percent of whites do. And while 88 percent of blacks see racism as a "major factor" in black incarceration rates, 44 percent of whites see it the same way.[5] The racial divide over the magnitude and importance of racism in America will only be made deeper as unsubstantiated claims of racism against Obama critics become more numerous.

One particularly egregious case of race baiting by Obama supporters involved the resignation of federal "green jobs" czar Van Jones, appointed by Obama in August of 2009 to be a special advisor on the creation of jobs related to the development of "clean energy." Conservative critics, most notably Glenn Beck of Fox News, gleefully pointed out some facts about Jones's background that the mainstream media ignored: Jones signed a 2004 petition supporting the "9/11 truther" movement, which suspects Bush administration complicity in the 9/11 terrorist attacks; Jones was a self-professed communist during much of the 1990s; he supported cop killer Mumia abu-Jamal; in 2008 Jones accused "white polluters" of "steering poison into the people of color communities"; and early in 2009, speaking to a friendly crowd in Berkeley, California, Jones called Republicans "assholes," a phrase that would seem to contradict Obama's promise to "change the tone" in Washington.[6]

The public backlash against Jones made his continuation as "green jobs" czar untenable, and he resigned on September 6th, 2009. Black critics and other liberal pundits responded with outrage. Black columnist Mary Mitchell of the *Chicago Sun-Times* wrote that "Jones is being sacrificed in the same way the Reverend Wright was sacrificed," referring to Obama's belated break with the radical preacher during his campaign for president. "Beck and people like him can't seem to accept that John McCain lost the election and a black man and the people of his choosing are running the country." Probably without meaning to,

Mitchell shed light on the vast differences of perception dividing blacks and whites, excusing Jones's signature on the "9/11 truther" petition thusly: "As ridiculous as that might sound, a lot of black people distrusted Bush to the point that they thought anything was possible."[7]

No behavior on the part of Obama opponents, however bizarre or isolated, seems to fall outside the prism of race for Obama's supporters. In September of 2009 Obama gave his twenty-sixth speech on health care reform to a nationwide audience in front of the U.S. congress. During an interval after a portion of the speech in which Obama insisted that his proposal would "not apply to those who are here illegally," South Carolina Republican Congressman Joe Wilson blurted out "You lie!" Despite the lack of incriminating evidence and an immediate and thorough apology from Wilson, who clearly violated congressional etiquette, Obama supporters were adamant in attributing the outburst to Wilson's racism. Wilson "kind of winked at that element" of society that has shown disrespect to Obama because of his race, black Georgia Democrat Hank Johnson insisted. "He said it's o.k. We will probably have folks putting on white hoods and white uniforms again, riding through the countryside intimidating people," Johnson said. Another black lawmaker, Diane Watson of California, said she believed that Obama wouldn't have been heckled during his speech if he were white. "No other president in history has been called out in a joint session," Watson said. Congresswoman Eddie Bernice Johnson (D-Texas) chalked up the anger toward president Obama to racial tensions. "As far as African Americans are concerned," she claimed, "we think most of it is [racism]. And we think it's very unfortunate. We as African American people of course are very sensitive to it." Congresswoman Barbara Lee (D-CA), head of the Congressional Black Caucus, said that "today is about the civility and decorum of the House" and added that we "can't sweep race under the rug -- racism is still a factor and must be addressed." White Obama supporters also stumbled over each other to accuse Wilson and Obama opponents of racism. Columnist Maureen Dowd of the *New York Times* wrote "fair or not, what I heard was an unspoken word in the air: 'You lie, boy'!" Even former president Jimmy Carter said of Wilson's outburst "I think it's based on racism. There is an inherent feeling among many in this country that an African American should not be president." Under pressure from the Congressional Black Caucus, the House of Representatives passed a resolution along party lines rebuking Congressman Wilson for a "breach of decorum," the first time in the 220 year history of that body that such a rebuke was issued.[8]

Blacks have thus far shown no inclination to criticize Obama's fitness for or performance in office, and even the most serious disagreements they have with him on policy seem to matter little. Obama's support for "live birth" abortions while serving in the Illinois legislature didn't seem to bother black voters, a majority of whom are pro-life.[9] Black voters in California had no problem voting for a constitutional amendment banning gay marriage (70 percent voted for

California's Proposition 8), then voting for Obama, who publicly opposed the amendment. This too is consistent with a long established pattern: the unshakable commitment to big government and the Democratic party driven by black status anxiety renders the social positions of black elected officials irrelevant. In the words of writer Jeff Goldstein, "a sense of perceived 'commonality' based almost entirely on skin color and the requisite party affiliation that marks one as 'authentic' is what is, unfortunately, driving the voting habits of many blacks."[10]

Black circling of the wagons around the president promises to be a staple of the Obama era. Jesse Jackson's tears of pride during Obama's victory celebration in Chicago on election night, after he was overheard on a studio mike saying he wanted to "cut [Barack Obama's] balls off" the previous July, indicates that when push comes to shove even potential adversaries of Obama within black leadership circles will consider any differences among them mere family squabbles.

Word in February of 2009 that the predominantly non-white Ludlum Elementary School in Hempstead, New York became the first in the country to be renamed "Barack Obama Elementary School" (followed by schools in California, D.C., Maryland, New Jersey, Minnesota, and Pennsylvania), and that Perry County, Alabama, where a majority of its 12,000 residents are black, has created an annual "Barack Obama Day," give little hope blacks will evaluate Obama's presidency with cool disinterest. They are too heavily invested in its success. When Obama nominated Judge Sonia Sotomayor, the first Latina, for a seat on the Supreme Court, approval of the nomination was higher among blacks (85 percent) than it was among Hispanics (58 percent). Three months into Obama's term, a *New York Times* poll found that black Americans remained among Obama's staunchest supporters, with 70 percent saying the country is headed in the right direction, compared with 34 percent of whites.[11] The survey took place during a period in which the stock market remained well below its levels at the start of the year, the national unemployment rate had reached a twenty-five year high of 8.9 percent (before moving even higher), and Obama's national approval ratings were plummeting. While the nation's overall approval rating for the president dropped by around seventeen points over the first year of his term, Gallup analyst Jeffrey Jones noted that the one exception to this trend was among blacks, whose support for Obama had averaged 93 percent during his first year in office, and had been at or above 90 percent nearly every week during that period.[12]

There is little doubt that overwhelming black support for Obama is based on racial solidarity. Blacks had suffered the most of all voting blocs during the recession of 2007-2010, encompassing Obama's first two years in office. The jobless rate for young black men and women between sixteen and twenty-four years of age reached 30.5 percent in October 2009, while the rate for all races in that age group was 19.1 percent. The national unemployment rate for all groups was 10.2 percent while for blacks it was 15.7 percent. These disparities in employment aren't as stark as the racial disparities in income and wealth. Median net worth for black households dropped from $9,300 in 2007 to $2,200 in 2009, far less than the $98,000 owned by the typical white household. Median household income for blacks fell 7.2 percent from 2007 to 2009, significantly more than the 4.2 percent decline for whites, or the 4.9 percent for Hispanics, according to the Census Bureau.[13]

It is true, of course, that blacks have given Democratic presidents more intense support than whites. Bill Clinton averaged 55 percent job approval during his presidency, including 52 percent among whites, a much higher 76 percent among all non-whites, and 82 percent among blacks. But Clinton governed during a period of robust economic growth in which the black unemployment rate dropped to almost seven percent for the first time in several decades. "The political upshot is clear," wrote a blogger on the *National Review's* "Agenda" blog. "You'd expect that the hardest hit workers would be least inclined to give President Obama the benefit of the doubt. Instead, a large portion of the hardest hit workers are ardent Obama supporters."[14]

The racial divide goes even deeper than presidential approval ratings, according to Ron Brownstein of the *National Journal*. Brownstein noted an Allstate/*National Journal*/*Heartland Monitor* poll from September 2009 revealing sharply divergent attitudes between whites and non-white adults. Both whites and non-whites, for example, worried that young people won't match earlier generations' living standards, but whites were much more pessimistic about their own prospects. Two-thirds of whites believed that living standards for "people like me" won't grow as fast as they did for previous generations. Only about one-fourth of blacks and two-fifths of Hispanics agreed. Whites were not only more anxious, but also more alienated. Big majorities of whites said the prior year's turmoil had diminished their confidence in government, corporations, and the financial industry. Non-whites were also sour on the private sector but were much less disillusioned with government. Asked which institution they trust most to make economic decisions in their interest, a plurality of whites older than thirty years of age picked "none." By contrast, a majority of blacks and a plurality of Hispanics chose elected officials in Washington. On other questions about government's role, whites and minorities veered apart. Only four in ten whites said they support the health care reform legislation wending its way through congress in the fall of 2009, compared with three-fourths of non-whites. And just 30 percent of whites, compared with 45 percent of non-whites, said that an Obama-like agenda of public investment in education and technology offers the nation its best chance at long term prosperity. Far more whites than non-whites would bet on a conservative approach of tax cuts and deregulation. The starkest finding of all was that three-fifths of non-whites (including three-fourths of blacks) believed that Obama's agenda will increase opportunities for people like them; but a plurality of whites -- 38 percent -- said his agenda will decrease their opportunities. "That statistic clearly reflects Obama's pull," Brownstein concluded. "In the long term, it's difficult to overstate the challenge either party would face in governing a country where the white majority and burgeoning non-white minority are moving in such diametrical directions. Red, as in 'danger ahead,' is the color that should be flashing from these results."[15]

The impact on race relations of black stridency when it comes to President Obama is difficult to assess, but there are signs of problems. In March 2009 frustrated black lawmakers staged a walkout after the Georgia state legislature decided to delay a vote on a resolution that would have honored Obama as a politician with an "unimpeachable reputation for integrity, vision and passion" and made him an honorary member of the black caucus. Supporters of the resolution, who said it would have been the first such action in the country, claimed white Republican legislators were trying to snub the nation's first black president. "It drips with racism," said state representative Al Williams, a Democrat who joined about two dozen black lawmakers outside the chamber.[16]

Skeptics and well wishers alike were cheered by polling before and after the election that found the percentage of blacks who said race relations were "generally good" increased from 29 percent in July 2008 to 59 percent in April 2009. But the temporary convergence of blacks and whites toward an optimistic view of race relations said more about the historic enormity of electing the first black president than it does about public policy preferences. By June, in the fifth month of Obama's presidency, the optimism had dissipated considerably. A CNN/*Essence Magazine*/Opinion Research Corporation poll found that 55 percent of blacks believed racial discrimination was a serious problem, an increase from 38 percent during the 2008 presidential campaign, and about the same percentage as in 2000. A Rasmussen poll in October 2010 found that the initial boost in racial optimism generated by Obama's election had disappeared, especially among blacks. Just 36 percent of voters said relations between blacks and whites were getting better, down from 62 percent in July of 2009. Thirty-nine percent of whites thought black-white relations were getting better, but just 13 percent of blacks agreed.[17]

While most Americans may not be aware of it, black and white Americans have sharp differences in opinion and outlook, and Obama's presidency will likely make more people conscious of them. A report from the National Association for the Advancement of Colored People in 2007 found that two-thirds of blacks felt the federal government should make reparations payments to the descendants of slaves. A mere 7 percent of whites agreed. The report also found that a strong majority of blacks (80 percent) said they would "likely" or "definitely" support a candidate who defends affirmative action, while less than half of whites held this view. When "racial preferences" is substituted for the more opaque "affirmative action," an overwhelming majority of whites are opposed.[18] A *Washington Post*-Kaiser Foundation poll of black men conducted in 2006 found that half claimed to have been treated unfairly by the police, and a clear majority said the economic system is "stacked against blacks." Sixty percent reported they are often the targets of racial slights or insults, two-thirds said they believe the courts are more likely to convict black men than whites, and a quarter claimed they have been physically threatened or attacked because they are black. Obviously, these experiences and perceptions lead to huge racial differences of opinion on matters like mandatory sentencing, the death penalty, felon re-enfranchisement, and racial profiling. This is in line with racial differences of opinion over the role of government in welfare, housing, and education, which surveys also find.[19]

The intensity with which blacks cling to an identity grounded in racial grievance gives little hope that electing America's first black president will uproot it. For many blacks, writes Hoover Institute psychologist Shelby Steele, "to say simply that one is no longer racially aggrieved will surely feel like an act of betrayal that threatens to cut one off from community, family and history."[20] The kind of defensiveness that derives from this identity makes it difficult for blacks to dispense with the notion that levels of racial discrimination remain prohibitively high. Shortly after Obama's inauguration, the Pew Center for the People and the Press conducted its bi-annual survey of American attitudes and beliefs. It found that only 30 percent of blacks agree that discrimination is rare. And while large majorities of both whites (59 percent) and blacks (66 percent) disagree, about twice as many blacks "completely disagree" that discrimination is rare (30 percent vs. 14 percent of whites).[21]

The chasm is wider for the black leadership class, which finds it almost impossible to relinquish the model of political grievance they inherited from the postwar civil rights generation. There is much to lose if they do: political power and access; massive social service bureaucracies with endless patronage opportunities; non-profit institutions, private philanthropies, think tanks, university departments, centers, museums, and libraries awash in public and private dollars. There are television programs, public radio stations, film production companies, magazines, and newspapers, all organized around the centrality of racism in American life. To be sure, a large cache of inoffensive jargon now exists to camouflage the enormous sums of money committed to sustaining the ideology of black victimization. In 2008, the Foundation Coalition, an umbrella group of California's largest foundations, pledged hundreds of millions of dollars to support "capacity building" and "leadership development activities" of minority led institutions. The "criteria for philanthropy at its best" set forth by the authoritative National Committee for Responsive Philanthropy says that "non-profits should provide at least 50 percent of their grant dollars to benefit lower-income communities, communities of color, and other marginal groups." But whatever the phrases or terms deployed, the implication is clear: significant portions of the nation's commercial and cultural capital must be set aside to address the uniquely debilitating circumstances of black Americans.[22]

Obama's election has done nothing to curb racial defensiveness, apparent in even the highest profile black celebrities, many of whom have been lionized by white audiences, producers, and critics throughout their careers. When pop superstar Michael Jackson died amid drug abuse allegations in June of 2009, Black Entertainment Television held a tribute at which black rapper Sean "Diddy" Combs complained about racially biased media coverage, telling a CNN reporter "The way you're all reportin' on this man's life. You know, we didn't do Elvis like that. We didn't do JFK like that. This man is like, you know, one of the greatest heroes for us. He's one of the reasons Barack Obama is president." Jamie Foxx, who won a best actor Oscar for his roll as music great Ray Charles in 2004's *Ray*, angrily claimed Jackson for the black race, which generously shared the racially ambivalent performer with white America. Before the live, mostly black BET audience, Foxx harangued the media for assuming that Jackson's history of skin bleaching and plastic surgery was an effort to erase his black identity. "He belongs to *us*," Foxx pronounced authoritatively. "And we shared him with everybody else. They talk about how he looks in the media. It don't matter what he look like."[23]

The month after Jackson's death, an even more bewildering episode involving elite black rage transpired: the arrest for disorderly conduct of famed Harvard University black studies professor Henry Louis

Gates, Jr. Gates was arrested in his Cambridge home after a female passer-by noticed Gates and his driver attempting to pry open the front door of Gates' home. Believing it to be a burglary, the Samaritan called Cambridge police, who arrived to find Gates "exhibiting loud and tumultuous behavior," repeatedly shouting at a policeman as onlookers gathered on the street in front of his house watched, refusing to initially provide identification, and generally being uncooperative. Gates, who had locked himself out of his house after spending a week in China, maintained that he was "racially profiled" by a "rogue policeman" who "couldn't stand a black man standing up for his rights." Accounts of the event differ, but neither side denies that when asked to step outside of his home so the police could explain what they were doing there, the typically demure college professor yelled "Yeah, I'll speak with your mama outside." The entire incident became a national scandal on July 22nd, 2009 when President Obama rather unceremoniously waded into the matter at a news conference on health care reform, saying the Cambridge city police "acted stupidly" and prompting calls for an apology from police unions and their supporters around the country. Gates himself demanded an apology from Sgt. James Crowley, the arresting officer who, it turns out, had taught a class on race and police work at the Lowell Police Academy for five years. The class, which Crowley taught with a black police officer, instructed about sixty police cadets per year in the subtleties of policing "communities of color." Cadets spent twelve hours in the class, and Crowley was hand picked to teach the class by former Cambridge police commissioner Ronny Watson, who is black. The officer had also been credited earlier in his career with performing emergency cardiac care in a failed attempt to resuscitate black NBA basketball great Reggie Lewis, whose widow praised the law officer for doing everything he could to save her husband.[24]

But whether or not the Cambridge police acted properly in arresting Gates (the charges were quickly dropped), the incident was notable for the spectacle of someone with Gates' status immediately striking the pose of victim. A friend of president Obama's and one of the most highly paid academics in America, Gates flatly claimed that Crowley "presumed that I was guilty because I was black. There was no doubt about that." The fact that, at the time of his arrest, the city of Cambridge had a black mayor and was located in a state with a black Governor in a country with a black president (all three of whom came out vocally on Gates' side), had no bearing on Gates' perception. Neither did the fact that one of the arresting officers was black or that the Cambridge police department has been said to be as diverse as the city it serves: "[W]e have a black commissioner, female deputies, black deputies, gay officers," one officer was quoted as saying.[25] Nor had Gate's own quite favorable treatment by the academy and society at large weighed on the perception of his own powerlessness. Gates was the first black to receive the Andrew W. Mellon Foundation Fellowship and, in 2002, he was selected to give the Jefferson Lecture, the most prestigious honor in American humanities. Gates sits on the boards of many notable arts, cultural, and research institutions, and has had tens of millions of grant dollars lavished upon him as Director of the W. E. B. Du Bois Institute for African and African American Research at Harvard, which Gates himself called "the largest, finest, and richest research institute for African and African American studies in the world." Yet in his interaction with Sgt. Crowley, Gates saw himself not as an academic superstar, but as a representative of the aggrieved black underclass.[26]

Gates broke sharply with the belief that Obama's election represented a new post-racial America, using the publicity stemming from his arrest to assure Americans that the country was still immersed in racial bigotry despite having elected a black president. "What is most important," Gates told an interviewer, "is that this be a 'teaching moment'; a chance to disabuse Americans of the notion that we live in a 'post-racial society' because of the election of Barack Obama. America is just as classist and just as racist as it was the day before the elections."[27]

The Gates episode was only the most visible evidence since Obama's rise to power that many high status blacks have much more to gain from identity politics than from a color blind America. From the start of Obama's presidential campaign black intellectuals have been in a kind of panic about the possibility that electing a black president might put an end to the racial spoils regime. Paul Street, author of the book

Barack Obama and the Future of American Politics, told a CNN reporter before the election that Obama risks becoming an Oval Office version of talk show host Oprah Winfrey. "They're cited as proof that racism is no longer a significant barrier to black advancement and interracial equality," Street said. "This isn't new. Go to the nineteenth-century, and Southern aristocrats would point to a certain African American landowner who was doing well to prove that whites are not racist."[28]

Andra Gillespie, an assistant professor of political science at Emory University, has insisted that Obama's success doesn't mean America has become a post-racial society. Gillespie makes the point that systemic racism, not individual racism, is the primary cause of inequality in America, and that having a black president does nothing directly to ensure improvement for substandard public schools and "disproportionate" rates of black imprisonment. "Electing a black president does not mean that America is ready to take on systemic racism," Gillespie told one blogger. "People could say if Barack [Obama] can succeed and someone can't get off of the stoops in the hood, it's their fault, and it has nothing to do with systemic racism." Gillespie's fear was echoed by Glen Ford, executive editor of the online journal *blackagendareport.com*, who wrote that Obama's presidency might offer some white Americans an easy solution to the country's most stubborn dilemma. "Millions of whites came to believe Obama could solve the 'race problem' by his mere presence, at no cost to their own notions of skin privilege," Ford wrote in an essay in January of 2008.[29]

The notion that many whites voted for Obama, or didn't object all that much to his election, precisely because it might result in a measure of racial redemption did not escape the view of some conservative writers as well. Shelby Steele has written that Obama tapped into a deep longing on the part of whites to escape the stigma of racism. "In running for the presidency . . . [Obama] knew whites were stigmatized as being prejudice, and that they hated this situation and literally longed for ways to disprove the stigma."[30]

Steve Sailer, a columnist for the *American Conservative* magazine, has written that some whites who supported Obama were driven by a desire to purchase some "White Guilt Repellent" and put racial issues behind them. "They hope that when a black finally moves into the White House, it will prove to African Americans, once and for all, that white animus isn't the cause of their troubles. All blacks have to do is to act like President Obama -- and their problems will be over."[31]

Until the Gates affair, Obama had skillfully crafted an image of racial neutrality which helped him avoid becoming the nation's first "black" president, someone specifically identified as serving black interests or symbolizing black cultural affinity. The fact that blacks and whites on the campaign trail saw Obama's racial identity differently is testimony to his success in playing to both sides of a still deep political and cultural divide. Nia-Malika Henderson has written that Obama benefited during the campaign and afterward from "dog-whistle politics." "His language, mannerisms and symbols resonate deeply with his black supporters, even as the references largely sail over the heads of white audiences," Henderson wrote, pointing to Obama's pre-inaugural visit to Ben's Chili Bowl, a landmark for Washington's black community. When Obama was asked by a cashier if he wanted his change back he replied, "Nah, we straight." According to Henderson, the video of this exchange became an internet craze on black oriented web sites, yet the white reporter on pool duty misquoted Obama as saying, "No, we're straight." Henderson never considered that a white pool reporter could edit black slang out of reported Obama quotes in an effort to make Obama more palatable to whites. But it is true that Obama often uses coded references to black history that have special meaning to blacks, but not to most whites. While campaigning in South Carolina, for example, Obama attempted to extinguish the persistent rumors that he is Muslim by telling a predominantly black crowd that "They try to bamboozle you, hoodwink you," an unmistakable reference to the speeches of Malcolm X. "Beyond speech," writes Henderson "blacks have picked up certain of Obama's mannerisms, particularly his walk, that signal authenticity. Bush had his cowboy strut, and Obama has a swagger -- a rhythmic lope that says cool and confident and undeniably black."[32]

Typically, there is great risk in cultivating support among two very different voting blocs with this kind of signification. President Bush, who used certain phrases in order to connect deeply with Christian Evangelicals while not offending more secular voters, fostered tremendous resentment when his actions -- the nomination of his old friend and political centrist Harriet Meiers for the Supreme Court -- did not live up to his words. While he withdrew the nomination, Bush never fully regained his standing with devoutly Christian voters. But Obama does not face this risk. Blacks have already demonstrated a willingness to permit him extremely wide latitude when it comes to specific policies. The sensation of having a black person occupy the oval office, a black person not only of body but of mind, is too euphoric for most blacks to turn sharply against the President.

Thus far Obama has taken several crucial, though comparatively subtle, steps that have served to meet the demands of identity politics. They include his early foray into Latin America, dominated as it was by an attempt to make common cause with the non-whites of that region; his selection of the first Latina, and racial preference champion, for the Supreme Court; his black Attorney General's call for a national "dialogue on race," and his decision to drop charges of "voter intimidation" against the New Black Panther Party; Obama's racially exclusionary video appeal to non-whites in a Democratic National Committee ad for the 2010 elections; his decision to sue the state of Arizona over its immigration enforcement law, labeling it "racial profiling"; and Obama's own comments in support of professor (and, apparently, gangbanger) Henry Louis Gates, Jr.

As the 2012 election shapes up Obama has shown that he intends to indulge the racial grievance proclivities of black and, perhaps more broadly, Hispanic voters. In May of 2011, Obama drew the ire of police departments nationwide when he and his wife Michelle played host at the White House to the rapper Common, who had praised convicted cop killers, and the poet Jill Scott, who had previously condemned inter-racial marriage. The day before this poetry reading event, Obama spoke to a predominantly Hispanic crowd in Texas to paint the Republicans as anti-immigrant. In front of a majority Hispanic audience Obama chided those who insist on strengthening border security before passing a broad amnesty for illegal immigrants, saying "Maybe they'll need a moat. Maybe they'll want alligators in the moat."[33]

In April of 2011 Obama attended the Reverend Al Sharpton's National Action Network's Twentieth Anniversary and National Convention. Sharpton has long been known for his confrontational marches and his demands for corrective action for perceived racial injustices. Many politicians have avoided appearing with Sharpton because of his role in several disturbing racial episodes, the most notorious being the 1987 Tawana Brawley case. Brawley, a black Wappinger, New York teenager, claimed she was abducted and sexually assaulted by at least three white men, some of them police officers. A grand jury refused to indict anyone, and Sharpton and other local civil rights leaders were found guilty of defamation as a result of pointing fingers at a specific police officer. Obama's decision to shore up his support among blacks by rubbing shoulders with Sharpton could prove controversial as the election draws closer, but was designed to sure up his base among black activists.[34]

More problematic may be Attorney General Holder's approach to the redistricting process for congressional and state legislative seats under way with the release of the 2010 census. All redistricting plans produced by states must meet the "one person, one vote" equal protection standard established by the Supreme Court, which means that districts are supposed to be as even in population as possible. But redistricting must also comply with the Voting Rights Act, and Holder's Civil Rights Division released a 2011 report indicating that sixteen states will now have the burden of proving their redistricting plans will not have any "discriminatory effect," a very broad standard. Under the Justice Department's "Guidance Concerning Redistricting Under Section 5 of the Voting Rights Act," Holder could deny "pre-clearance" of redistricting plans if it finds "direct or circumstantial evidence" of a "discriminatory purpose." Former Justice Department official Hans Spakovsky has concluded from this that "the Holder Justice Department's opposition to race neutral enforcement of the law over the last two years suggests that redistricting may touch off contentious court battles over the rule of law."[35]

These racially tinged activities, while ostensibly taken to appease black voters, run the greater risk of alienating whites, many of whom made a critical "bargain" with Obama which they believe included his dispensing with the angry, left wing politics of urban America. As early as the Gates affair, there was evidence that Obama's race neutral veneer was not going to wear well. In entering the Gates affair in support of a racial narrative that presumes racism on the part of white males, Obama proffered a viewpoint at odds with the majority of non-black voters. The visceral demands for an apology from the president for saying the Cambridge police "acted stupidly" from so many quarters suggests that most non-blacks subscribe to a narrative far more racially neutral, a narrative that allows for the possibility that minority males are disproportionately stopped by police because they are more likely to commit felonies, and that at least some complaints about racism by privileged blacks may stem from an exaggerated sense of racial entitlement.[36]

Even before the Gates affair, Obama had taken racially risky steps, such as the kind that have emboldened the Congressional Black Caucus, a group that brooks little concern for how its radical positions -- not to mention its name and exclusive membership rules -- might look to white Americans. In early April, 2009, his second full month in office, Obama ended limits on family travel and money transfers by Cuban Americans in the United States to Cuba, and permitted some telecommunications business trade between the two countries. The same week, six members of the Congressional Black Caucus traveled to Cuba and met with its Marxist rulers Raúl and Fidel Castro. Now, according to the authoritative *Black Book of Communism*, more than 100,000 Cubans have served time for political offenses in Cuba's equivalent of the Soviet Gulag Archipelago since Castro came to power in 1959. Among those singled out for persecution have been human rights activists, homosexuals, and religious believers.[37] But that didn't stop long time Castro apologist and black caucus member Bobby Rush from explaining after meeting Raúl Castro that what "endeared me to him was his keen sense of humor, his sense of history and his basic human qualities." As the *Miami Herald* reported, the black representatives found Castro to be "very engaging, very energetic . . . very talkative."[38]

Obama also donned the cloak of the "black president" at the Summit of the Americas in April 2009. Though Obama is not a descendant of slaves, lived a relatively privileged life growing up in Indonesia and Hawaii, and attended a prep school and two Ivy League colleges, he drew on his race as evidence of his affinity for the region's poor.[39] Obama associated himself closely with Latin America's indigenous, black and mixed race underclass and politely sat through strong anti-U.S. criticism from hostile leaders like Venezuela's Hugo Chávez and Bolivia's Evo Morales. In his opening speech, Obama said "We have to stand up against any force that separates any of our people from that story of liberty -- whether it's crushing poverty or corrosive corruption; social exclusion or persistent racism or discrimination. Here in this room, and on this dais, we see the diversity of the Americas."[40]

In the long run, though, Obama's nomination of Latina jurist Sonia Sotomayor to the Supreme Court may do the most to threaten his image as a "post-racial" healer. The nomination and subsequent senate approval of this second circuit court judge, a woman who has spoken of her preference for the "better conclusions" arrived at by Latina judges over white judges, who believes that inherited physiological differences are central to a judge's ability to reason, and who has favored the distribution of jobs on the basis of race, symbolizes Obama's troubling lack of imagination in envisioning how a post-racial America should look. "In selling himself as a candidate to the American public he is a gifted bargainer," writes Shelby Steele, "beautifully turned out in post-racial impressionism. But in the real world of Supreme Court nominations . . . he chooses a hardened, divisive and race focused veteran of the culture wars he claims to transcend."[41]

Chapter 6

OBAMA'S RADICALISM AND THE DAMAGE TO NATIONAL UNITY

Evaluating presidential qualifications is a difficult exercise that rarely escapes the pitfalls of political partisanship. People get promoted in electoral politics from a wide variety of circumstances without the benefit of competitive qualifying exams, so few subjective measures are available. Yet the uniqueness of Barack Obama's candidacy and the role played by racial sympathy may have permanently compromised the protean, but nevertheless real criteria by which presidents have historically been selected. America's civic life, in particular the unifying power of the presidency, will be seriously eroded as a result.

This is not to imply that Barack Obama did not "earn" the presidency. Anyone capable of conducting a successful campaign for the most powerful office in the world -- dispensing with the Clinton political machine along the way – likely possesses talents in excess of what would be necessary for the job. But Obama's ability is not in question. What is in question is the basis upon which that ability was evaluated by the public. For, as author James Fallows has explained -- in rather direct contrast to Obama's self-proclaimed skill as a "uniter" -

- "America's radius of trust is expanded not by racial unity but by the belief that everyone is playing by the same rules."[1]

There is ample evidence that Obama did not -- and even now does not -- need to play by the same rules as previous presidential candidates or presidents. In terms of experience, for example, every single elected president of the past century has served more than six years as a federal legislator or has served in an executive capacity in a federal agency -- including the military and as Vice President -- or as governor of a state. Obama has done none of these things, necessitating his supporters to lead with the salvo that Obama possesses a "first class temperament." And while every major party presidential nominee in American history until recently was, in part, selected on condition that they not possess black skin, none has ever benefited from their whiteness in a head-to-head race against a non-white, as Obama benefited from his blackness (Obama won 54 percent of voters who said race was a factor in their vote and 58 percent who said race was the most important factor -- see Figure 4). Certainly, at any rate, no candidate in the postwar era has ever had a close public relationship with a preacher of ethnic and religious intolerance, as Obama had had with Jeremiah Wright. It is also worth noting that the Wright imbroglio is far from the only event or activity in Obama's life about which almost nothing was known before the campaign and about which strenuous efforts were made by the Obama campaign and a friendly media to ignore. The media's lack of curiosity in Obama's enigmatic background as a "community organizer" and as a back bench Illinois legislator, among other things -- Stanley Kurtz has called 1996 to 2004 "Barack Obama's Lost Years" -- seems to run counter to the intense public scrutiny that typically goes with the vetting of presidential candidates.

One needn't be a conspiracy theorist to be astounded by how few details about Obama's past were known with certainty at the time of his election and continuing through his term in office. When he became a serious presidential contender, Obama's public record was trifling, and what it did entail was ambiguous. Obama managed to squeeze 850 pages of autobiography from his personal history, but that effort did not result in a reliable factual record. Indeed, Obama has shown a disturbing inclination to misrepresent his past and to hide his motives for doing so. We know now, for example, that the description in his first book of how he came to be a community organizer is mostly fiction. In his job with an "international consulting" company, Obama explained in *Dreams from My Father,* he had his "own office, my own secretary, money in the bank," before leaving for a low paying entry level position with a Chicago non-profit.[2] But the image of Obama as a principled, self-sacrificing servant of the masses turns out to be mostly false. Dan Armstrong, one of Obama's former co-workers and a supporter, has written that "I certainly know what he did there, and it bears only a loose resemblance to what he wrote in his book . . . it wasn't a consulting house." According to Armstrong, by all accounts a credible source, Obama's job was to get copy from overseas correspondents and edit it so that it fit into a standard outline, a form of copyediting. "I'm sure we all wished that we were high priced consultants to multinational corporations," Armstrong continued, "But we also enjoyed . . . bonding over the low salaries and heavy workload." Not unexpectedly, this wholly unnecessary embellishment was unearthed by bloggers at *Sweetness and Light,* and was mostly ignored by the mainstream media.[3]

If the media ignored inconsistencies in Obama's biographies they also paid a curious inattention to the parts of his life that were conspicuously left out of them. Little is known, for example, about the four years from 1995 to 1999 that Obama served as the first chairman of the board of the Chicago Annenberg Challenge (CAC) education foundation, or his additional years on that board until 2001. It would stand to reason that a presidential candidate with no executive experience would want to publicize even the most insignificant leadership activities in his past. But Obama makes no mention of his role at CAC in either of his two autobiographies. That may be because University of Illinois archives show that Obama and former Weather Underground terrorist William Ayers worked as a team to advance the CAC agenda, including shoveling $100 million into the hands of "community organizers" like ACORN and other radical activists. Ayers founded CAC with two other education "reformers" in an effort to translate his radicalism into practice. Although funding came from politically diverse sources (Walter Annenberg, now deceased, was a former Nixon appointed ambassador), one of CAC's own in-house evaluations noted that CAC was a "founder-led foundation." This made Ayers the most powerful individual at the foundation, allowing him to hand select Obama as its first board chairman. Essentially, CAC's approach to education subordinated achievement in math and science to the imperative of political activism, to making, in Ayers own words, "new generations of militant activists and organizers." Predictably, the effort failed miserably to help inner city students. In-house evaluators comprehensively studied the effects of its grants on the test scores of Chicago public school students and found no evidence of educational improvement: "There were no statistically significant differences in student achievement between Annenberg schools and demographically similar non-Annenberg schools. This indicates that there was no Annenberg effect on achievement," the report found. The report also indicated that the campaign failed because CAC's heavily politicized "community organizer partners" didn't know much about improving educational performance.[4]

In the simplest terms, the Chicago Annenberg Challenge stood as Barack Obama's most important executive experience prior to his being elected president and it was, by its own account, largely a failure. Yet aside from a question by moderator George Stephanopoulos during a single primary season debate sponsored by ABC, the three broadcast networks paid no attention to Obama's leadership role with CAC, or to his relationship with Ayers. Out of 1,365 broadcast evening news stories about Obama prior to the end of the primaries, only two mentioned Ayers. During the general election, broadcast networks did not present a single in-depth report on Obama's relationship with Ayers.[5]

It is no surprise that Ayers would pick Obama to preside over the distribution of monies to organizations that would include Ayers' own "Small School Network." Obama had already burnished his radical political credentials by announcing his run for the Illinois state senate in 1995-1996 at Ayers' town house in Hyde Park, and by joining the New Party, a creation of the Democratic Socialists of America. The New Party was a mid-1990s effort to build a socialist coalition to the left of the Democratic party, uniting wealthy white leftists, racial minorities, militant unionists, and idealistic young people. New Party luminaries include radical historian Howard Zinn, linguist and anti-Zionist Noam Chomsky, the feminist Gloria Steinem, and best selling anti-capitalist author Barbara Ehrenreich. ACORN was clearly the main force behind the New Party chapter in Chicago, where the party won its biggest victories. In 1995, the newsletter of the Chicago Chapter of Democratic Socialists of America, *New Ground,* noted "In Chicago, the New Party's biggest asset and biggest liability is ACORN." And Obama's ties to ACORN run deep. In 1992, ACORN hired Obama to run a voter registration effort known as the "motor voter" program, which fought to make voter registration automatic for any resident who drives a car, even those who can't prove citizenship or who have served time for a felony. He later became a "trainer" for ACORN, as well as its lawyer in election law cases, leading Chicago ACORN leader Toni Foulkes to refer to Obama during the 2004 U.S. senate primary as "the candidate we hold dear." Foulkes explained that she asked Obama to participate "in our leadership training sessions to run the session on power every year," though it is unclear whether the $190,000 ACORN received from the Woods Foundation between 2000 and 2002 (years Obama served on that foundation's board) had anything to do with the invitation, or with Obama's exhortation, when running for president, that "I've been fighting alongside ACORN on issues you care about my entire career."[6]

Nevertheless, while big media outlets like the *Los Angeles Times*, MSNBC, and the *New York Times* all featured reports on the speculation, later proven false, that Republican Vice Presidential candidate Sarah Palin's husband Todd had once belonged to the Alaska Independence Party (which wanted Alaska to secede from the U.S.), the story of Obama's very real membership in the New Party and his long association with ACORN was never fully rendered. This was despite the fact that Obama's presidential campaign paid more than $800,000 to ACORN for "get-out-the vote efforts" at almost the same time the group came under at least eleven separate investigations across the country for voter fraud. ACORN was convicted of falsifying signatures in a voter registration drive in Washington State in 2007. In 2009, a Democrat controlled congress withdrew federal funding to ACORN after video tape emerged showing ACORN staff giving advice on how to get government funding for such illegal activities as prostitution and committing fraud.[7]

Given that Obama's primary claim on the presidency was his compelling life story, the media showed surprisingly little interest in several other parts of Obama's life that might have concerned voters, including his foreign excursions. Nowhere in his biographies does Obama mention his 1981 trip to Pakistan, where he stayed with influential political leaders from that country at a time when a State Department advisory warned U.S. citizens against travel to Pakistan.[8] There was also a strange disinterest in Obama's 2006 trip to Kenya where, as a sitting U.S. senator, Obama criticized the incumbent government (a U.S. ally) and barnstormed with a Marxist candidate he supported. It is highly unusual for an American elected official to directly interfere in a foreign election. But only later was it discovered that the candidate Obama supported made a secret agreement with Islamists to convert Kenya to *sharia* law if the party won. Upon losing the election Obama's candidate presided over a political party that rioted, committed murder, and displaced thousands of Kenyans.[9]

Some of the missing details of Obama's life are doubtlessly trivial. Obama probably has benign explanations for not providing more information about them. But there is a troubling sense of calculation emanating from the gaps in the official record. Given that President George W. Bush and Sens. Al Gore and John Kerry paid no political price for releasing their mediocre college grades, for example, it is unclear why Obama has prohibited the release of his academic records from Occidental College, Columbia University, and Harvard University, including his master's thesis from Columbia and other written work. It is possible the critic Andrew Breitbart is correct when he postulates that Obama may have "committed himself to a radical curriculum . . . and sought to keep this biographical information from his political enemies . . . for fear that they would paint the former . . . follower of the Rev. Jeremiah Wright as something other than an advocate of racial reconciliation." But Obama could easily put an end to all speculation simply by releasing his transcripts. That he hasn't yet done so is a testament to his inexplicable penchant for secrecy, and the latitude the media and much of the public have been willing to cede him.[10]

One of the functions of the media is to protect the public from fraudulent statements made by public figures. The unwillingness of the media to fulfill this role in the case of Obama has led to significant, and probably needless, public tension. Obama's prolonged resistance to releasing the long version of his birth certificate, for example, served not only to raise legitimate speculation about the circumstances surrounding his birth, but to give fodder to anti-Obama extremists. According to Vanderbilt University Law Professor and Obama supporter Carol Swain, "I think that by not releasing it [the full birth certificate], it makes people much more passionately opposed to the president . . . Moreover, for a president who was elected on the basis of his personal background, it is troubling that Obama himself would want to withhold such basic information." Before Obama finally released his full birth certificate under pressure from billionaire builder Donald Trump in 2011, even a supporter like professor Swain concluded that his fierce resistance to doing so "suggests there's something that the president has decided not to share with the public."[11]

While the long form of Obama's birth certificate offers solid proof, as did most of the evidence available previously, that Obama was born in Hawaii and is an American citizen, eligible to hold the office of president, it does nothing to explain Obama's curious relationship to Islam. This relationship would, of course, constitute a potentially important measure of presidential outlook that voters should want to know and that, in Obama's case, remains ambiguous.

Obama doesn't appear to have chosen Islam as his formal religion at any time in his adult life. But questions about his Islamic background, his relationship to his mother's husbands, and hence even any other name he might have once formally been known by remain subjects of speculation. Before the release of the long form birth certificate, former CIA officer Larry Johnson speculated that the full record from the State of Hawaii might have been amended in 1968 to show that Obama was adopted by the Indonesian Muslim Lolo Soetoro and became formally known for a time as "Barry Soetoro."[12]

It is not clear why Obama refused to yield information that could have put these matters to rest earlier, or why the media did not demand it. But it was not unreasonable to assume that it had something to do with Obama's desire to keep his past association with Islam malleable for political advantage, something he has done with impunity. When he was running for the Democratic nomination, Obama's middle name "Hussein" was a celebrated asset. "Well, I think if you've got a guy named Barack Hussein Obama, that's a pretty good contrast to George W. Bush," Mr. Obama told PBS's Tavis Smiley on October 18th, 2007.[13] When his vaguely Islamic mien became burdensome, Obama set about branding any mention of his middle name an insidious form of intolerance. It was "just making stuff up," Obama said during his battle for the Democratic nomination with Hillary Clinton, for people "to say that, you know, maybe he's got Muslim connections." "The only connection I've had to Islam," the candidate insisted, "is that my grandfather on my father's side came from [Kenya]. But I've never practiced Islam." The nation's most circulated daily newspaper *USA Today* went so far as to claim that Obama's Kenyan grandmother is a Christian -- even though a year earlier the *New York Times* had described the same woman, 85 year old Sara Hussein Obama, as a "lifelong Muslim" who proclaimed "I am a strong believer of the Islamic faith."[14]

Andrew C. McCarthy, a former federal prosecutor who tried the Islamist terrorists responsible for planning and executing the 1993 attack on the World Trade Center, has written that most of the available information suggests Obama was raised as a Muslim for at least some of the years he was in Indonesia, the world's most populous Muslim country. It is also likely that he attained Indonesian citizenship, something that would had to have been done through adoption by his mother's second husband, the Indonesian Muslim Lolo Soetoro Mangunharjo. While his citizenship in that country would have lapsed when he left as a young boy, the records of the Catholic school and the public school Obama attended during his last year in Indonesia identify him as a Muslim. As Obama relates in *Dreams from My Father*, he took Koran classes. Children in Indonesia generally attend religious instruction in accordance with their family's chosen faith. Moreover, acquaintances recall that Obama occasionally attended Friday prayers at the local mosque, and Maya Soetoro-Ng, Obama's half-sister (born after Lolo and Ann moved the family to Jakarta), told the *New York Times* "My whole family was Muslim, and most of the people I knew were Muslim." In fact, back in March 2007 when Obama was still selling his Muslim bonafides to the far left of the Democratic party, the candidate shared with *New York Times* columnist Nicholas Kristof his memories of the muezzin's Arabic call to prayer: "one of the prettiest sounds on earth at sunset." Kristof marveled at the "first rate accent" with which Obama was able to recite its first paragraph.[15]

Nevertheless, Obama vehemently denied any Muslim connection after winning the Democratic nomination. "My father was basically agnostic, as far as I can tell, and I didn't know him," Obama claimed. The media -- whose curiosity about the background of candidates for national office seemed to know no bounds when it came to George W. Bush's service in the Texas Air National Guard or the sexual behavior of Alaska Governor Sarah Palin's daughter -- did not press him, and once safely elected Obama continued to manipulate his Islamic influence. "The president himself experienced Islam on three continents," an administration spokesman announced early in Obama's term in an effort to explain why Obama is especially qualified to strengthen U.S. ties to the Muslim world. "You know," said the spokesman, "growing up in Indonesia, having a Muslim father." In his first interview as president, granted to the Muslim newspaper *Al Arabiya* in January of 2009, Obama told the Muslim world "I have Muslim members of my family. I have lived in Muslim countries." After the speaker of the Turkish parliament had introduced him by his full name of "Barack Hussein Obama" on his first European tour, Obama said: "The United States has been enriched by Muslim Americans. Many other Americans have Muslims in their family, or have lived in a Muslim majority country -- I know, because I am one of them."[16]

As McCarthy has observed, the point of detailing Obama's relationship to Islam is not to portray Obama as a "stealth Muslim Manchurian candidate." The point is to demonstrate how unlikely it would be for almost anybody else to get elected president on the basis of their personal life story when so much remains unknown about that story. If Obama was treated differently because of his race, and if that fact shielded voters from observing that Obama held views that are far outside the mainstream of American political life, then America's radius of trust will have undergone significant diminution.

And there is indeed a widespread perception that Obama was "given a pass," especially by a media intoxicated with a candidate they considered to be prophetic. As already noted, in the heat of the campaign in the fall of 2008, by a margin of 70 percent to 9 percent, Americans said most journalists want to see Obama, not John McCain, win the presidential election. The passage of time has only strengthened this perception. Results from a national Sacred Heart University survey released in September of 2009 found that 89.3 percent of Americans believe the national media played a "very or somewhat strong role" in helping to elect President Obama. Just 10 percent suggested the national media played little or no role.[17] Apparently, even significant numbers of Democrats and Obama supporters saw the same bias that Republican voters did.

One might expect the Republican National Committee Chairman Michael Steele to complain that Obama "was not vetted . . . was not vetted because the press fell in love with the black man running for the office."[18] But Obama is undoubtedly the first U.S. president that can tell those gathered at his first annual White House Correspondents

Association dinner "I am Barack Obama. Most of you covered me. All of you voted for me."[19]

A consequence of this overt favoritism is that the unifying power of the presidency becomes attenuated, rendering obsolete one of the office's most important functions and one that has helped make the American political system uniquely successful. It was President Lincoln, after all, who said that "a house divided against itself cannot stand," and upon whom the responsibility of unifying a nation torn apart by slavery ultimately fell. The president, along with the vice president, is the only officer of the national government elected by a nationwide constituency. Unlike senators and congressmen, the president must ideally win by appealing to the broad middle, and by building a majority governing coalition. Because of racial sympathy, Obama was not required to make substantial pieces of his past available for public scrutiny to the extent that other presidential candidates previously had been. Obama was, in other words, not forced by the vetting process to earn the confidence of the "broad middle." Since there is reason to believe that he might not have earned that confidence, this portends a period of polarization and divisiveness, a period that has already begun as voters have discovered how Obama governs and his vision for America. Only midway through his first year in office, polling data revealed deep divisions. A Pew Research Center poll in April of Obama's first year found that the president's job approval was the most polarized for any new president in forty years. The study, entitled "Partisan Gap in Obama Job Approval Widest in Modern Era," found that the difference in Obama's approval ratings between Republicans and Democrats (61 percentage points) was the greatest ever recorded by that poll. By January 10th of 2010, Gallup reported that the 65 percentage point gap between Democrats' (88 percent) and Republicans' (23 percent) average job approval ratings for Barack Obama was easily the largest for any president in his first year in office, "greatly exceeding the prior high of 52 points for Bill Clinton." By February 4th, 2011 the Gallup organization would release a report entitled "Obama's Approval Ratings More Polarized in Year 2 Than Year 1," which found "An average of 81 percent of Democrats and 13 percent of Republicans approved of the job Obama was doing as president during his second year. That 68 point gap in party ratings is up from 65 points in his first year and is easily the most polarized second year for a president since Dwight Eisenhower." A December 14th, 2009 Rasmussen poll found racial polarization was as intense as the partisan divide. Obama earned approval from 37 percent of white voters and 98 percent of black voters.[20]

America was deeply divided before Obama came on the national scene. Astute observers of American politics understand that Obama's campaign promises of post-racialism, "hope and change," and non-partisanship could never, even under the best circumstances, have been perfectly realized. But the artifice constructed around Obama, the careful and deliberate deception that obscured his personal and professional history, his radical ideology, and his lack of appropriate credentials for high office, will make the trauma associated with political disappointment more severe than the standard presidential disillusionment of times past.

Chapter 7

AMERICA THE ORDINARY, OBAMA THE GREAT

Obama may be the first U.S. president to reject the notion of "American exceptionalism," the idea that America occupies a special place in world history, that the ideals it was founded upon represent something new in the governance of human beings, and that the future of freedom in the world hinges on its strength. For most of its history the U.S. has been led by people whose worldview and desire to lead was shaped by this idea. Ronald Reagan, for example, believed the nation's unique form of success lay in its Puritan roots, the notion derived from orthodox Protestantism that God had made a covenant with the Americans to lead the other nations of the world -- to be, in John Winthrop's famous words, a "shining city upon a hill." Revolutionary era figures like Thomas Paine argued that the American Revolution derived from a tradition of republicanism that had been repudiated by Europe, a national identity based on laws and not the ambitions of men. In this view, the most important things about America have not been what it inherited from Europe, but how America developed once liberated from European rule: its bounty, its frontier spirit of "rugged individualism," the absence of an inherited class structure, the nearly unlimited potential for wealth creation, its high degree of social mobility, its rejection of blood and inheritance as a basis for citizenship, its penchant for local government and guarantee of individual liberties, its multitude of voluntary institutions buffering the individual from government power. These are the ingredients, critics ranging from Alexis DeToqueville to historian Frederick Jackson Turner have argued, that went into making America the most powerful and culturally dominant country in the world, a complex country with the most appeal to the largest number of people from other parts of the world, the staunchest defender of free markets and democracy, the most religiously devout of developed nations, the protean "hyperpower" that seeks "exit strategies" when it sends troops to another nation and worries incessantly about the damaging effects of "foreign entanglements."[1]

There have always been opponents of this idea, mostly of European origin. European intellectuals naturally come at the subject from an angle of cultural snobbery. For them America is the *enfant terrible,* the New World upstart that ungratefully left its weathered but more culturally mature parent behind in the struggle for global power. In the nineteenth century Oswald Spengler worried that Germany would devolve into "soulless America," with its worship of "technical skill, money and an eye for facts." British critic Matthew Arnold fretted about the global forces that would Americanize England. "They will rule [Britain] by their energy but they will deteriorate it by their low ideas and want of culture." More recently, French diplomats have taken to scornfully condemning U.S. "arrogance."[2]

Other civilizations too have produced critiques, formed mostly around America's materialism. Critics in Asia and the Middle East have argued that America has solved the crisis of scarcity, but not the problem of culture, which allows for a very high standard of living but also for high levels of crime, illegitimacy, drug abuse, promiscuity, and general vulgarity. Some see this critique, combined with America's military and economic might, at the core of radical Islam's revulsion toward the United States. "American culture is a kind of syphilis or disease that is destroying the Islamic community," they say. "We don't object to how you Americans live, but now you are spreading your way of life throughout the universe."[3]

Conservative critics in the United States ranging from Henry Adams, T.S. Eliot, and Ezra Pound at the turn of the twentieth century to the Reverend Jerry Falwell, Robert Bork, and Patrick J. Buchanan at the turn of the twenty-first century also believe that America has experienced a severe moral meltdown at the hands of the two main forces of secularism: capitalism and socialism (euphemisms really, in the cases of Eliot, Pound, and Buchanan, for "Judification"). Even exceptionalists in the neoconservative camp, most notably the optimistic but philosophically cautious Daniel Bell and Irving Kristol, have acknowledged the damage that free market capitalism can do to a nation's moral foundation, and offered not three but "two cheers for capitalism." But contemporary conservatives generally see the founding of America and its primary doctrines as one of the great events in world history, and many of the true traditionalists among them seek merely the reestablishment of an older, and in their view superior social order, "the country we grew up in."[4]

Today it is in the universities that opposition to American exceptionalism has become institutionalized. The late Columbia University "orientalist" Edward Said, for example, believed that the United States is little more than the repository for half baked European ideas about the cultural superiority of the west. Other scholars, perhaps most prominently the recently deceased radical historian Howard Zinn, point to the obvious moral stains of America's past -- slavery, racial segregation, Indian removal -- and see its true character peeking through the thin veneer of its Protestant work ethic, its checks and balances, its electoral college, its Bill of Rights. Still others, noting the ruin of Rome, Hellenic Greece, the Ottoman's, and the British -- empires that all at one time or another claimed for themselves special dispensation from the natural laws of civilizational rot and decay -- argue that history will prove false the notion of America's "chosenness."[5] American academics largely crib from the neo-Marxism of influential European intellectuals who, noting the decline of their own continent, insist on the folly of nationalism and call for rule by global bureaucracy. They see little use for the values given institutional heft through the American nation state, and believe that American power derives not from its high ideals, better political system, or more efficient markets, but rather from treachery, avariciousness, and violence. For many academics, America stands as the last great redoubt for retrograde notions about love of country, metaphysical religious belief, and all particularisms -- the vulgar, Neanderthal voice for the superiority of western values against the enlightened global community proffering the equality of all civilizations and the natural brotherhood of men.

Barack Obama drank deeply from the well of academic "postnationalism" during his years at Columbia University and Harvard Law School, and during his time as a lecturer at the University of Chicago Law School. Given his Ivy League background, his self-conscious effort to be seen as an intellectual, and his proclivity for talking down to bible owning, gun toting Americans, it is little wonder that some critics see Obama as really "all faculty lounge."[6] But Obama may indeed be the first president in U.S. history to openly deny American exceptionalism. In early 2009, while attending the European summit of the Group of Twenty major economic powers, Obama was asked if he believed in American exceptionalism. He replied, "I believe in American exceptionalism, just as I suspect that the Brits believe in British exceptionalism, and the Greeks believe in Greek exceptionalism," an answer which on its face is ambivalent enough, but when taken in combination with his actions as president leaves little doubt about his position on the matter. Throughout his first year in office Obama made strenuous efforts to inflate the status of other civilizations in relation to the United States, refusing to address even the most obvious distinctions between tyrannies and democracies, and to reinforce the view of America as an abuser of power that needs to be chastened. Examples of these efforts abound. On his first world tour as president Obama told foreign audiences essentially that America no longer sought to be the dominant actor in world affairs, that he was sorry for America's arrogance and dismissiveness, and that he was there to "listen." Speaking to the Muslim newspaper *al-Arabiya*, Obama promised that America will henceforth "start by listening, because all too often the United States starts by dictating." In Strasbourg, France in early April of 2009, Obama told a town hall audience that America "has failed to appreciate Europe's leading role in the world." In Turkey several days later Obama flummoxed students of U.S. history when he told the Turkish parliament "We will convey our deep appreciation for the Islamic faith, which has done so much over the centuries to shape the world -- including in my own country." In his address to Latin American leaders at the Summit of the Americas on April 17, 2009, Obama told countries ruled by dictators (Cuba, Venezuela, and Bolivia), economic basket cases (Haiti, Equador, and Dominica), and tiny island countries (Grenada and Aruba) "I pledge to you that we seek an equal partnership. There is no senior partner and junior partner . . . The United States will be willing to acknowledge past errors where those errors have been made." In his video taped address to Iran of March 2009, the first of his olive branches to the radical mullahs, Obama became the first U.S. president to respectfully call that nation what only its self-appointed leaders alone believe it to be, "The Islamic Republic of Iran." At his first G-20 meeting of world leaders in April 2009 Obama told a press conference he prefers for the United States to be less dominant than it was immediately following World War II. "[I]t is very important for us to be able to forge partnerships as opposed to simply dictating solutions . . . if there's just Roosevelt and Churchill sitting in a room with a brandy, that's an easier negotiation. But that's not the world we live in, and it shouldn't be the world that we live in." In his first address as president to the United Nations in September of 2009, Obama insisted to a general assembly that included Libya's Moammar Gadhafi, Iran's Mahmoud Ahmidinejad, and Zimbabwe's Robert Mugabe, that "No world order that elevates one nation or group of people over another will succeed."[7]

Obama's strategy for remaking America and the world includes generous doses of national self-prostration, most of it seemingly for the purpose of convincing the rest of the world of America's presumed new willingness to subordinate national sovereignty to the will of the global community. Other presidents too, in particular Woodrow Wilson, believed America's best interests lay in "not a balance of power, but a community of power" founded on "the moral force of the public opinion of the world." But other presidents, if for no other reason than political viability, appealed to international authority with the interests of their own nation in mind. In Wilson's case, the hope was to strengthen global cooperation as a way to keep the U.S. out of World War I. For Obama, the emphasis seems not to be on making the world "safe for democracy," but on keeping the world safe from America. In his first speech to the United Nations as president, Obama made a point to say that what was wrong with our foreign policy under his predecessor George W. Bush was that "America has acted unilaterally, without regard for the interests of others," causing former U.S. Ambassador to the United Nations John Bolton to wonder if the president's job was to look out for "the interests of others" or defend the interests of his compatriots. Bolton called this speech "a post-American speech by our first post-American president."[8]

The most troubling demonstration of Obama's "post-Americanism" came during the May 2010 visit to the United States by Mexican president Felipe Calderon. There, at a greeting ceremony on the White House South Lawn, Obama told Calderone that his presence there was proof that "in North America and the world in the twenty-first century, we are defined not by our borders, but by our bonds."[9] The Mexican president's visit was spurred by the passage several weeks earlier of a law by the state of Arizona which attempted to stanch the flow of illegal immigrants from Mexico by requiring local police to question suspects about their immigration status. Like most presidents of Mexico before him, Calderone was keenly aware of the importance of keeping open the spigot of illegal migration to the U.S., which helps rid

Mexico of some of its worst residents and provides billions of dollars in revenue from Mexican nationals sending money home. For these reasons, Calderone condemned the law as discriminatory and warned that Mexico would reject any effort to "criminalize migration."[10]

Seemingly unaware that the U.S. president represents all U.S. citizens, even those from states with laws he opposes, Obama sided with Calderone against the freely elected legislators of Arizona. Despite an Associated Press-GfK poll that found 42 percent of Americans favoring the law and 24 percent opposed (another 29 percent said they were neutral), Obama stated that the Arizona law amounted to racial profiling, that it was "a misdirected expression of frustration" and that "In the United States of America, no law-abiding person -- be they an American citizen, a legal immigrant, or a visitor or tourist from Mexico -- should ever be subject to suspicion simply because of what they look like."[11]

Arizona public officials and representatives pointed out that Obama had accused Arizonans of racial intolerance for passing a law that essentially "piggybacked" the federal law and was proposed in the first place only because of federal unwillingness to enforce that law. But the President's comments were more perverse than that. Obama was essentially condemning the citizens of his own country for their treatment of illegal immigrants in front of the president of a foreign country cited only three weeks earlier for massive abuse of illegal immigrants. In April of 2010 the human rights group Amnesty

International called the abuse of migrants in Mexico a "major human rights crisis," and accused some officials of turning a blind eye or even participating in the kidnapping, rape and murder of migrants.[12]

In the end, though, even Calderone acknowledged U.S. sovereignty on the matter, explaining that "In Mexico, we are and will continue being respectful of the internal policies of the United States and its legitimate right to establish in accordance to its Constitution whatever laws it approves."[13] Obama offered no such defense of U.S. sovereignty. With Calderone at his side Obama said "We're examining any implications [of the Arizona law], especially for civil rights." Days later a top U.S. Department of Homeland Security official said his agency will not necessarily process illegal immigrants referred to them by Arizona authorities. On Tuesday, July 6th, 2010, Obama's Justice Department sued Arizona over the state's immigration law, an assertion of federal power that set up a rare clash with a state on one of the nation's most divisive political issues.[14]

Another troubling demonstration of Obama's moral ambiguity when it comes to comparing U.S. policy with that of other countries occurred on his tour of Asia in November of 2009. In China Obama strained credulity in his attempt to mitigate any criticism of China's human rights record by comparing it with America's own. Every leading human rights agency in the world has denounced the widespread trafficking of women and forced abortions of mostly female fetuses, some in the ninth month of pregnancy, that regularly take place in

China. Yet Obama told a town hall style meeting that "it is important for us to affirm the rights of women all around the world" but that "we will always do so with the humility and understanding that we are not perfect . . . If you talk to women in America, they will tell you that there are still men who have a lot of old fashioned ideas about the role of women in society." Thus, in Obama's view, does the hapless, beer swilling American male who opposes modified strength tests for female firefighters become the moral equivalent of one of the world's great human rights violators.[15]

Obama has repeatedly denounced American policies he views as manifestations purely of national self-interest and has promised to end or reverse actions that previous presidents have deemed necessary to protect the United States. To take one example of this presidential second guessing, Obama delivered a speech in Prague during his first trip to Europe where he offered a not-so-subtle apology for America's use of nuclear weapons in World War II. "As the only nuclear power to have used a nuclear weapon," Obama said, "the United States has a moral responsibility to act" in furtherance of total disarmament, thus drawing a moral equivalence between the U.S. nuclear arsenal and the potential possession of such weapons by saber rattling Islamist regimes and suicidal terrorist groups. For Obama, America's use of nuclear weapons in World War II has made it the nation most culpable for nuclear proliferation, burdening it with a special "moral responsibility." America obvious restraint in using its nuclear arsenal only one -- to stop the fascist Japanese war machine -- and that arsenal's success at keeping the tyranny of communism in check and offering protection to vulnerable allies, has little bearing on Obama's calculation. For him, U.S. nuclear weapons serve no other purpose than to bully other countries and make them feel unsafe. So Obama has set about reducing the U.S. arsenal, signing the 2010 "START II" nuclear reduction pact with Russia, and reducing the U.S. arsenal's effectiveness by declaring (unilaterally) in his "Nuclear Posture Review," that the U.S. will not retaliate with nuclear weapons against countries that attack it with chemical or biological weapons.

None of this should be surprising. When asked by a reporter to do so, Obama was neither able nor willing to articulate any justification for America's use of two nuclear bombs against imperial Japan, bombs that put an end to a war that had killed tens of millions and threatened to kill millions more. For Obama, America's decades long effort to achieve military and strategic victory over its enemies through nuclear superiority is evidence not of its scientific prowess, its resourcefulness, or its obvious self-restraint (America could destroy the world many times over with its nuclear weapons), but of its militarism, its jingoism, and its penchant for violence. America's nuclear weapons have long been the primary deterrent to Soviet/Russian expansionism and the plans of other tyrannical regimes, thereby saving American lives by obviating the need for even more conventional warfare. But Obama continues to see the United States as the primary culprit in the creation of the world's greatest threat to humanity -- nuclear proliferation. "Earlier this week," Obama announced to great fanfare upon the signing of the START II with Russia, "the United States formally changed our policy to make it clear that those [non]-nuclear weapons states that are in compliance with the Nuclear Non-Proliferation Treaty and their non-proliferation obligations will not be threatened by America's nuclear arsenal."[16] Given that no non-nuclear, non-terrorist supporting country has ever expressed concern about being bombed by the U.S. with nuclear weapons, there seems no logical reason for this pronouncement, other than Obama's need to publicly excoriate his own country, a need which far outweighs any presumed presidential imperative to acknowledge the virtues of America's indispensable nuclear stewardship.

The Root of Obama's Anti-Exceptionalism: Race

It would be a mistake to view Obama's rejection of American exceptionalism as purely intellectual. It is imbedded deeply in his personal and racial identity, and in the black nationalism that has shaped black identity in general. As with all other things in American life, black history has been central to the formation of the contemporary multicultural conceit that says America just isn't all it's cracked up to be.

"Black Power," the secular name given to calls for black solidarity and separation from white society, gained ascendancy in the late 1960s and '70s when a series of urban race riots shook America to its core. Black Power leaders challenged the faith of integrationists like James Forman, Bayard Rustin, and Ralph Bunche in the redemptive power of American individualism, positing that equal rights absent the necessary political power to ensure special accommodations for blacks was an illusion. "Integration," said Black Power advocate Stokely Carmichael, "is a subterfuge for the maintenance of white supremacy." As Harold Cruse explained in his influential *The Crisis of the Negro Intellectual*, "the individual in America has few rights that are not backed up by the political, economic, and social power of one group or another." White politicians quickly agreed to pay "riot insurance" to black militants like Reverend Milton Galamison, Rhody McCoy, and Sonny Carson in New York in the form of community control of government agencies and jobs, racial preferences, expanded social programs, and the gerrymandering of electoral districts to increase the number of black office holders. It was, in the wake of the riots, far easier for white urban liberals to hand out government largesse to blacks as a form of reparations than it was for them to convince the white middle class (including themselves) to integrate with them. In their challenge to the belief in a color blind America, black radicals scored an impressive victory for their view that the "color line" in America was permanent and that the disenfranchisement of black Americans remained the most fundamental and enduring fact of American life. This represented not only a sustained attack on America as an idea, but on the assumptions, attitudes, and habits of its vaunted white middle class, the very symbol of America's success. Individualism and personal merit, radical black organizations like the African American Teacher's Association and the Student Non-Violent Coordinating Committee (SNCC) insisted, were a "myth" perpetuated by whites to create "black versions of the white middle class." Since the "color line" prevented blacks from joining the mainstream, the logic went, the whole idea that there is or should be a "mainstream" had to be discredited. Instead, blacks were encouraged to see "middle class" habits as racist and corrupt, and to see political power distributed along racial lines as the only way to ensure black advance.[17]

It is not hard to see how seamlessly the anti-Americanism of the academic leftists fits with the precepts of Black Power, or their natural confluence in the modern practice of "multiculturalism." Like black nationalists, for whom the middle class culture of thrift and work is a myth designed to sustain racial hierarchy, and for whom nation states represent obstacles to achieving a higher level of solidarity with other non-white peoples of the world -- the multiculturalist also sees nation states as mostly artificial constructs constituting one more obstacle toward true human brotherhood. For the multiculturalist it is only power that determines the hierarchy of nations, not any intrinsic set of cultural virtues. Any attempt to define a universal standard for how well a society meets the needs of its citizens is bound to fail, since human "needs" themselves are subjective. In the realm of world affairs, multiculturalism translates into a disdain for unilateral action in the name of national self-interest, a belief in the sanctity of international institutions and collective decision making, and a sense of obligation, bordering on guilt, toward the undeveloped world. The guilt the multiculturalist feels toward the undeveloped world stems from the notion that since no society is intrinsically "better" than any other, the vast equalities between nations that exist must be the result of mean spirited plunder and aggression on the part of the powerful against the weak.

This association of American power with international suffering is why, in late 2010, when several Muslim countries exploded in political unrest, Obama was quick to side with opponents of long time American allies like Hosni Mubarak in Egypt, but slow to join with opposition forces rising up against long time American foes, such as Bashar al-Assad in Syria and Moammar Gadhafi in Libya: allies of the U.S., in the multiculturalist mind, are clearly creations of the aggressive wielders of power in the world, while assuredly more oppressive dictators not aligned with the U.S. are less obviously the beneficiaries of unfair power advantages. It is also why when addressing Iran during a speech from Cairo in June 2009, Obama spoke openly about America's role in a 1953 Iranian coup, the first American president to do so. "In the middle of the Cold War, the United States played a role in the overthrow of a democratically elected Iranian government," Obama told the Cairo audience. "[T]here is in fact a tumultuous history between us." For Obama, Iran's descent into a brutal, terrorist-supporting theocracy based on tenth century moral codes is a natural response to the CIA's (rather inconsequential, it turns out) intervention in the 1950s. Clearly, Obama's suspicion of American intelligence agencies, which led to Justice Department investigations into CIA interrogation methods in 2009 -- methods that were subsequently vindicated by the killing of Osama bin Laden -- has deep ideological roots.[18]

Black Power is merely the domestic application of multiculturalism, the replacement of a unified American identity based on national ideals with a belief in the equal importance of subnational, racial, ethnic, cultural, sexual, and gender identities. The academic multiculturalists re-write American history with a bias against the western (and hence, white) origins of and contributions to American life, using the experience of the black "other" as proof that the American promise of liberty, prosperity, and the pursuit of happiness is an illusion.

Black identity has been broadly shaped by Black Power and multiculturalism. While blacks have been more central to the formation of American life and culture than any other single group, they are also more ambivalent about their American identity. In September of 2008 an ABC News poll found that only 46 percent of blacks consider themselves "American" before they consider themselves "black" (this increased to 51 percent immediately after Obama's election). Ninety-one percent of whites said they were "American" first. To contrast these numbers with a more discreet, mostly white American subgroup, a 1998 poll of American Jews found that only 13 percent feel that being Jewish is the single most important way in which they identify themselves.[19]

Black ambivalence about America may also explain why a Pew Research Center poll in 2005 found 78 percent of blacks describing themselves as "very patriotic" while 93 percent of whites said the same thing, or the transformation of black civil rights groups from among the most aggressively anti-immigrant forces in the country to one of the most pro-immigrant: the shift in America's immigration flow from mostly white before 1965 to mostly non-white afterward has converged with the shift in civil rights objectives from racial integration to black (or, if need be, non-white) power.[20]

Black Power's emphasis on "collective work and responsibility," "cooperative economics," and a "black value system" has translated into a public policy preference for "fairness" through social leveling, redistribution of income through taxation, a suspicion of free market individualism, and a preference for broad government interventionism among blacks. A Pew Research Center poll also found that 71 percent of blacks believe government should do more to help the needy even if it means more government debt, compared to 56 percent of whites. Eighty-one percent of blacks said the government "should guarantee food and shelter," compared to 61 percent of whites. These preferences are reflected not only in voting patterns, but in employment patterns as well. So, for example, while blacks continue to trail whites, Hispanics, and Asians in the rate at which they create new businesses, they are overrepresented in government employment. Blacks make up approximately 11.4 percent of the civilian labor force, yet they constitute roughly one-third of all state and local government employees, and 17 percent of the federal government work force.[21]

It is at least as much from his strident effort to absorb the black experience in America as it is from his years at Harvard that Obama has come to the belief that America's moral failures discredit its claims for the universal goodness of its ideals. Obama himself no doubt prefers living in a democratic republic, but his own interpretation of the black experience has made it difficult for him to claim for it any greater moral authority than radical Islam, Russian authoritarianism, or Chinese market communism. That is why, when speaking to the Turkish parliament, Obama compared American racism to the Armenian genocide of 1915, explaining "The United States is still working through some of our own darker periods in our history . . . Our country still struggles with the legacies of slavery and segregation, the past treatment of Native Americans." In Obama's view, America's nineteenth century struggle with slavery, over which it fought its bloodiest war and which has defined its politics for 150 years, is the moral equivalent of the twentieth century Turkish slaughter of one million Armenians, which Turkey has not officially acknowledged.[22]

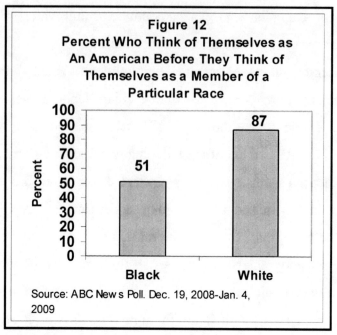

Figure 12
Percent Who Think of Themselves as An American Before They Think of Themselves as a Member of a Particular Race

Source: ABC News Poll. Dec. 19, 2008-Jan. 4, 2009

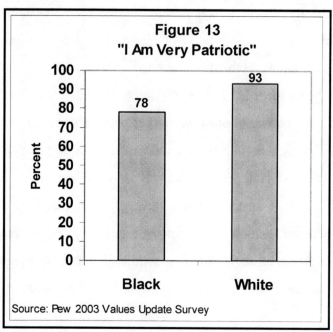

Figure 13
"I Am Very Patriotic"

Source: Pew 2003 Values Update Survey

That Obama should admonish his own country for its legacy of slavery, without irony, while visiting the one nation more responsible than any on earth for the institutionalization of slavery is one thing. (Constantinople's slave market was the world's largest and slavery was so entrenched in Turkey that it continued into the twentieth century). That he should do it without even tipping his hat to America's central role in abolishing slavery around the world, in defining it as a universal evil, and in committing hundreds of thousands of its son's lives to ending it, is indicative of something much larger: his strict adherence to multicultural moral relativity and the rejection of American exceptionalism.

Obama personifies the linkage of the Black Power appeal to the non-white base with the elite "post-nationalism" of European and American intellectuals: he is a member of the great excluded people who give lie to the American Dream, as well as a member of the global intellectual class whose expertise will overturn the American dominated international system. As University of Virginia political scientist James Ceasar has written, "Although Obama never conceived himself as playing a universal role when he launched his presidential bid, he awakened at some point in the campaign to the realization that he was no longer running merely for president of the United States. He was being selected for the much grander 'office' of leader of a new world community." It took a member of the positively giddy elite media -- Evan Thomas of *Newsweek* -- to make clear what many of Obama's supporters had in mind when they latched onto his candidacy: a new era in which the archaic belief in the primacy of the nation, the claims of American exceptionalism, and bold faced patriotism will be buried in the graveyard of discarded lies. "Well, we were the good guys in 1984," Thomas said after Obama's speech at the 65th anniversary of the Normandy invasion. "Reagan was all about America . . . Obama is 'we are above that now.' We're not just parochial, we're not just chauvinistic, we're not just provincial. We stand for something. I mean in a way Obama's standing above the country, above -- above the world, he's sort of God -- He's going to bring all different sides together."[23]

With supporters like Thomas, Obama should probably be forgiven for believing that while he had no part in America's past indiscretions, its redemption has only been made possible by his election to the presidency. Obama's high regard for himself and what he represents is not in itself a detriment to the nation. At the very least, and to his credit, Obama has shown a disarming sense of humor about his famous ego, telling the audience at his first White House Correspondence Association dinner that "I would like to welcome you to the ten day anniversary of my first 100 days. During the second 100 days, we will design, build and open a library dedicated to my first 100 days. My next 100 days will be so successful, I will complete them in seventy-two days. And on the seventy-third day, I will rest."[24]

But Obama's worldview is a striking combination of personal ego and multicultural non-judgmentalism, reflecting a deep suspicion of American power and an even deeper certainty that he embodies the necessary corrective to its past abuse. Obama started his first trip to Europe by stating "I would like to think that with my election, we're starting to see some restoration of America's standing in the world." In Latin America he reiterated "I think my presence here indicates, the United States has changed over time."[25] At his victory speech in Chicago's Grant Park on November 4th of 2008, Obama pronounced "We may not get there in one year or even in one term. But, America, I have never been more hopeful than I am tonight that we will get there." "For those disappointed to hear that Obama might need more than a year to fix America's problems, or who believe there may have been more than a few commendable things about America prior to Obama's becoming president, he added that comfort could be taken simply from the fact of his election. "If there is anyone out there who still doubts that America is a place where all things are possible . . . who still questions the power of our democracy, tonight is your answer."[26]

As president, Obama has continued to portray his administration as a palliative for the world's grievances with America, often treating those grievances uncritically. "I took office at a time when many around the world had come to view America with skepticism and distrust," Obama told the audience at his first presidential appearance before the United Nations General Assembly in September 2009, setting the stage, one might suppose, for a withering defense of America's role in world affairs. But instead of reminding United Nation's delegates of America's post-World War II Marshall Plan to rebuild Europe, the successful deterrence of Soviet expansionism, the Berlin Airlift, the billions of dollars spent on fighting AIDS in Africa, tsunami relief, defeating Nazism and communism, stopping ethnic cleansing in the Balkans, removing Sadaam Hussein from power, vanquishing the Taliban, and keeping the fires of the global economy stoked by opening U.S. markets on unilaterally generous terms, Obama argued on behalf of only his first nine months in office. "For those who question the character and cause of my nation, I ask you to look at the concrete actions we have taken in just nine months" Obama told the General Assembly. In a chamber crowded with authoritarian dictators and terrorist supporters, Obama reserved the only use of the word "torture" for indicting his own country and slapping himself on the back for stopping it. "On my first day in office, I prohibited without expectation or equivocation the use of torture by the United States of America." And so goes, as one political pundit has suggested, Obama's well known dialectic: pre-Obama America is a nation of many flaws and failures. The world responds with understandable but misguided prejudice. I, Obama, will fix it. "How great a world we all should see, if only all were more like me."[27]

Obama's belief that his election was the moment of America's vindication was also on display when, on behalf of the city of Chicago, he made a special plea to the International Olympic Committee in Copenhagen in October of 2009. The president's unprecedented appearance before the IOC was itself testimony to his inordinate faith in the power of his own personality. By his tenth month in office Obama had given a record five prime time televised addresses on various topics. But in his ultimately unsuccessful attempt to persuade the IOC to hold the 2016 Olympic games in Chicago, Obama stressed his international pedigree and what he feels is the global necessity of his election. "Nearly one year ago," Obama told the IOC, "on a clear November night, people from every corner of the world gathered in the city of Chicago or in front of their televisions to watch the results of the U.S. presidential election . . . Their interest sprung from the hope that in this ever shrinking world, our diversity could be a source of strength, a cause for celebration; and that with sustained work and determination, we could learn to live and prosper together during the fleeting moment we share on this Earth." Again, in James Ceasar's words, "Only the most rare of persons, after being the object for over a year of such unrelenting adulation, could have resisted the temptation to think that the world revolved around him . . . His [Obama's] speeches and remarks are filled with references to himself in a ratio that surpasses anything yet seen in the history of the American presidency."[28]

The moral imperative of Obama's election is a sentiment the president shares with his wife Michelle, who also has little use for America's past and small regard for its achievements. Speaking in

Milwaukee, Wisconsin during the Democratic primary she referred to Obama's campaign as "the first time in my adult life I am proud of my country because it feels like hope is finally making a comeback." Shortly after that speech, in an attempt at damage control, the first lady gave an interview with the *New Yorker* magazine in which she stated America is "just downright mean," "guided by fear," a nation of "cynics, sloths, and complacents." Mrs. Obama also expressed the belief that things had not improved in at least forty years. "We have become a nation of struggling folks who are barely making it every day. Folks are just jammed up, and it's gotten worse over my lifetime. And, doggone it, I'm young. Forty-four!"[29]

Americans have withstood their fair share of presidential ego. Obama is joined in his generous estimate of his own importance by a long line of predecessors. It was Bill Clinton, after all, who openly lamented the absence of a world crisis during the 1990s for denying him the opportunity to be a "great" president. Still, for his age (forty-seven when he took office) and his modest professional achievements prior to his election, Obama's impression of himself seems unusual even in the rarified precincts of presidential self-esteem. Obama's warning to the United Nations General Assembly in September, 2009 is symptomatic. "Consider the course that we're on if we fail to confront the status quo: extremists sowing terror in pockets of the world, protracted conflicts that grind on and on, genocide, mass atrocities, more nations with nuclear weapons, melting ice caps and ravaged populations, persistent poverty, and pandemic disease." The notion that any or all of these events may have causative factors independent of his leadership seems never to have crossed Obama's mind.

Even if Obama is chastened in office it will be harder for many voters to reconcile his impoverished view of American power and its importance for global stability with their own obvious pride of country, a powerful sense of national self-worth that, remarkably, preceded Obama's election. A 2005 Pew Research Center survey found that 63 percent of Americans supported the idea that U.S. policies should try to "keep it so America is the only military superpower," while opposing the idea of "Europe, China, or another country" gaining parity with the United States.[30] A Zogby poll in 2003 found that 93 percent of Americans see the following statement as either "very accurate" or "somewhat accurate": "America is a good friend and ally of people who desire freedom and individual human rights." A Rasmussen national telephone survey found that 75 percent of U.S. voters declare themselves proud of America's history. The poll found that 64 percent view the United States as a positive role model for human rights. The same percentage of voters say the world would be a better place if other nations "Followed America's example." Earlier Rasmussen surveys found that roughly six out of ten voters believe that American society is generally fair and decent.[31]

Obama possesses a sophisticated understanding of American history and has been careful to pay homage to America's "promise," to hold up his personal story as a symbol of America's potential and to speak of it as one "that could only happen in the United States of America." He is politically astute enough to include a sentence or two in every speech to counterbalance his criticism of the nation he leads. But the primary implication of his oratory and writing, what separates it from what past American presidents have thought and said, is that the United States is not exceptional, that it is a country morally compromised by its racist past, the unequal distribution of its wealth, and its aggressive military action abroad and is, therefore, woefully incomplete. In this view American greatness is a project in the making, a process of striving for something not yet achieved. In a moment of candor, at a campaign rally in Elkhardt, Indiana in August of 2008, a young girl asked Obama why he wanted to be president. Obama answered, somewhat confusedly, "America is . . . uh, is no longer, uh . . . what it once was. What it could be . . . And I say to myself, I don't want that future for my children."[32]

That for Obama the virtuous America must become something other than what it already is, his fealty to the goodness of many of America's highest ideals in the abstract, but not to its present form, has been on almost constant display since he became a serious presidential contender. It is revealed in its most basic form in Obama's campaign theme of "hope" and "change." Hope implies an expectation that something one wishes for will be obtained, a longing that has not yet been fulfilled. This is most likely the main reason why left leaning political campaigns are so often grounded in the idea of hope. Famous liberal historian and Kennedy white house official Arthur Schlesinger, Jr. titled his 1963 book, which emphasized the responsibility of liberals to build something better in the future, *The Politics of Hope*.[33] Jesse Jackson ended his rousing speech to the 1988 Democratic National Convention with the almost obsessive chant "Keep hope alive. Keep hope alive! Keep hope alive! On tomorrow night and beyond, keep hope alive!" And the most influential speech in Obama's life, delivered by his mentor and preacher Reverend Jeremiah Wright of Trinity United Church in Chicago, was entitled "The Audacity of Hope."

It is significant that like the left wing preachers Jackson and Wright, Obama sees hope for America as divinely inspired. But for Obama America's future is inspired by the punitive side of Protestant Christianity, not the optimistic side that Ronald Reagan clung to. America for Obama is not a shining city on a hill, but a nation conceived in original sin, guilty of offenses against the world for which it must now atone. Hope, for the hard left in America, is not optimistic about America's ability to achieve significant reform. It reflects alienation from the American creed, from the sunny optimism of free people in their ability to solve problems, alienation from the confidence in existing institutions to redress grievances and expand opportunity. "Hope" and "Change" are slogans used by forlorn radicals to rally sympathizers to the cause of remaking America in an entirely new image, one that casts off some of the most enduring and treasured American values. It is an image that has been rejected time and again by Americans, the vast majority of whom acknowledge human imperfection, but prefer a variety of decentralized incremental reforms, not a "one size fits all" centralized revolution imposed from Washington. By contrast, the meaning of America's hope for Obama reflects a presumed mandate to remake the world in the service of the left's two most oft stated goals, "equality" and "justice." As the writer Jean Kaufman has observed, "Obama views himself as the special instrument through which America can finally purify herself, join the world of other nations as an equal rather than a leader, and go forth in sin no more. You might say that Reagan believed in American exceptionalism, whereas Obama believes in Obama's exceptionalism."[34]

Chapter 8

E PLURIBUS PLURIBUS: *OBAMA AND THE HISPANIC FACTOR*

Obama's presidency in terms of both the policies he supports and in his personal embodiment of multicultural ideals has troubling implications for group life in America. Culturally diverse from its beginning, the United States has been held together by the common ideals of individual rights, free enterprise, and merit based advance. Even with the advent of Black Power and identity politics in the post-1960s era, the classic American belief in talent, hard work, and Horatio Alger like pluck as the engines of mobility gained dominion over the idea that opportunities and status should be distributed on the basis of race, ethnicity, creed, or group. Whether supportive of affirmative measures to redress racial discrimination or not, most Americans take the black predicament to be a special circumstance, an outlier peculiar to United States history which required greater latitude in terms of recognizing individuals as members of a protected class. But it was not expected that newcomers would be assimilated to the same racial spoils regime. For the most part the American electorate, in polls as well as in public referenda, has stood for individual rights and a common creed against multi-lingualism, racial preferences, and politically defined racial groups organized to fight for material gains. Even liberal "blue" states like California (1996), Washington (2000), and Michigan (2006) have passed ballot initiatives banning race based preferences (though heavy Obama driven black/Hispanic turnout in 2008 resulted in the defeat of one such measure in Colorado). A Quinnipiac University poll in June of 2009 found that Americans oppose by 70 percent to 25 percent giving some racial groups preference for government jobs to increase "diversity." For private sector jobs Americans are opposed to preferences by a margin of 74 percent to 21 percent. That no "accident of birth" should determine the social status of an individual is an ideal the majority of Americans still cling to.[1]

But there are many who do not believe in the primacy of this ideal, and Obama is now first among them. In the words of Charles Krauthammer, Obama "is a leveler . . . for him the ultimate social value is fairness. Imposing it upon the American social order is his mission."[2] When, in the summer of 2008, Republican presidential candidate John McCain came out in favor of an Arizona "civil rights initiative" prohibiting racial and gender preferences in state government, Obama told a conference of UNITY, a group committed to the hiring and advancement of "journalists of color," that he was "disappointed" and favors affirmative action "when properly structured." In the fall of 2008, when asked whether his proposals would increase taxes on small businesses, Obama famously told Samuel Joseph Wurzelbacher (aka

"Joe the Plumber") that "My attitude is that if the economy's good for folks from the bottom up, it's gonna be good for everybody. I think when you spread the wealth around, it's good for everybody." During the presidential campaign, Obama went on record supporting the issuance of driver's licenses to illegal immigrants, a policy widely regarded as a sop to Hispanics. When the state of Arizona passed a strict anti-illegal immigration law in May of 2010, the Obama administration declined to commit to prosecuting violators of America's immigration laws referred to them by Arizona officials, a clear indication of Obama's willingness to apply the rule of law unevenly in ways that favor protected groups.[3]

As president, Obama has been more than willing to divide Americans by race and ethnicity in order to conquer at the polls. Not only did Obama make his racially exclusionary video address urging "young people, African Americans, Latinos, and women who powered our victory in 2008 to stand together once again." He also, without the slightest humility, invoked the battle against nineteenth century chattel slavery to describe his own struggle against a disapproving electorate. In Madison, Wisconsin in 2010, Obama told a crowd of Democrats upset at a perceived lack of economic progress to think of the patience of American slaves. "You know, the slaves sitting around a fire singing freedom songs, they weren't sure when slavery would end, but they understood it was going to end." For Obama, electoral victory means his racial demographic (non-whites and women) must overwhelm the other racial demographic (white men and old people) at the polls.[4]

There may never be an appropriate time for the president of the United States to favor government mandated diversity. But it seems especially risky for a nation in the midst of an unprecedented mass migration of newcomers from all over the world. Since the early 1990s, something on the order of one million people -- many of them poor and from parts of the world where individual rights and markets are not highly valued -- have come into the United States annually, with probably a half million more on top of that if illegal entries are included. There have been previous mass migrations of people who originate from countries that reflect close to nothing of America's political or cultural heritage, notably the 1880-1920 migration of eastern and southern Europeans. But it has been the singular success of the United States to have convinced newcomers to adopt American notions of individualism and merit based success as their own. Rights and liberties, yes, but individual effort and responsibility too.

It took massive "Americanization" efforts in our public schools and elsewhere, and a singular commitment to the English language, to achieve this. The effort involved local, state, and national governments, private organizations, and businesses. Americanization became a key element in the "progressive" phase of American politics, promoted by Theodore Roosevelt, Woodrow Wilson, and other leaders. In almost every city with a significant immigrant population the chamber of commerce had an Americanization program.[5]

Today, it is not clear the country is succeeding, or even trying to succeed, in this Americanizing effort. Nor is it as clear as it once was what "Americanization" means. A recent "index of immigrant assimilation" compiled by the conservative Manhattan Institute found that while most newly arrived immigrants in 2006 advance economically and become citizens at about the same rate as newly arrived Italian, Greek, and Polish immigrants in 1910, this is not true of many Hispanics, especially the eleven million plus natives of Mexican origin.[6] A Pew Hispanic Center/Kaiser Family Foundation 2002 National Survey of Hispanics found that "Hispanics who are American citizens are still more likely to identify themselves primarily by country of origin [or parent's origin] (44 percent) than to identify primarily as an 'American' (33 percent)." Among Hispanics who are third generation or higher, i.e. those who were born in the United States and whose parents were born in the United States, the report found that only 57 percent consider themselves primarily Americans. This number includes the large number of Hispanics whose families have been in U.S. territory for hundreds of years, and so might actually be lower among the newer arrivals.[7]

There are several reasons why large numbers of residents of Mexican descent, and to a lesser degree some other Hispanic groups, fail to adopt English, become citizens, and advance more quickly economically. Incentives to do so are weak. Coming from a border country, many Mexican migrants expect to return to Mexico, and many do. Moreover, there is a strong language network among the forty-seven million people of Hispanic descent in the United States (the Pew Research Center estimates that the Hispanic population will grow to 128 million by 2050), reducing the need to learn English. Many Mexican and other Central Americans are also here illegally, which hinders their efforts to become citizens.

More importantly, perhaps, is that most Hispanic organizations now constitute part of the multicultural coalition, pushing hard for bilingual/bicultural education, the rights of illegal immigrants, and affirmative action. Many of them, including the National Council of La Raza ("The Race"), are modeled on the major black civil rights groups and eschew the notion that newcomers should be made to conform to a particular cultural standard.

Political pressure on Hispanic leaders emanating from well heeled foundations, government agencies, urban pressure groups, and academia to follow the path of blacks in politicizing their grievances and developing a culture of rejection are considerable. Bilingualism, for example, which initially began as a well intentioned effort to cushion the path toward English mastery, has become in the eyes of many of its proponents a means of keeping Spanish language and culture separate and alive.[8]

Obama appears eager to encourage this form of separatism. Two weeks before the congressional elections of 2010, Obama told the "Piolínpor la Mañana" program, a Univision Spanish language radio show, "if Latinos sit out the election instead of saying, we're gonna punish our enemies and we're gonna reward our friends who stand with us on issues that are important to us, if they don't see that kind of upsurge in voting in this election, then I think it's gonna be harder - and that's why I think it's so important that people focus on voting on November 2."[9] For Obama, Republicans are primarily the white "enemies" of Hispanics who most multiculturalists count as "non-white," not the loyal opposition to the Democrats.

During the presidential campaign in July of 2008, Obama lamented legislative efforts to make English the official language of the United States and said Americans should instead focus on making sure their children learn Spanish. "I don't understand when people are going around worrying about, we need to have English only" Obama told supporters in Powder Springs, Georgia. "Now, I agree that immigrants should learn English, I agree with this. But understand this, instead of worrying about whether immigrants can learn English, they'll learn English, you need to make sure your child can speak Spanish."[10]

Obama also seems determined to promote the identity politics of the Hispanic elite. In his first Supreme Court nomination as president, Obama selected Sonia Sotomayor, a second district circuit court judge and, apparently, a believer in racial determinism. In 2001, the first

Latina Supreme Court nominee told an Hispanic group, "We need diversity because inherent physiological or cultural differences . . . make a difference in our judging." In the same speech she made this now famous remark about innate ability: "I would hope that a wise Latina woman with the richness of her experiences would more often than not reach a better conclusion (as a judge) than a white male who hasn't lived that life." This is a clear rejection of the view that individuals are to be judged on their merit, not by their ethnic or racial background. As a judge, Sotomayor sat on a panel that rejected the complaint of a group of white New Haven firefighters who scored high on a promotional exam but were denied promotion by the city. The city argued it was denying promotions to all candidates in order to stave off a "disparate impact" lawsuit by low scoring blacks. In a 5 to 4 decision, Sotomayor's panel was overturned by the U.S. Supreme Court on June 29, 2009. All of the justices, even the four dissenters, rejected Sotomayor's holding in the case. In her opinion for the dissenters, liberal Justice Ruth Bader Ginsburg acknowledged the "disparate impact" law's requirement that employment exams be reflective of job performance, and demanded the city prove the test did not meet that criterion. Sotomayor's panel never considered whether or not the test reflected job performance.[11]

It is not correct, then, to say that Hispanics as a group have not assimilated. Many Hispanics have assimilated rather well. It is just not always clear whether the American subcultures they have assimilated to are conducive to civic well being. Hispanic elites have adopted the identity politics of black leadership, academic institutions, and other sponsors of multiculturalism. They subscribe to the belief that acknowledging group suffering and discrimination is a higher value than rewarding individuals for their credentials. Judge Sotomayor once complained that "We (Latinos) have only ten out of 147 active circuit court judges and thirty out of 587 active district court judges. Those numbers are grossly below our proportion of the population." Sotomayor did not bother to estimate the number of Hispanics who are qualified to hold such posts. In her view, and presumably Obama's as well, proportional group representation trumps individual achievement.[12]

Just as the Hispanic elite have adopted the identity politics of the black civil rights establishment, there is a disturbing tendency on the part of poor Hispanics to assimilate to the norms of the urban poor. Like other immigrants, most Hispanics start off poor and move up the socioeconomic ladder through the generations. Forty-seven percent of first generation Hispanic children are poor, a rate that falls to 26 percent by the second generation. But by the third generation, just when other immigrant groups flood into the middle class, Hispanic progress comes to a halt. Its poverty rate drops only two points, with 24 percent of Hispanic kids growing up poor. The economic stagnation is associated with other social pathologies. Hispanic women have one of the highest rates of out-of-wedlock births among racial groups (51.3

percent in 2007). Moreover, the large proportion of Hispanic children being raised by a single parent rises over time: 69 percent of first generation Hispanic children live in married couple families compared with 73 percent of second generation children but just 52 percent in the third generation or higher. Crime rates also rise for the American born children of Mexican immigrants. Many Hispanics, in other words, are "assimilating down" rather than up. It is not surprising that with many of its members experiencing downward mobility, Hispanics as a group are less than enthusiastic about free market individualism. The 2002 Pew-Kaiser poll found that 60 percent of Hispanics said they "would prefer to pay higher taxes to support a larger government that provides more services" compared to 35 percent of whites.[13]

Hispanic attitudes toward cultural assimilation and speaking English are similarly ambivalent. Although 73 percent of Hispanics say that it is very or somewhat important for Hispanics to change so that they blend into the larger society, 93 percent say that it is very or somewhat important for Hispanics to maintain their distinct cultures. Furthermore, nearly nine out of ten (88 percent) Hispanics say that it is very or somewhat important for future generations of Hispanics living in the United States to speak Spanish. Only 55 percent of Hispanics believe an immigrant must speak English to "say they are a part of American Society" and only 54 percent say an immigrant must become a U.S. citizen to say the same.[14]

Obama is not just a proponent of multicultural policies. In being elected president, he has also been the most luminous beneficiary of the multicultural *zeitgeist*. Presidential elections are complicated things. Rarely does one factor determine the outcome. At the end of the day Obama's election was a referendum on the previous eight years and the deep economic recession that began in late 2007. The alarming financial meltdown, the collapse of financial powerhouse Lehman Brothers in September of 2008, and the nationalization of American International Group permitted the most ideologically left wing candidate in American history to put together a winning coalition. But the important question is not whether external events guaranteed the election of a generic Democrat. The chance that they did appears high. The more meaningful question is whether Obama -- or someone with an identical background -- could have won in 2008 if he was white, and the answer to that question seems to be a resounding "no."

The motivations of blacks and Hispanics in voting for Obama are fairly obvious. But during the 2008 Democratic primary race it also became clear that many whites were attracted to the idea of electing a black president, certainly more whites than were interested in Obama's actual record or holding him accountable for it. Many white Obama voters were motivated almost as much by Obama's race as were black Obama voters. Shelby Steele and others have pointed out that many whites saw voting for Mr. Obama as proof that they were personally void of any racism. Many others were motivated by the election's potential to prove to blacks that white racism isn't the primary impediment to black progress anymore. Whatever the case may be, Obama's race was central to his historic election to the presidency. Kwame Anthony Appiah, a philosopher and theorist of racial identity at Princeton University, has said of Obama's candidacy, "Senator Obama can only serve the function of moving us along in our racial politics because he counts as black. If we were moving beyond race altogether, he couldn't serve that function. He's an instance of the politics of recognition, not a move beyond it."[15]

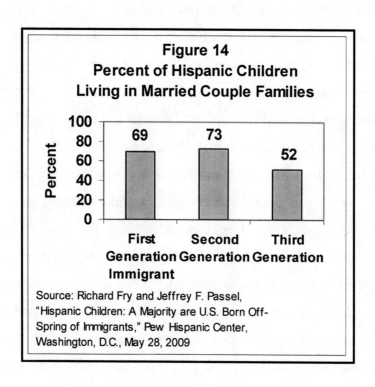

The likelihood that high numbers of blacks and whites voted for Obama because he is black, albeit with different anticipated outcomes, has set the stage for an era of anxiety and disappointment. Many white voters who now feel largely vindicated from the wrongs of America's past, stand to experience substantial regret as they come to discover that the pragmatic, post-racial candidate they voted for has turned out to be neither. If Obama continues on the road he has chosen early in his presidency, it will become obvious that Obama's vision for America -- that of a furtive and declining superpower with a tainted past committed to the drawing down of its defenses, the regulation of success, the expansion of the welfare state, and the distribution of spoils and privileges by race -- is not one the white voting public shares with the president. Cracks among centrists and independents, large numbers of whom voted for Obama, appeared early in his presidency. In January, 2009 just 13 percent of respondents in the *Wall Street Journal/NBC News* poll strongly disagreed with the notion that Mr. Obama shared their positions on the issues. That doubled to 25 percent by August, 2009. The proportion of Americans who strongly disagree that the president is willing to work with people whose viewpoints are different from his own nearly doubled, to 21 percent from 12 percent in April. Jonathan Weisman, chief investigator for the survey, reported that "the theme that Mr. Obama has played favorites with minorities surfaced in a number of voter interviews."[16]

For blacks, alienation will come in the discovery that significantly fewer Americans than might have been reflected in the election results share their vision of a more collectivist America or support Obama's far reaching agenda to attain it. This has already had a sobering effect. According to a Gallup report from November 9th of 2009, only 11 percent of blacks thought race relations would get a lot better with the election of Obama, compared with 23 percent in the summer of 2009, leading black columnist Charles Blow to conclude "The Age of Obama, so far at least, seems less about Obama as a black community game changer than as a White House gamesman. It's unclear if there will be a positive Obama Effect, but an Obama Backlash is increasingly apparent. Meanwhile, black people are also living a tale of two actions: grin and bear it."[17]

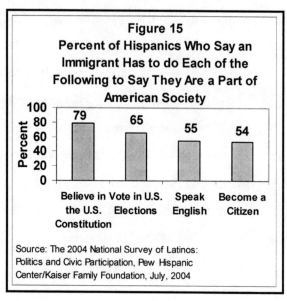

And what of Obama's underreported background as a "community organizer"? Supporters and pundits continue to emphasize Obama's admirable personal qualities as a father and husband, believing this will be transformative for black families, close to 70 percent of which are headed by single mothers. But knowledge that Obama built his career on a foundation of political agitation, blaming "the system," and shaking down private sector wealth on behalf of indigent "victims" will also leave a lasting impression. Blacks, and to a lesser extent Hispanics, stand to suffer if Obama's personal success reinforces the belief, now widespread within these groups, that racial solidarity in the pursuit of political power is the pathway to economic mobility. For a group of citizens that already views free market entrepreneurship with great skepticism, this could prove to be even more debilitating.

The rest of America will also be affected. As political economist George Gilder has written, "A society or a global system that misunderstands wealth creation and wishes to level society by penalizing success will make life poorer for everyone."

Nevertheless, Obama has pursued policies that seem not to have even a rudimentary concern for wealth creation or confiscatory tax levels. In his first two years in office, in the middle of a serious recession, Obama saddled the country with an enormous and still incalculable health care mandate on businesses and individuals. In the guise of economic "stimulus" and other emergency programs, federal spending rose a mind-numbing 37 percent from 2008 to 2010. Spending for all governmental levels was 42.7 percent of Gross Domestic Product (GDP) in 2010, up from 36.4 percent only two years before. The federal budget deficit alone (how much the government borrows each year) skyrocketed a whopping $1.8 trillion in the single year between 2008 and 2009 and in 2010 stood at 10.6 percent of GDP. This is up from 3.2 percent in 2008. To put this increased financial burden in greater context, the total federal debt per person in the United States rose from $32,800 in 2008 to $46,600 in 2010. As a percentage of gross domestic product, total government debt rose from 86.8 percent in 2008 to 117.5 percent in 2010. Even during World War II, the nation's total government debt never reached higher than 109 percent of GDP.[18]

By April of 2011, two years into Obama's term as president, these policies appeared to be having their desired effect. A *USA Today* study found that Americans depended more on government assistance than at any other time in the nation's history. A record 18.3 percent of the nation's total personal income was a payment from the government for social security, medicare, food stamps, unemployment benefits and other programs. In May of 2011 the U.S. Department of Agriculture reported that 44.2 million, or 1 in 7 Americans, were receiving food stamps, the highest ever. In 2010 wages accounted for the lowest share of income -- 51 percent – since the government began keeping track in 1929. By April of 2011, both the labor force participation rate and the ratio of people in the workforce as a percentage of the population eligible to work reached twenty-five year lows (64.2 percent and 58.4

percent, respectively). The trend of government dependency showed few signs of easing, even though an economic recovery was said to be nearly two years old. For the single month of February 2011 wages accounted for 50.5 of total income.[19]

Far from empowering blacks, the 2008 presidential election will likely create an even more aggrieved class of black victims. With the encouragement of white elites and a compliant media, many blacks have invested Obama personally with almost Promethean capabilities. Failure or criticism of the administration will not go down easily. The possibility that blacks will interpret the normal give and take of democracy, the ups and downs of presidential administrations, standard partisan politics, and the mundane tasks of day-to-day governance as, in fact, purposeful racial obstructionism is strong. Even the time honored tradition of rendering the president in caricature on posters, billboards, and Halloween masks has the potential to deeply offend black Obama supporters. In the summer of 2008 just the image of Obama's face on a poster in the makeup of actor Heath Ledger's "Joker" in the movie *Batman* turned the inimitable non-racial Joker into a symbol of racism. "By using the 'urban' makeup of the Heath Ledger Joker, instead of the urbane makeup of the Jack Nicholson character," Philip Kennicott of the *Washington Post* explained, "the poster connects Obama to something many of his detractors fear but can't openly discuss. He is black and he is identified with the inner city, a source of political instability in the 1960s and '70s, and a lingering bogeyman in political consciousness."[20]

Obama as "The Joker." Seen in Livermore, CA Greenville Rd., 2008. Photo by Dave Parker.

Racially polarized presidential approval ratings, followed by the possibility of electoral defeat for Obama, could engender severe resentment among blacks, evidence for many of them that whites won't let even the most gifted black man in America succeed.

Chapter 9

CONCLUSION: WHAT WAS LOST

No modern president has been elected with the emotional fervor upon which Obama has risen to power. Obama's supporters have infused his presidency with a missionary zeal that makes rational analysis difficult and sincere opposition dishonorable. Elites of all races, through the media outlets and college classrooms where they predominate, have worked tirelessly to define support for Barack Obama as the measure of moral decency, and to exile opponents to the realm of "Palin style" dolthood or "Birch style" bigotry. Fierce opposition to Obama's health care reform proposals in 2009 triggered responses from Obama supporters that are illustrative of this unseemly campaign. Congressman John Dingell (D-Michigan) said on national television that opponents of health care reform remind him of the Ku Klux Klan. Columnist Cynthia Tucker told Chris Matthews of MSNBC's *Hardball* that 45 to 65 percent of health care reform protesters showing up at town hall meetings in the summer of 2009 were racist. *New York Times* columnist Paul Krugman wrote that "the driving force behind the town hall mobs is probably the same cultural and racial anxiety that's behind the 'birther' movement, which denies Mr. Obama's citizenship." These attacks came at a time when a Rasmussen poll showed that 62 percent of unaffiliated (independent) voters opposed the Obama health care reforms.[1]

Even if the Obama presidency is ultimately a smashing success, mitigating the failure of those charged with reflecting on politics impartially on the public's behalf, much has been lost with his election. The studied refusal of Obama supporters to see anything in his candidacy but the highest possible moral purpose has resulted in a serious diminution of what has historically gone into the making of a president. Given Obama's demonstrated lack of achievement in either business or government, his unprecedented lack of executive experience, and the virtual celebration of his candidacy by a fawning media, it will be nearly impossible to insist on a well developed resume from future presidential contenders. State governorships, city mayoralties, and even U.S. senate seats have seen experienced candidates with well honed executive skills usurped by candidates with only celebrity name recognition and personal wealth or charisma. The former governor of California, and former bodybuilder and movie star, Arnold Schwarzenegger, New York City media mogul and Mayor Michael Bloomberg, and the current U.S. senator from Minnesota, former comedian Al Franken, are only the most obvious examples of this. But the U.S. presidency has, until now, been held to a higher standard. More time in the public eye and more scrutiny has been required for Americans to grant permission to fill the shoes of Lincoln and Washington, to occupy an office that reflects the national conscience and is endowed with more symbolic and formal power and esteem than any other. This is the true value of executive and federal government experience for presidential candidates: it is not that the skills learned in these positions can't be learned elsewhere. It is that executive experience somewhere in the public eye creates witnesses to an individual's character, beliefs, feelings and, ultimately, actions and achievements, something that even the most "straight talking," honest, and forthright political campaign can not do.

It is exceedingly strange, in fact, that besides Reverend Jeremiah Wright, nobody of any prominence ever really stepped forward during the 2008 presidential race to vouch for Obama's professional capabilities. Hoover Institute scholar Shelby Steele has observed that "without self-disclosure on the one hand or cross-examination on the other, Mr. Obama became arguably the least known man ever to step into the American presidency."[2] It is true that Obama's wife Michelle made a speech at the 2008 Democratic convention focusing on Obama's personal qualities. The Clintons made tortured gestures of reassurance in Obama's "readiness to lead." But unlike John Kerry, who accepted the Democratic nomination with a dozen mates from his Vietnam days at his side, or George W. Bush, who had legions of Texas politicians, Democrats and Republicans, praising him at the podium, such testimonials about Obama were completely absent. As columnist Charles Krauthammer wrote after the convention, "Eerily missing at the Democratic convention this year were people of stature who were seriously involved at some point in Obama's life standing up to say: I know Barack Obama. I've been with Barack Obama."[3]

Even Bill Clinton wondered during the Democratic primary about the impact of "electing a president based on one year of service before he's running?" When talk show host Charlie Rose responded that "experienced" politicians have made their share of blunders, Clinton answered "That's like saying that because 100 percent of the malpractice cases are committed by doctors, the next time I need surgery, I'll get a chef or a plumber to do it."[4]

As effective and talented a leader as Obama may yet turn out to be, in the wake of his election, it is not clear if any particular background, skill set, prior behavior or level of public familiarity will be expected of future presidential aspirants. This signals a clear break with the informal understanding of the recent past that the highest office in the land be reserved for those who have submitted a reasonable portion of their lives to public scrutiny. Given that Obama was a U.S. senator for just under two years before beginning his run for president, the office of the U.S. president now reflects the absence of standards and the culture of celebrity endemic to so many areas of American life. It was the submission to these standards that gave the public confidence that the office of the president, independent of the individual holding that office, was properly representative of the nation at large. They were the basis upon which a nation of exceptional diversity was able to establish the trust necessary to allow the gradual consolidation of executive power in one person's hands. They are why America's foremost monument to character and leadership remains Mount Rushmore, which features the facial carvings of four very different presidents. It is unlikely the presidency will continue its crucial role in America's democracy if future ads for the office read "no experience necessary."

Youthful drinking binges, divorce, military deferments, pot smoking, infidelity, and psychological instability have all been character issues that have impacted modern presidential campaigns. But the one standard that has remained consistent has been that major party presidential nominees be free of any association with racial hatred or the condoning of anti-American violence. After Obama's deeply troubling associations (Reverend Jeremiah Wright, Professor Rashid Khalidi, and domestic terrorist Bill Ayers), on what basis can voters insist that a candidate for president demonstrate a lifelong commitment to rejecting extremism? Given Obama's deep entanglement with politically radical and corrupt organizations like ACORN, the Trinity United Church of Christ, and the Woods Fund of Chicago, can any amount of cynical pandering to local voting blocs and interest groups eliminate a prospective candidate from serious presidential contention? Obama's election has obliterated anything resembling a consensus on these matters we may have previously had. That Donald Trump -- a loud, brutish, and bombastic reality t.v. show celebrity with no demonstrated competence in electoral governance but many demonstrated character flaws -- may one day be taken seriously as a presidential candidate owes to no one so much as it does Barack Obama, whose own candidacy seriously eroded the standards for presidential qualification.

The election of the country's first black president was supposed to usher in a post-racial era of group amity and trust, a permanent state of color blindness that has been the nation's unrealized dream since its founding. Obama came to the American people bearing the long sought after gifts of racial conciliation and color blindness, but instead has brought the country to a dangerous racial precipice. America's obsession with race, reflected in the 2008 presidential vote, allowed Barack Obama to get elected despite holding views that are anathema to most mainstream voters. As a result, Obama's agenda poses a direct challenge to the belief of many Americans in the value of their "earned success," of individualism, free enterprise, and self-government. Large swaths of the American public sense they are witnessing changes to the nation's governmental and private institutions that are really transformations of the American character, changes in the way America defines the responsibilities of citizenship that will undermine the nation's exceptional nature. Obama's presidency has forced a recognition among whites of how deeply radical politics has become entwined with "being black," and laid bare the painful and irreconcilable political differences that still separate blacks and whites.

So deep are the divisions that now encumber race relations in the United States that no less a giant of American sociology than Harvard's Nathan Glazer insisted recently that racial matters have moved beyond the realm of discussion. The election of Barack Obama to the presidency marked "a paradox in the long history of race in America," Glazer has written. "There was a time not so long ago when we had trouble having a dispassionate, constructive discussion of these matters in public; now we seem unable to have any discussion at all."[5]

Statements like this coming from the sleepy groves of academe may not raise eyebrows. But when two long time Democratic pollsters, Patrick Caddell and Douglas Schoen, take to the *Wall Street Journal*, as they did on July 28th, 2010 to call President Obama "cynical" and "racially divisive," it's a thunderbolt that America can no longer ignore. With Obama's presidency the vast political differences between blacks and whites in America has now emerged as an explosive frontline issue.

Critics who spoke of a post-racial America if Obama became president ignored the fact, laid out in his two autobiographies and throughout his career, that Obama embodies the ambivalence that many blacks feel toward the "American creed" of individualism, free enterprise, and American "exceptionalism." Whites were content to cede the politics of racial grievance to blacks so long as the changes it required (e.g. affirmative action, multicultural school curricula) were on the margins and primarily local in nature. But Obama's aggressive agenda to change the vital structure of American life to reflect the more collectivist, less individualistic creed of the far left does not sit well with the broad white middle class, though it does with most blacks. An initial boost in racial optimism with Obama's election has declined into a rueful pessimism, most distinct among blacks. A Rasmussen poll in October 2010 found that 39 percent of whites think black-white race relations are getting better, but just 13 percent of blacks agree. Only 12 percent of all voters agreed in September of 2009 that opposition to the health care overhaul was motivated by racism, but among blacks, 27 percent felt that way and 48 percent were undecided. Rather than eliminating race as a significant issue in American politics, the Obama presidency has made it the central cleavage in American life for years to come.[6]

The political economist Thomas Sowell once compared Obama's imminent election victory to baseball great Paul Waner's 3,000th hit. Waner, a star for the Pittsburgh Pirates in the 1920s and '30s, requested the official scorer not count his softly hit, misplayed ground ball to second base as a "hit" because it was, in Waner's view, really a fielding error. Waner believed the 3,000th hit of a career should be a legitimate one, and the official scorer complied with his wish, marking it down in the record book as an error. When Waner eventually smacked his 3,000th hit several days later, the achievement was much more satisfying than if it were reached through a "gimme." I assured Waner that there would be no question marks or asterisks in the history books near his name. So too, Sowell believed, the election of a black man to the presidency would be a great and inevitable achievement. But that Barack Obama should be that black man is probably the political equivalent of counting a fielding error as a hit. Prior to the 2008 vote Sowell wrote, "It is only a matter of time before there is a black president . . . The issue is whether we want to reach that landmark so badly that we are willing to overlook how questionably that landmark is reached."[7]

Though treated like something miraculous by the punditry, the election of a black president would seem to follow naturally from an ever expanding circle of opportunity for all Americans. If there was anything miraculous about the election of Barack Obama as America's first black president it is how much the nation was willing to overlook to achieve it.

INDEX

"Obama Effect", 76, 258
"riot insurance", 228
1953 Iranian coup, 71, 230
60 Minutes, 62, 67, 146
9/11 - terrorist attack, 24, 63, 67, 68, 69, 174, 175
ABC News, 147, 158, 159, 231
ABC's Good Morning America, 10, 147
Abigail Thernstrom, vii, 3, 43, 111, 124, 280
abortion, 129, 130, 131, 134, 135, 145, 161
ACORN, 13, 103, 104, 201, 203, 204, 267
Admiral Mike Mullen, 22
affirmative action, 15, 37, 48, 103, 139, 182, 246, 250, 269
Afghanistan, 13, 23, 28, 63, 81, 83, 168, 170
African American Teacher's Association, 229
Ahmed Ghailani, 63
Al Arabiya, 210
Al Gore, 125, 128, 135, 149, 205
Al Jazeera, 65
al Qaeda, 24, 25, 27, 63, 69
Al Sharpton, 44, 127, 193
Alaska Independence Party, 204
Alexander Hamilton, 45
Alexis DeToqueville, 216
Alicia Keys, 113
Allen West, 88
Alvin Poussaint, 93
American Enterprise Institute, 45
American exceptionalism, 215, 218, 219, 227, 235, 236, 244
American power, 15, 20, 21, 22, 25, 33, 39, 59, 82, 219, 230, 237, 241

Americanization, 248, 249
Anderson Cooper, 157
Andre Carson, 9
Andrew Breitbart, 206
Andrew C. McCarthy, 208
Angela Merkel, 72
Anita Dunn, 61
Arnold Schwarzenegger, 166, 264
Arthur Schlesinger, 243
Artur Davis, 93
assimilation, 93, 249, 254
Association of Community Organizations for Reform Now, 13, 103
Atlantic Monthly, 161
Audacity of Hope, 127, 152, 243
Baltimore Sun, 159
Barbara Ehrenreich, 203
Bashar al-Assad, 230
Batman, 261
Bayard Rustin, 91, 228
Berlin, 24, 29, 72, 238
Berlin Wall, 72
Bill Bradley, 142
Bill Clinton, 4, 127, 140, 149, 150, 179, 213, 240, 266
Black Entertainment Television (BET), 113, 185
black grievance, 44, 48, 92
black nationalists, 96, 98, 99, 229
Black Power, 154, 227, 229, 231, 232, 235, 245
black rage, 37, 42, 43, 44, 185
black Republican, 87, 88, 114
Black Values System, 97
Bob McDonnell, 79
Bob Schieffer, 78, 152
Bobby Rush, 4, 196
Booker T. Washington, 35, 155

Index

Born Again (Christians), 128, 134
Bosnian, 28
Brandenburg Gate, 72, 73
Brent Staples, 43
Brian Williams, 69
British Petroleum, 67
Bush Doctrine, 65
Campaign Finance Institute, 143
Carol Swain, 206
Castro (Raul and Fidel), 195, 196
Cathleen Falsani, 96
Center for Media and Public Affairs at George Mason University, 149, 150
Charles Blow, 258
Charles Bolden, 65
Charles Gibson, 158
Charles Hill, 59
Charles Krauthammer, vii, 20, 33, 58, 160, 246, 266
Charles Rangel, 6, 172
Charlie Rose, 266
Chicago Annenberg Challenge (CAC), 102, 201, 202
Chicago Magazine, 101
Chicago Reader, 97
Chicago Sun-Times, 96, 98, 174
Chicago's Grant Park, 237
China, 21, 82, 186, 224, 241
Chris Cillizza, 110
Chris Matthews, 156, 263
Christine "Roz" Samuels, 110
Christopher Hitchens, 162
CIA - Central Intelligence Agency, 62, 68, 69, 70, 71, 207, 231
City of New Haven, 62
Civil Rights Act, 7, 46, 90, 122
civil rights protest model, 35
Clark Hoyt, 148
CNN, 7, 27, 43, 112, 117, 156, 157, 163, 164, 182, 185, 189
Cocoa Tea, 113
Col. Moammar Gadhafi, 22, 23, 24, 25, 82, 221, 230

Colin Powell, 87, 114, 127
Columbia University, 206, 218, 219
community organizer, 200, 202, 259
Community Reinvestment Act (of 1977), 103
Congressional Black Caucus, 6, 10, 93, 176, 195
Congressional Budget Office, 56
Creigh Deeds, 79
Crisis of the Negro Intellectual, 228
Crispus Attucks, 45
Current Population Survey, 117
Cynthia Tucker, 263
Czech Republic, 30, 33
Daily Breeze, 108
Daily Caller, 158
Dan Armstrong, 200
Dana Redd, 110
David Brooks, 139
David Cameron, 22
David Dinkins, 123
David Horowitz, 4, 280
David Paterson, 5, 280
David Paul Kuhn, 80, 120, 142
David Scott, 110
Deepwater Horizon, 67
Democratic party, 38, 80, 86, 89, 122, 177, 203, 209
Democratic Socialists of America, 203
Department of Homeland Security (DOHS), 66, 224
Der Spiegel, 67
Deval Patrick, 5
Dinesh D'Souza, vii, 94
Dmitri Medvedev, 30
Don Imus, 44
Donald Trump, 207, 267
Dorothy Rabinowitz, 71
Douglas Schoen, 269
Douglas Wilder, 123
Dreams from My Father, 94, 154, 200, 209

Dual Language Exchange, 104
E.D. Hirsch, 44
E.J. Dionne, 1, 280
Earl Ofari Hutchinson, 108
East Africa Journal, 94
Ebonya Washington, 87
Ed Schultz, 78
Edison Media, 117
Edward Brooke, 114
Edward Said, 218
Eliot Spitzer, 5, 164
Ellis Cose, 37
enhanced interrogation, 62, 68, 69
Environmental Protection Agency (EPA), 58
Eric Holder, 4, 63
Ethics and Public Policy Center, 105
Eugene Genovese, 35
Evan Thomas, 235, 280
Evangelicals/Christians, xiii, 128, 129, 192
Exxon Valdez oil spill, 67
Ezra Pound, 217
Fareed Zakaria, 27
FDR, 49
Federal Election Commission, 143
Federal Reserve (Board), 60
Felipe Calderon, 222
Franklin Delano Roosevelt, 49
Fred Siegel, 36, 92
Frederick Jackson Turner, 216
Fugitive Days, 101
fundraising, 143
Gallup, 7, 54, 73, 76, 77, 135, 173, 178, 213, 258
GDP, 49, 52, 260
General David Petraeus, 83
George Gilder, 259
George P. Schultz, 59
George Stephanopoulos, 158, 202
George W. Bush, 3, 13, 14, 23, 24, 62, 81, 115, 116, 138, 143, 146, 149, 150, 162, 205, 208, 210, 222, 265

George Wallace, 160
Gerald David Jaynes, 40
Geraldine Ferraro, 108
Global War on Terror (GWOT), 64
Gloria Steinem, 203
God and Country Festival, 136
Gross Domestic Product, 49, 260
Grutter v Bollinger, 105
Guantanamo Bay, 24, 62, 67, 68, 69
Hamilton College, 75
Harold Cruse, 228
Harold Washington, 123
Harriet Beecher Stowe, 45
Harriet Tubman, 45
Harry Truman, 72, 73
Harvard University, 57, 185, 206
health care reform, 7, 8, 56, 93, 172, 175, 180, 186, 263
Heath Ledger, 261
Henry "Scoop" Jackson, 72
Henry Adams, 217
Henry Louis Gates, Jr., 186, 192
Hillary Clinton, 5, 22, 108, 109, 135, 153, 157, 164, 208
Hispanics, xiv, 16, 116, 178, 179, 180, 233, 247, 249, 251, 252, 253, 254, 255, 259
Horatio Alger, 245
Hosni Mubarak, 230
Howard Dean, 38
Howard Kurtz, 1, 280
Howard Zinn, 203, 218
Howell Raines, 43
Hugo Chavez, 20
Hurricane Katrina, 43
immigrants, 13, 103, 164, 166, 193, 222, 223, 224, 247, 249, 250, 251, 253
immigration, 48, 117, 166, 192, 222, 224, 232, 247
International Olympic Committee, 239
Iran, 13, 21, 33, 71, 82, 221, 230

Index

Iraq, 14, 23, 24, 27, 28, 81, 83, 115, 148, 168
Islamism, 71
Islamist, 70, 208, 225
J.C. Watts, 114
James Ceasar, 235, 239
James Forman, 228
James Hund, 95
Janet Napolitano, 66
Japan, 33, 73, 226
Jay Cost, 128, 140
Jayson Blair, 43
Jeremiah Wright, 98, 99, 105, 121, 153, 163, 172, 199, 206, 243, 265, 267
Jesse Jackson, 43, 93, 108, 123, 127, 177, 243
Jim Martin, 119
Jim Rutenberg, 113
Jimmy Carter, 125, 176
Joel Kotkin, 139
John Bolton, 222
John Dingell, 263
John Kennedy, 72
John Kerry, xiii, 110, 117, 125, 128, 135, 138, 141, 142, 143, 149, 166, 167, 168, 205, 265
John Lewis, 110
John McCain, 23, 113, 114, 115, 117, 130, 147, 151, 163, 168, 170, 174, 211, 246
John McWhorter, 96, 114
John O'Sullivan, 126
Jon Meacham, 1
Jonah Goldberg, 3, 280
Jonathan Weisman, 257
Jordan, 33
Jose Rodriguez, 69
Joseph C. Phillips, 114
Journolist, 158, 159
Juan Williams, 3, 172, 280
Justice Department (DOJ), 54, 63, 68, 194, 224, 231

Kaiser Family Foundation, 53, 249
Karith Foster, 44
Karl Rove, 159
Kay Hymowitz, 47
Ken Blackwell, 88
Kenneth Feinberg, 59
Kevin Jennings, 61
Khalid Sheik Mohammed (KSM), 63
Khalil Gibran International, 46
Kim Jong Il, 20
Kuwait, 28, 33
Kwame Anthony Appiah, 256
Kwanzaa, 96
Lanny Davis, 157
Larry Johnson, 207
Larry King, 129, 163
Latinos, 84, 247, 251, 253
Laura Ingraham, 137
Leon Panetta, 69
Lester K. Spence, 114
liberals, 44, 78, 138, 139, 140, 143, 144, 228, 243
Libya, 22, 82, 221, 230
Lolo Soetoro, 94, 207, 209
Louis Farrakhan, 98, 106, 108, 127
Louise Lucas, 109
Lyndon Baines Johnson (LBJ), 92
Lynn Swann, 88
Mahmoud Ahmidinejad, 221
Malcolm X, 14, 113, 154, 155, 191
Manning Marable, 93
Mao Tse-Tung, 61
Margaret Thatcher, 72
Mark Halperin, 147
Mark Lloyd, 60
Mark Steyn, 153
Martin Luther King, Jr., 36, 45, 112, 155
Mary Frances Berry, 84
Matthew Arnold, 216
Maulana Karenga, 96
Maxine Waters, 6
Maya Soetoro-Ng, 209

Mayor Michael White, 110
media bias, 146, 151
Medicaid, 7, 52, 53, 56
Meet the Press, 115
Melvin Watt, 6
Mexican, 222, 249, 254
Miami Herald, 196
Michael Bloomberg, 264
Michael Dawson, 108, 109
Michael Gerson, 3
Michael Isikoff, 70
Michael Pfleger, 99, 105
Michael Steele, 10, 88, 211
Michael Tomasky, 159
Mighty Sparrow, 113
Milton Galamison, 228
More Perfect Union (speech), 153, 156, 160
Muhammad Ali, 113
mujahedeen, 28
multiculturalism, 229, 231, 253
Muslim extremists, 24
Muslims, 27, 28, 48, 210
NAACP, 154, 171
Nancy Pelosi, 9, 135
Nathan Glazer, 269
Nathan Silver, 141
Nation of Islam (NOI), 98, 106, 108, 154
National Association for the Advancement of Colored People, 10, 182
National Council of La Raza, 250
National Election Pool (exit poll), 86, 110
National Public Radio, 3, 150, 156
National Review, 3, 126, 179, 280
National Security Strategy, 64
National Voter Registration Act ("motor voter"), 54
National Welfare Rights Organization (NWRO), 103
NATO, 22, 24

NBC News, 2, 69, 257
New Ground, 203
New Haven firefighters, 252
New Party, 203, 204
New START, 30, 31, 32
New York Times, 2, 43, 70, 101, 113, 114, 121, 146, 148, 150, 156, 158, 165, 169, 176, 178, 204, 208, 209, 263, 280
New Yorker, 169, 240
Newsweek, 1, 70, 150, 235, 280
Nicholas Kristof, 209
Nicholas Lemann, 139
Nicolas Sarkozy, 22
Noam Chomsky, 203
Nobel Peace Prize, 21, 80
Nuclear Posture Review, 32, 226
Obamacare, 56, 57
Occidental College, 206
Oprah Winfrey, 113, 189
Osama bin Laden, 20, 24, 69, 82, 231
P. Diddy, 113
Pakistan, 23, 63, 69, 95, 205
Patient Protection and Affordable Care Act, 56
Patrick Caddell, 269
Patrick J. Buchanan, 160, 161, 162, 217
Paul Krugman, 121, 263
Paul Tsongas, 142
Paul Waner, 270
Peter Bernholz, 50
Pew Center for the People and the Press, 112, 183
Pew Hispanic Center, 116, 249
Pew Research Center, 75
Poland, 30, 33
Pope John Paul II, 72
Pradeep Ramamurthy, 65
presidency, the, vii, 1, 10, 11, 28, 29, 48, 49, 74, 78, 79, 100, 120, 122, 132, 150, 163, 171, 177, 179, 182, 189, 190, 198, 205, 212, 236, 239,

245, 256, 257, 263, 264, 265, 267, 268, 269, 270, 271
Prince George's County, 38
Qatar, 33
Ralph Bunche, 228
Ralph Ellison, 42
Randall Ballmer, 162
Rashid Khalidi, 148, 267
Rasmussen polling, 57, 182, 213, 241, 264, 270
Realclearpolitics, 128, 141
Reihan Salam, 139
Republican party, 88, 115, 162
Reverend James T. Meeks, 99
Reverend Jerry Falwell, 217
Rhody McCoy, 228
Rick Warren, 129
Robert Bork, 217
Robert Mugabe, 221
Robin Williams, 40
Rod Blagojevich, 4
Roger Wilkins, 34
Ronald Reagan, 31, 72, 215, 243
Ross Perot, 161
Russia, 20, 21, 30, 31, 82, 226, 227
Ruy Texeira, 139
S. Robert Lichter, 145, 146, 149
Sacred Heart University, 150, 211
Saddam Hussein, 24, 28
Saddleback Church, 129
Salim al Nurridin, 98
Samuel Joseph Wurzelbacher, 246
Sara Hussein Obama, 208
Sarah Palin, 115, 125, 168, 204, 210
Saudi Arabia, 33
Saxby Chambliss, 119
Sean Trende, 128, 140
Serbian nationalists, 28
Shelby Steele, 13, 94, 127, 139, 183, 190, 197, 255, 265
Shiloh Baptist Church, 100
Sonia Sotomayor, 61, 84, 178, 197, 251

Sonny Carson, 228
South Shore African Village Collaborative, 104
Soviet Union, 31
Spencer Ackerman, 159
Stanley Kurtz, 105, 200
Star Parker, 129
Stephen Thernstrom, vii
Steve Kroft, 62
Steven Sark, 161
Student Non-Violent Coordinating Committee, 229
Sweetness and Light, 201
Syria, 230
T.S. Eliot, 217
Taiwan, 33
Taliban, 28, 63, 238
Tavis Smiley, 78, 109, 208
Tea Party, 9, 10, 122
Texas Air National Guard, 146, 210
The Politics of Hope, 243
Thomas F. Schaller, 40
Thomas Friedman, 2
Thomas Paine, 215
Thomas Schaller, 159
Thomas Sowell, vii, 61, 270
Tim Russert, 108
Tim Scott, 88
Time magazine, 2, 147
Tom Bradley, 123
Toni Foulkes, 204
Tony Powell, 44
Trinity United Church of Christ, 97, 98, 152, 164, 267
Turkey, 27, 33, 220, 233, 235
U.S. Bureau of Labor Statistics, 76, 77
U.S. Census Bureau, 51, 116
U.S. House of Representatives (congress), 123, 135
Ulysses S. Grant, 45
United Nations, 17, 21, 25, 82, 221, 222, 237, 240

UNITY, xi, 198, 246
Vaclav Klaus, 58
Van Jones, 61, 174
Vicki Iseman, 148
Vietnam (war), 115, 166, 167, 168, 265
Vladimir Putin, 31
Voting Rights Act, 90, 122, 194
W.E.B. Du Bois, 35
Wallace Charles Smith, 100, 106
Warrant Ballentine, 137
waterboarding, 62, 69
Weather Underground, 101, 201
Whoopi Goldberg, 78
William Ayers, 13, 101, 201
William Jefferson, 6
Wilson Goode, 123
Woodrow Wilson, 221, 248
Woods Foundation, 204
World Trade Center, 68, 152, 209
World War II, 20, 27, 33, 45, 50, 73, 221, 225, 238, 260
Zimbabwe, 21, 221

NOTES

NOTES – Introduction

[1] E.J. Dionne, "A New Era for America," *Washington Post*, November 5, 2008.

[2] This title was later changed to *A Long Time Coming: The Inspiring, Combative 2008 Campaign and the Historic Election of Barack Obama*. Evan Thomas and Richard Wolffe, "Obama's Lincoln," *Newsweek*, November 15, 2008; Howard Kurtz, "A Giddy Sense of Boosterism," *Washington Post*, November 17, 2008.

[3] "Yes We Can," NBC Universal Networks, 2009.

[4] Don Van Drehle, "Why History Can't Wait," *Time*, December 17, 2008.

[5] Thomas L. Friedman, "The American Civil War Ended," *New York Times*, November 4, 2008.

[6] Juan Williams, "What Obama's Election Means for Race Relations," *Wall Street Journal*, November 10, 2008; Abigail Thernstrom, "One Journey Ends," *New York Post*, January 21, 2009; Gerson quoted in Gideon Rackman, "The Man is the Message," *Financial Times*, January 20, 2009.

[7] Juan Williams, "What Obama's Victory Means for Racial Politics"; Abigail Thernstrom, "One Journey Ends," *New York Post*, January 21, 2009; Jonah Goldberg, "What Obama Brings to Conservatives," *National Review*, January 21, 2009; David Horowitz, *Hating Whitey and Other Progressive Causes* (New York: Spence, 1999); David Horowitz, "How Conservatives Should Celebrate the Inauguration," *Frontpagemag.com*, January 20, 2009.

[8] Pierre Thomas and Jason Ryan, "Stinging Remarks on Race From Attorney General," *ABCNews.com*, February 1, 2009; "Rush Joins Senate Seat Circus," *NBCChicago.com*, December 31, 2008; John Blake, "Could an Obama Presidency Hurt Black Americans,"*CNNPolitics.com*, July 22, 2008.

[9] Kenneth Lovett, "Gov. David Paterson Blames Calls for Him to Step Aside on Race," *New York Daily News*, August 21, 2009; Kenneth Lovett, "Poll shows Gov. Paterson Far Behind Democratic Rival Andrew Cuomo," *Daily News*, August 16, 2009.

10 "Black Caucus Rises to Jefferson's Defense," *Associated Press*, June 8, 2006. Found on world wide web at <http://www.msnbc.msn.com/id/13212812/> (accessed August 20, 2010); Harold Jackson, "Allegations and Racism," *Philadelphia Inquirer*, August 15, 2010; Jonah Goldberg, "Race Card Payment Coming Due," *Realclearpoliltics.com*, August 13, 2010; "Rangel's Race Ruse," *New York Post*, August 22, 2010.

11 Mark Penn, "The Health Care Jam," *Realclearpolitics.com*, March 8, 2010; "Obama and the Democrats' Health Plan," *Realclearpolitics.com*, table on national polls. Found on world wide web <http://www.realclearpolitics.com/epolls/other/obama_and_democrats_health_care_plan-1130.html> (accessed April 10, 2010).

12 Andrew Breitbart, "Barack Obama's Helter-Skelter, Insane Clown Posse, Alinsky Plans to 'Deconstruct' America," *Bigjournalism.com*, April 2, 2010; Thomas Sowell, "Race and Politics," *Realclearpolitics.com*, April 6, 2010; "Rep.: Protesters Yell Racial Slurs," *CBSNews.com*, March 20, 2010; Jesse Washington, "Wrong Video of Health Protest Spurs 'N-Word' Dispute," *Associated Press*, April 13, 2010; Ben Jealous, "Denouncing and Repudiating the Tea Party's Racism," *Blackstarnews*, July 18, 2010. Found on world wide web at http://blackstarnews.com/news/135/ARTICLE/6691/2010-07-18.html (accessed August 20, 2010); Kenneth T. Walsh, *Family of Freedom: Presidents and African Americans in the White House* (Boulder, Colo.: Paradigm Publishers 2010).

13 "Michael Steele's Lame Excuse," *New York Post*, April 7, 2010.

14 Shelby Steele, "The Obama Bargain," *Wall Street Journal*, March 18, 2008.

NOTES – Chapter 1

[1] Charles Krauthammer, "Decline Is a Choice: The New Liberalism and the End of American Ascendancy," *Weekly Standard*, October 19, 2009.

[2] "Full Text of Obama's Strasbourg Town Hall with Questions," *Los Angeles Times*, April 3, 2009.

[3] Joshua Hersh, "Oh, Hill No!," *The Daily*, March 17, 2011.

[4] Seth Forman, "Obama's Scary Discomfort with American Power," *American Thinker*, March 29, 2011.

[5] "Obama: America a Superpower 'Whether We Like It or Not'," *Foxnews.com,* April 15, 2010.

[6] Stephen Schwartz, "America Defends Muslims," *Weekly Standard,* February 12, 2003.

[7] Charles Krauthammer, "The Selective Modesty of Barack Obama," *Washington Post,* July 9, 2010; George Will, "As the Oceans Rise," *Newsweek,* June 7, 2008.

[8] John Guardino, "The Obama Doctrine," *FrumFiles.com,* December 14, 2009; "Obama Constitution Quote in Context." Found on world wide web at <http://www.youtube.com/watch?v=a_xNyrzB0xI&feature=player_embedded> (accessed October 22, 2009).

[9] Jim DeMint, "The Treaty is Mad," *National Review,* July 29, 2010.

[10] Dinesh D'Souza, "President Ronald Reagan: Winning the Cold War," *American History* (October 2003); DeMint.

[11] DeMint.

[12] Tunku Varadarajan, "Obama is Weakening America," *The Daily Beast,* April 6, 2010; Dick Cheney, "Concerns About America's Foreign Policy Drift," *Realclearpolitics.com,* October 22, 2009; Jack Kelly, "President Obama's Nuclear Naïveté," *Realclearpolitics.com,* April 11, 2010; Fred Kaplan, "How Revolutionary is Obama's Nuclear Posture," *Slate,* April 10, 2010; Charles Krauthammer, "U.S. Shouldn't Play Nice on Nukes," *Washington Post,* April 9, 2010.

[13] Barack Obama, *Dreams from My Father: A Story of Race and Inheritance* (New York: Three Rivers Press, electronic version 2004), 6. Quoted by Gregory Chang, "Quotes on Race, *Dreams From My Father.*" Found on world wide web at <http://www.stop-obama.org> (accessed on September 11, 2009).

[14] Bruce Wright, *Black Robes, White Justice* (New York: Carol Publishing, 1987), 65; Lena Williams, "In a '90s Quest for Black Identity, Intense Doubts and Disagreements," *New York Times,* November 30, 1991, A-1, A-26. Cited by Dinesh D'Souza, *The End of Racism* (New York: Free Press, 1995), 480.

[15] Richard Alba and Victor Nee, *Remaking the American Mainstream: Assimilation and Contemporary Immigration* (Cambridge, MA: Harvard University Press, 2003); Miriam Cohen, *Workshop to Office: Two Generations of Italian Women in New York City, 1900-1950* (Ithaca, NY: Cornell University Press, 1992); Thomas Guglielmo, *White on Arrival: Race, Color, and Power in Chicago, 1890-1945* (New York:

Oxford University Press, 2003); Thomas Kessner, *The Golden Door: Italian and Jewish Immigrant Mobility in New York City* (New York: Oxford University Press, 1977); Joel Perlmann, *Italians Then, Mexicans Now: Immigrant Origins and Second-Generation Progress, 1890-2000* (New York: Russell Sage Foundation, 2005).

[16] Genovese is quoted in D'Souza, *End of Racism*, 484; Eugene Genovese, *Roll, Jordan, Roll* (New York: Vintage, 1976).

[17] Ellis Cose, *The Rage of a Privileged Class* (New York: HarperCollins, 1993).

[18] Genovese is quoted in D'Souza, 484; D'Souza, 483-484; John Ogbu, "A Cultural Ecology of Competence Among Inner-City Blacks," in Margaret B. Spencer, Geraldine K. Wilkins, and Walter R. Allen, eds., *Beginnings: The Social and Affective Development of Black Children* (Hillsdale, NJ: Lawrence Earlbaum Associates, 1985), 66; John Ogbu, *Minority Education and Caste* (New York: Harcourt, Brace, Jovanovich, 1978); Elijah Anderson, "The Code of the Streets," *The Atlantic* (May 1994): 82; author calculations using U.S. Census Bureau American Community Survey 2005-2009 PUMS data and American Factfinder.

[19] Stephan Thernstrom and Abigail Thernstrom, *America in Black and White: One Nation, Indivisible* (New York: Simon and Schuster, 1997), 34; Gerald Jaynes and Robin M. Williams, eds., *A Common Destiny: Blacks and American Society* (Washington, DC: National Academy Press, 1989), 6-9.

[20] Thomas F. Schaller, "My Run In With Dave 'Mudcat' Saunders, The Democrats' Dixie Huckster," *The American Prospect*, June 21, 2006.

[21] Daniel Aaron, "The Hyphenate Writer and American Letters," *Smith Alumnae Quarterly* 55, no.4 (July 1964): 215, 217.

[22] Ralph Ellison, "Brave Words for a Startling Occasion," in *Shadow and Act* (New York: Random House, 1964), 104-105.

[23] Brent Staples, *Parallel Time: Growing up in Black and White* (New York: Pantheon Books, 1994), 259; "Raines Comes Clean -- But Soils Times Reputation," *Timeswatch.org*, May 15, 2003; Stephan Thernstrom and Abigail Thernstrom, 494-500.

[24] Stephan Thernstrom and Abigail Thernstrom, 496-498; Seth Forman, "Beyond Social Dependency and Political Grievance," *Society* (July/August 2006): 34.

[25] "Imus Takes His Lumps on Sharpton's Show," *SFGate.com*, April 9, 2007.

[26] Quoted in Sol Stern, "E. D. Hirsch's Curriculum for Democracy: A Content Rich Pedagogy Makes Better Citizens and Smarter Kids," *City Journal* (Autumn 2009).

[27] Greg Toppo, "Teens Losing Touch With Historical Reference," *USA Today*, August 1, 2008; Victor Davis Hanson, "The Forces of Division Have Started to Raise Their Ugly Heads Again," *The Corner* blog at *Nationalreview.com*, March 16, 2008; "Failing Our Students, Failing Our Nation," International Studies Institute, National Civic Literacy Board, 2007. Found on world wide web at <http://www.americancivicliteracy.org/2007/summary_summary.html> (accessed October 25, 2010); Khalil Gibran International Academy, *Wikipedia.com*. Found on world wide web at <http://en.wikipedia.org/wiki/Khalil_Gibran_International_Academy> (accessed May 21, 2010).

[28] Thomas Sowell, *Economic Facts and Fallacies* (New York: Basic Books, 2008), 162-170; "America in Black and White: Explaining the Racial Gap in Poverty," Smart Library on Urban Poverty. Found on world wide web at<http://www.poverty.smartlibrary.org/NewInterface/segment.cfm?segment=2466> (accessed September 15, 2009); Julia B. Isaacs, *The Economic Mobility of Black and White Families*, Economic Mobility Project, Pew Charitable Trusts, 2008.

[29] Kay Hymowitz, "The Black Family: 40 Years of Lies," *City Journal* (Summer 2005).

[30] Forman, "Beyond Social Dependency," 34; "Black Families Headed by Married Parents on the Rise, Census Finds," *Jet*, May 12, 2003.

[31] "Most Americans Proud of U.S. History, Say Other Nations Should Follow America's Lead," *Rasmussen Reports*, July 2, 2009.

[32] Peter Bernholz, "How Likely is Hyperinflation," *The American*, December 15, 2009.

[33] "Will: Obama Said Stimulus Would Cap Unemployment at 8 Percent," Politfact.com, July 11, 2010. Found on world wide web at <http://www.politifact.com/truth-o-meter/statements/2010/jul/13/george-will/will-obama-said-stimulus-would-cap-unemployment-8-/> (accessed May 12, 2011).

[34] Peter Ferrara, "Reagonomics vs. Obamanomics: Facts and Figure," *Forbes*, May 5, 2011.

[35] Seth Forman, "Krugman Misleads On Government Spending, Economic Growth," *Weekly Standard*, "The Blog", October 15, 2010.

[36] John F. Cogan and John B. Taylor, "Where Did the Stimulus Go?," *Commentary* (January 2011).

[37] "A Shovel-Empty Waste of $787 Billion," *Investor's Business Daily,* May 18, 2011; Timothy Conley and Bill Dupor, "The American Recovery and Reinvestment Act: Public Sector Jobs," Ohio State University, May 17, 2011. Found on world wide web at <http://web.econ.ohio-state.edu/dupor/arra10_may11.pdf> (accessed May 19, 2011).

[38] John F. Cogan and John B. Taylor, "Where Did the Stimulus Go?," *Commentary* (January 2011).

[39] Richard Wolf, "Record Number in Government Anti-Poverty Programs," *USA Today,* August 30, 2010.

[40] Wolf; Fred Lucas, "Obama Will Spend More on Welfare in the Next Year Than Bush Spent on Entire Iraq War, Study Reveals," *CNSNews.com*, September 22, 2009.

[41] Richard Wolf, "Welfare Agencies Boost Voters," *USA Today,* July 28, 2010; Steven Rosenfeld, "Justice Department Stands Behind Voter Registration Law," *Daily Kos,* June 24, 2010.

[42] Jeffrey H. Anderson, "By 17 Percentage Points, Americans Support Repeal," *Weekly Standard,* May 16, 2011.

[43] *Ibid.;* Jeffrey H. Anderson, "Obamacare Less Popular than Any Time Since it Became Law," *Weekly Standard,* January 27, 2011.

[44] Charles Krauthammer, "Obama's Ultimate Agenda," Washington Post, April 3, 2009; Charles Krauthammer, "Obama Proposes a European U.S.," *Washington Post*, February 27, 2009; Ben Smith, "Barack Obama's Biggest Critic: Charles Krauthammer," *Politico.com*, May 20, 2009

[45] Hill quoted in Varadarajan, "Obama is Weakening America."

[46] Stevenson Jacobs and Vinnee Tong, "Under Prodding of Pay Czar, No '09 Salary or Bonus for Departing Bank of America CEO," *Associated Press,* October 16, 2009; George Melloan, "Government Deficits and Private Growth," *Wall Street Journal*, November 23, 2009.

[47] Cliff Kincaid, "Controversial New Video of Obama's Pastor," Gopusa.com, November 2, 2009; Thomas Sowell, "Dismantling America," *Realclearpolitics.com*, October 27, 2009.

[48] Stuart Taylor, "Sotomayor and 'Disparate Impact'," *National Journal*, May 30, 2009; Stuart Taylor, "Identity Politics and Sotomayor," *National Journal*, May 23, 2009.

[49] Sowell, "Dismantling America."

[50] David Sunday, "Obama Fires Back at Cheney on *60 Minutes*," *Video Café*, March 22, 2009. Found on world wide web at <http://videocafe.crooksandliars.com/david/obama-fires-back-cheney-60-minutes> (accessed on November 25, 2009); Stephen Hayes, "Miranda Rights for Terrorists," *Weekly Standard Blog*, June 10, 2009.

[51] "Eric Holder Lindsay Graham: Eric Holder Jon Kyle: Holder Senate Questioning on 9/11 Civil Trials," *Maggiesnotebook.blogspot.com*, November 18, 2009.

[52] Thomas Jocelyn, "Ghailani Verdict a Miscarriage of Justice," *Weekly Standard*, November 17, 2010.

[53] Scott Wilson and Al Kamen, "'Global War On Terror' Is Given New Name," *Washington Post*, March 25, 2009.

[54] *Ibid.*

[55] "Obama Nixes 'Islam, Jihad' From U.S. Documents," *Associated Press*, April 7, 2010.

[56] "NASA Chief: Next Frontier Better Relations with Muslim World," *Foxnews.com*, July 5, 2010.

[57] "NASA to Focus on Muslim Outreach," *Judicialwatch.org*, February 17, 2010; "Napolitano Avoids Terror Terminology," *CBSNews.com*, February 24, 2009; "Interview with Homeland Security Secretary Janet Napolitano," *Der Spiegel*, March 16, 2009; Kenneth Bazinet and Michael Mcauliff, "President Obama: I'm in charge of Oil Spill Cleanup," *New York Daily News*, May 27, 2010.

[58] Charles Krauthammer, "A Travesty in New York," *Washington Post*, November 20, 2009; Sunday, "Obama Fires Back."

[59] Josh Meyer, "Attorney General Eric Holder Opens CIA Abuse Investigation," *Chicago Tribune,* August 25, 2009; Marc Thiessen, "Obama Owes Thanks, and an Apology, to CIA Interrogators," *Washington Post,* May 4, 2011.

[60] "Transcript of Interview with CIA Director Panetta," MSNBC.com, May 3, 2011. Found on world wide web at <http://www.msnbc.msn.com/id/42887700/ns/world_news-death_of_bin_laden/> (accessed May 4, 2011); "Detective Work on Courier Led to Breakthrough on Bin Laden," *New York Times,* May 2, 2011; Michael Isikoff, "Bin Laden's Death Rekindles 'Enhanced' Interrogation Debate," MSNBC.com, May 2, 2011.

[61] Peter Grier, "Obama Orders Guantanamo Tribunals to Resume," *Christian Science Monitor,* March 7, 2011.

[62] Dorothy Rabinowitz, "Obama Blames America," *Opinionjournal.com,* April 22, 2009.

[63] William Kristol, "Anti-Obama, Pro-America: What is the Loyal Opposition to Do?," *Weekly Standard,* November 23, 2009; Gregor Peter Schmitz, "Obama Reacts to Debate in Berlin," *Spiegel Online International,* July 10, 2008; Josh Mayer, "FBI Planning a Bigger Role in Terrorism Fight," *Los Angeles Times,* May 28, 2009.

[64] James Kirchik, "Squanderer in Chief," *Los Angeles Times,* April 28, 2009; "Obama Stumbles Again," *Powerlineblog.com,* November 14, 2009.

[65] Jeffrey M. Jones, "Obama's Approval Slide Finds Whites Down to 39%," Gallup Organization. Found on world wide web at <http://www.gallup.com/poll/124484/Obama-Approval-Slide-Finds-Whites-Down-39.aspx> (accessed November 25, 2009); Frank Newport, "Blacks and Whites Continue to Differ Sharply on Obama," *Gallup.com,* August 3, 2010; Jeffrey M. Jones, "Obama Approval Averages 45% in September," (October 4, 2010). Found on world wide web at <http://www.gallup.com/poll/143354/Obama-Approval-Averages-September.aspx?utm_source=alert&utm_medium=email&utm_campaign=syndication&utm_content=morelink&utm_term=Politics> (accessed October 4, 2010).

[66] "Black Unemployment Spikes to 16%," *Black Enterprise,* January 8, 2010; *Vanishing Work Among Teens 2000-2010,* Center for Labor Market Studies, Northeastern University, July 2010.

[67] Martha Irvine, "Black Teens More Optimistic Than Peers of Other Races," *Associated Press,* April 29, 2010.

[50] Blog Entries, June 9, 2010, *MrFormansPlanet.com*.

[68] Duncan Currie, "The Optimism Gap," *National Review Online,* September 1, 2010; Pew Research Center, *How the Great Recession Has Changed Life in America,* June 30, 2010; Pew Research Center, *Blacks Upbeat about Black Progress, Prospects A Year After Obama's Election,* January 12, 2010.

[69] "Blacks' Optimism About Their Standards of Living Tops Whites," Gallup, July 8, 2010. Found on the World Wide Web at <http://www.gallup.com/poll/141191/blacks-optimism-standards-living-tops-whites.aspx> (accessed September 1, 2010); Ronald Brownstein, "Obama's Approval Rating: Some Encouraging Signs for the President," *National Journal,* March 18, 2011.

[58] Melissa Harris-Lacewell, "Will a Racial Divide Swallow Obama?," *The Nation,* November 2, 2009; "Tavis Smiley: 2012 Will Be `The Most Racist' Election Ever'," *Realclearpolitics.com,* April 26, 2011.

[71] David Paul Kuhn, "Exit Polls: Unprecedented White Flight from Democrats," *Realclearpolitics.com,* November 3, 2010.

[72] Text of Obama's Nobel Peace Prize Speech, *Associated Press,* December 12, 2009; William Kristol, "A Note to My Fellow Hawks," *Weekly Standard,* August 31, 2010; John Podhoretz, "Barack Obama: Neocon," *New York Post,* September 1, 2010.

[59] Robert Kagan, "Armed for Reality," *Washington Post,* December 13, 2009; William Kristol, "A Nobel War Speech?," *Weekly Standard,* December 21, 2009.

[60] Richard Lowry, "Obama Said Nothing of Significance," *Realclearpolitics.com,* December 12, 2009; Michael Rubin, "The Afghanistan Withdrawal: Why Obama was Wrong to Announce a Withdrawal Date," Michaelrubin.org, March 8, 2010.

[61] Karl Rove, "Obama's `Come Home, America' Speech," *Wall Street Journal,* September 2, 2010.

[62] Ben Smith, "Obama Seeks to Reconnect," *Politico.com,* April 26, 2010; Patrick H. Caddell and Douglas E. Schoen, "Our Divisive President," *Opinionjournal.com,* July 28, 2010.

NOTES – Chapter 2

[1] On exit polling issues see endnote 5 for Chapter 3.

[2] John J. Miller, "What a Steele," *National Review Online,* August 31, 2004; David Bositis, "Black Elected Officials: A Statistical Summary: 2000," Joint Center for Political and Economic Studies, Washington D.C., 2000; Ebonya L. Washington, "How Black Candidates Affect Voter Turnout," Yale Economic Applications and Policy Discussion Paper No. 16, Department of Economics, Yale University, (January 2006).

[3] Dan Balz and Matthew Mosk, "The Year of the Black Republican?," *Washington Post,* May 10, 2006; Bill Berkowitz, "Black Voters Nix Black Republicans." Found on World wide web at <http://www.bendweekly.com/pdf_version.php?id=3271> (accessed July 15, 2009); "Minority Candidates Rack up Poll History," *Morning Star Online,* November 3, 2010.

[4] The late Daniel Patrick Moynihan has been credited with the following quote: "The central conservative truth is that it is culture, not politics, that determines the success of a society. The central liberal truth is that politics can change a culture and save it from itself." But Moynihan and others have spoken of the defeat of race as a determinant of fate as a great liberal victory. See world wide web<www.brainyquote.com> (accessed April 12, 2009).

[5] Bayard Rustin, "From Protest to Politics," *Commentary* (February 1965).

[6] Fred Siegel, "The Future Once Happened Here: Liberalism and the Decline of America's Big Cities," *Insideronline,* March 1, 1998.

[7] Shelby Steele, "Why the GOP Can't Win With Minorities," *Opinionjournal.com,* March 16, 2009; Dinesh D'Souza, *The End of Racism* (New York: Free Press, 1995), 204; Fred Siegel, "The Death and Life of America's Cities," *Public Interest* (Summer 2002); Manning Marable, "Clarence Thomas and the Crisis of Black Political Culture," in Toni Morrison, ed., *Race-ing Justice, En-gendering Power* (New York, Pantheon, 1992), 82; Lani Guinier, *Tyranny of the Majority* (New York: Free Press, 1970), 56; President Lyndon B. Johnson's Commencement Address at Howard University, "To Fulfill These Rights," June 4, 1965. Found on the World wide web at <http://www.lbjlib.utexas.edu/johnson/archives.hom/speeches.hom/650604.asp> (accessed January 10, 2009).

[8] Alvin F. Poussaint, *Why Blacks Kill Blacks* (New York: Emerson Hall, 1972), 19. Found in D'Souza, 484.

[9] Manning Marable, "Clarence Thomas and the Crisis of Black Political Culture," in Toni Morrison, ed., *Race-ing Justice, En-gendering Power*, 82. Found in D'Souza, 684; "Why We're not Post-Racial," *Wall Street Journal*, November 21, 2009.

[10] Barack Obama, *Dreams From My Father: A Story of Race and Inheritance* (New York: Three Rivers Press, electronic version 2004) 58, 157, 6, quoted by Gregory Chang, "Quotes on Race, *Dreams From My Father*. Found on world wide web at <http://www.stop-obama.org> (accessed September 11, 2009); Stanley Kurtz, "Barack Obama's Lost Years," *Weekly Standard* (August 11, 2008).

[11] Dinesh D'Souza, "How Obama Thinks," *Forbes,* September 27, 2010.

[12] Barack Obama, *Dreams From My Father: A Story of Race and Inheritance* (New York: Three Rivers Press, electronic version 2004) 58, 157, 6, quoted by Gregory Chang, "Quotes on Race, *Dreams From My Father*. Found on world wide web at <http://www.stop-obama.org> (accessed September 11, 2009); Stanley Kurtz, "Barack Obama's Lost Years," *Weekly Standard* (August 11, 2008).

[13] James Hund, *Black Entrepreneurship* (New York: Wadsworth Publishing, 1971), 119.

[14] John McWhorter, *Losing the Race: Self-Sabotage in Black America* (New York: Harper Perennial, 2001). Found in McWhorter's article "Toward a Usable Black History," *City Journal* (Summer 2001).

[15] Cathleen Falsani, Interview with State Sen. Barack Obama, 3:30 p.m., Saturday, March 27, Café Baci, 330 S. Michigan Avenue. Found on world wide web at <http://blog.beliefnet.com/stevenwaldman/2008/11/obamas-interview-with-cathleen.html> (accessed November 30, 2009); "Obama's Church," *Investor's Business Daily,* January 15, 2008; Jonathan Tilove, "Renewed Wright Imbroglio Exposes Fissure among Black Voters," *Realclearpolitics.com*, May 2, 2008.

[16] Falsani, "Interview."

[17] *Dreams From My Father* quoted by Chang, 142, 157; Entry from "Dreams From My Father," *Wikipedia.org*.

[18] Falsani, "Interview"; "Obama: Dem Race about More Than Race," *abcnews.com*, March 30, 3008; James Meeks entry in *Wikipedia.com;* "Phleger's Vile Sermon," *Vox Pop*, May 30, 2009. Found on world wide web at http://newsblogs.chicagotribune.com/vox_pop/2008/05/pflegers-vile-s.html (accessed December 22, 2009).

[19] Jonathan Seidl, "Obama's Easter Sunday Pastor Rails Against Racist Talk Radio (Compares Rush to KKK!)," Theblaze.com, April 25, 2011.

[20] Richard Noyes, "Barack Obama and Bill Ayers: Stanley Kurtz Makes the Connection," Media Research Center, September 23, 2009; Stanley Kurtz, "Obama and Ayers Pushed Radicalism On Schools," *Wall Street Journal*, September 23, 2008; Stanley Kurtz, "Obama's Challenge," *National Review*, September 23, 2008; Dinitia Smith, "No Regrets for a Love Of Explosives," *New York Times Book Review*, September 11, 2001; Marcia Froelke Coburn, "No Regrets," *Chicago Magazine*, August, 2001.

[21] Steven Malanga, "ACORN Squash," *Wall Street Journal*, August 26, 2006; Sol Stern, "Acorn's Nutty Regime for City's," *City Journal* (Spring 2003).

[22] Malanga, "ACORN Squash"; Steven Malanga, "Organizer In Chief," *City Journal* (Summer 2008); P.J. Gladnick, "Will MSM Report on Obama Membership in Socialist New Party?," *Newsbusters.com*, October 8, 2008.

[23] Steele quoted in Steven Sailer, "The Rise of Obama," *Washington Times*, December 25, 2007.

[24] Bonnie Goldstein, "Obama on Racism, 1990," *Slate.com*, March 19, 2008.

[25] Stanley Kurtz, "Barack Obama's Lost Years."

[26] Thomas Sowell, "Check The Record: Obama is No Reformer." Found on world wide web at <tsowell.com> (accessed October 8, 2009); Hank De Zutter, "What Makes Obama Run?," *Chicago Reader,* December 8, 1995.

NOTES – Chapter 3

[1] *Daily Breeze*, March 6, 2008; Earl Ofari Hutchinson, "Are Black Voters For Obama Racists?," *New American Media*, May 22, 2008.

[2] Jonathan Tilove, "Renewed Wright Imbroglio Exposes Fissures among Black Voters," *Realclearpolitics.com,* May 2, 2008.

[3] "Big Backer Goes from Clinton to Obama," *CNN.com*, February 18, 2008; "Black delegates under pressure to switch to Obama," *CNN.com*, February 19, 2008.

[4] Chris Cilizza, "5 Myths about an Election of Mythic Proportions," *Washington Post*, November 13, 2008.

[5] Abigail Thernstrom, "One Journey Ends," *New York Post,* January 21, 2009; "African Americans, Anger, Fear and Youth Propel Turnout to Highest Level Since 1960: Possible Pro-Democratic Realignment, GOP Disaster," American University News, Washington, D.C., December 17, 2008; CNN Election Center 2004 and 2008. Found on world wide web at <http://www.cnn.com/ELECTION/2008/results/polls.main> (accessed January 4, 2009); Dr. Michael McDonald, U.S. Elections Project, Department of Public and International Affairs, George Mason University. Found on world wide web at <http://elections.gmu.edu/voter_turnout.htm> (accessed February 15, 2009).

NOTE: This analysis relies on the National Election Pool (NEP) exit poll as reported by CNN for demographic breakdowns and total voter turnout numbers. The Pew Research Center also performs an analysis based on the U.S. Census Bureau's *Current Population Survey November Supplement* (CPS). CPS is used in this analysis for a limited amount of information on turnout rates for states and by race.

Generally, CPS total turnout numbers are significantly lower than the NEP exit poll. But the CPS is a household survey with a large margin of error. In Dr. Michael McDonald's words, "The CPS survey indicates that the national turnout rate and registration rate declined a slight 0.2 percentage points between 2004 and 2008. Using estimates of the voting-eligible population and the number of people who voted, I previously reported that the turnout rate increased by 1.6 percentage points between 2004 and 2008. I thus believe that the CPS decline is more apparent than real. The CPS is a survey and is prone to both statistical and non-statistical survey methodology errors, just like any other survey. When there are small changes in statistics from one election to the next, these survey errors are more likely to produce a discrepancy like the one here whereby the actual turnout rate increased slightly and the CPS turnout rate decreased slightly." (Found on Dr. McDonald's blog at <http://elections.gmu.edu/CPS_2008.html> (accessed May 20, 2009)).

In addition to these problems, Pew reporting on voter turnout is inconsistent. The findings of the Pew report from 2004 showed a large difference in voter turnout compared with two respected voter turnout research centers -- The Center for the Study of the American Electorate at American University and the United States Elections Project at George Mason University. In 2008, Pew's findings sharply contradicted a report put out by a separate arm of the Pew Research Center, the Pew

Hispanic Center. In November of 2008 the Pew Hispanic Center reported that Hispanics made up 9 percent of the 2008 presidential vote. In April, 2009 the Pew Research Center found the percentage of Hispanics to be 7.4 percent. See Mark Hugo Lopez, "The Hispanic Vote in the 2008 Election," Pew Hispanic Center, Washington, D.C., November 7, 2008; Mark Hugo Lopez and Paul Taylor, "Dissecting the 2008 Electorate: Most Diverse in United States History," Pew Research Center, Washington D.C., April 30, 2009.

[6] CNN/Opinion Research Corp., November 11, 2008. Found on world wide web at <http://www.cnn.com/2008/POLITICS/11/11/obama.poll> (accessed June 6, 2009); "Obama Boosts Leadership Image and Regains Lead Over McCain," Pew Research Center for the People and the Press, October 1, 2008. Found on world wide web at http://people-press.org/report/456/obama-regains-lead (accessed June 5, 2009); John Blake, "Could an Obama Presidency Hurt Black Americans?," *CNNPolitics.com*, July 22, 2008; "Post-Election Perspectives: Remarks by Andrew Kohut, President," Pew Research Center, 2nd Annual Warren J. Mitofsky Award Dinner, on Behalf of the Roper Center Newseum, Washington D.C., November 13, 2008.

[7] Jim Rutenberg, "Black Media in U.S. Go All Out For Obama," *New York Times*, July 27, 2009.

[8] David Carr, "Oprah Puts Her Brand on the Line," *New York Times,* December 24, 2007.

[9] "Black Republicans Consider Voting for Obama," *USA Today*, June 14, 2008.

[10] Alexander Bolton, "Colin Powell Splits With Son Over White House Race," *The Hill*, October 20, 2008; Ed Henry, "Powell Donates to McCain," *CNN*.com, August 9, 2009.

[11] Stephen Ohlemacher, "Colin Powell Endorses Obama," *Associated Press*, October 19, 2008; Mike Allen and Jonathan Martin, "Powell Endorses Obama," *Politico*, October 20, 2009.

[12] Mark Hugo Lopez, "The Hispanic Vote in the 2008 Election"; Robert Suro, Richard Fry, Jeffrey Passel, "Hispanics and the 2004 Election: Population Electorate and Voters," Pew Hispanic Center, June 27, 2009; Steven Malanga, "The Latino Voting Trickle," *City Journal* (Winter 2009).

[13] *Realclearpolitics.com* generic congressional polling average. Found on world wide web at

<http://www.realclearpolitics.com/polls/archive/?poll_id=14> (accessed on March 10, 2009).

[14] Jim Tharpe, "Chambliss Wins Second Term in U.S. Senate," *The Atlanta Journal-Constitution,* December 2, 2008.

[15] David Paul Kuhn, "Exit Polls: Unprecedented White Flight from Democrats," *Realclearpolitics.com*, November 4, 2011.

NOTES – Chapter 4

[1] "A More Perfect Union," Remarks of Senator Barack Obama, Constitution Center Philadelphia, Pennsylvania, March 18, 2008.

[2] Paul Krugman, "It's a Different Country," *New York Times,* June 9, 2008.

[3] Paul Krugman, "Fear and Favor," *New York Times,* October 3, 2010.

[4] David Bositis, *Black Elected Officials: A Statistical Summary: 2000,* (Washington D.C.: Joint Center for Political and Economic Studies, 2002); *Statistical Abstract of the United States: 2008,* U.S. Department of Commerce, U.S. Census Bureau, Washington, D.C., Tables 402, 255; Stephan Thernstrom and Abigail Thernstrom, *America In Black and White: One Nation, Indivisible* (New York: Simon and Schuster, 1997), 286-290.

[5] Stephan Thernstrom and Abigail Thernstrom, 295.

[6] Michael McDonald, United States Elections Project, Department of Public and International Affairs, George Mason University. Found on World Wide Web at <http://elections.gmu.edu/Turnout_2008G.html> (accessed on May 9, 2009); See also McDonald's review of 2008 Current Population Survey Voting and Registration Supplement, April 6, 2009; "Voting and Registration in the Election of 2008," Current Population Survey, U.S. Census Bureau, Washington D.C. (July 2009).

[7] Barack Obama, *Audacity of Hope* (New York: Vintage, 2008); Tony Blankley, "Obama's Blank Screen," *Washington Times,* January 27, 2009; John O'Sullivan, "A Sphinx without a Riddle?,"*Globe and Mail,* January 19, 2009.

[8] Shelby Steele, "Obama's Post-Racial Promise,"*Opinionjournal.com*, November 5, 2009; John O'Sullivan, "A Sphinx."

[9] Jay Cost and Sean Trende, "Election Review, Part I," *Realclearpolitics.com*, January 7, 2009.

[10] Star Parker, "Rick Warren is No Billy Graham," *Townhall.com*, January 5, 2009.

[11] The 2005 TIME 100: Rick Warren; Naomi Schaefer Riley, "What Saddleback's Pastor Really Thinks about Politics," *Wall Street Journal*, August 23, 2008.

[12] Transcript of Obama, McCain at Saddleback Civil Forum with Pastor Rick Warren, *Chicago Sun-Times,* August 18, 2008.

[13] Mike Allen, "McCain Protests NBC Coverage," *Politico.com,* August 17, 2008; Frank James, "Did McCain Cheat at Saddleback: Unlikely," *The Swamp*, August 18, 2008.

[14] Ben Smith, "'Punished with a Baby'," *Politico*, March 31, 2009.

[15] Dan Cox, "Young White Evangelicals: Less Republican, Still Conservative," Pew Research Center, Washington D.C., September 28, 2007.

[16] Lydia Sadd, "More Americans 'Pro-Life' Than 'Pro-Choice' for First Time," Gallup.com, May 15, 2009.

[17] Rich Lowry, "Obama is Lying About His Abortion Record," *Realclearpolitics*, August 18, 2009; "Obama Cover-up Revealed On Born-Alive Abortion Survivors Bill," Statement issued Monday, August 11, 2008 by the National Right to Life Committee (NRLC) in Washington, D.C. Found on World Wide Web at http://www.nrlc.org/ObamaBAIPA/ObamaCoverup.html (accessed September 20, 2009).

[18] Senator John F. Kerry, Transcript, *Washington Post,* November 7, 2003.

[19] Dan Cox, "Young White Evangelicals."

[20] "Growing Number of Americans Say Obama is a Muslim," Pew Forum on Religion and Public Life," August 18, 2010; Jeffrey H. Anderson, "Does Obama Think Our Rights Come From Our Creator," *Weekly Standard,* September 19, 2010; O'Reilly Factor Flash, *BillOreilly.com*, July 9, 2009.

[21] Joel Kotkin and Fred Siegel, "Gentry Liberals," *Los Angeles Times,* December 2, 2007; Nicholas Lemann, *The Big Test: The Secret History of the American Meritocracy* (New York: Farrar, Straus, Giroux, 2000); David Brooks, *Bobos in*

Paradise (New York: Simon and Schuster, 2001); John B. Judis and Ruy Teixeira, *The Emerging Democratic Majority* (New York: Scribner, 2004); Reihad Salam, "Park Avenue for Obama," *Forbes*, November 11, 2008.

[22]Steele, "Obama's Post-racial Promise"; Gideon Rachman, "The Man is the Message," *Financial Times,* January 22, 2009.

[23] Nathan Silver, "How Obama Really Won the Election," *Esquire*, January 14, 2009.

[24]*Realclearpolitics.com.* Found on World Wide Web at <http://www.realclearpolitics.com/epolls/2008/president/national.html> (accessed on May 18, 2009).

[25] Joel Kotkin, "The Three Geographies," *Politico*, July 2, 2008; Silver, "How Obama Really Won the Election."

[26]U.S. Census Bureau, American Community Survey, 2004, 2007.

[27] David Paul Kuhn, "Democrats' Year: Less Change than Chance," *Realclearpolitics.com*, January 2, 2009.

[28]Center for Responsive Politics, Washington, D.C., *Opensecrets.org*. Found on World Wide Web at <http://www.opensecrets.org/pres08/contrib.php?cycle=2008&cid=N00009638> (accessed on July 15, 2009).

[29] "Reality Check: Obama Received About the Same Percentage from Small Donors in 2008 as Bush in 2004," Campaign Finance Institute, Washington D. C., November 23, 2008. Found on World Wide Web at <opensecrets.org> (accessed on June 25, 2009).

[30] Joseph A. Schumpeter, *Capitalism, Socialism and Democracy* (New York: Harper & Row, 1942); Stephen Hess, *The Washington Reporters* (Washington, D.C.: Brookings Institution, 1981); S. Robert Licther, Linda Lichter, and Stanley Rothman, *The Media Elite* (New York: Hastings House, 1990), chapters 1-2; S. Robert Lichter, "The Media," in *Understanding America: The Anatomy of an Exceptional Nation*, ed. Peter H. Schuck and James Q. Wilson (New York: Public Affairs, 2008), 196.

[31] Rich Noyes, "The Liberal Media," Media Research Center, June 30, 2004.

[32] S. Robert Lichter, "The Media," 207.

Notes

[33] "Dan's Downfall: Forged Documents," Media Research Center, September 20, 2007; S. Robert Lichter, "Campaign 2004 -- Election Final: How TV News Covered the General Election Campaign," *Media Monitor* 18, no. 6 (November/December 2004), 1-6; S. Robert Licther and Stephen J. Farnsworth, "Television Coverage of the 2004 Presidential Election," *Presidential Studies Quarterly* (in press); S. Robert Lichter, "The Media," 211.

[34] Deborah Howell, "Obama Tilt in Campaign Coverage," *Washington Post*, November 9, 2008; Clark Hoyt, "What That McCain Article Didn't Say," *New York Times,* February 24, 2008; Lamar Smith, "Obama's Biggest Boosters Were the Media," *Washington Times*, November 25, 2008; Alexander Burns, "*TIME's* Mark Halperin: Extreme Pro-Obama Media Bias a 'Disgusting Failure'," *Politico.com*, November 22, 2008; William Tate, "Putting Money Where Mouths Are: Media Donations Favor Dems 100-1," *Investor's Business Daily*, July 23, 2008; "Winning the Media Campaign," Pew Research Center's Project for Excellence in Journalism, October 22, 2008.

[35] "Media Dodges Accusations of Bias in Campaign Coverage," *PBS News Hour*, July 25, 2008.

[36] Jim Rutenberg, Marilyn W. Thompson, David D. Kirkpatrick, and Stephen Labaton, "For McCain, Self-Confidence on Ethics Poses Its Own Risk," *New York Times,* February 21, 2008; Clark Hoyt, "What That McCain Article Didn't Say."

[37] "McCain Campaign Accuses L.A. Times of 'Suppressing' Obama Video," *Los Angeles Times*, October 29, 2008; "Barack Obama for President," *Los Angeles Times*, October 19, 2008.

[38] "Most Voters Say News Media Wants Obama to Win," Pew Research Center for the People and the Press, October 22, 2008.

[39] S. Robert Lichter, "Fox News: Fair And Balanced?," *Forbes.com*, November 16, 2009; "Trust and Satisfaction with the National News Media," Sacred Heart University Polling Institute, Fairfield, Connecticut, September 23, 2009.

[40] This is the title of a best selling book by Bernard Goldberg, *A Slobbering Love Affair* (New York: Regnery Publishing, 2009).

[41] "Obama's First 100 Days," Pew Research Center's Project for Excellence in Journalism, April 28, 2009; Howard Kurtz, "Boosting Obama," *Washington Post,* April 27, 2009; Robert Samuelson, "The Obama Infatuation," *Washington Post*, June

1, 2009; "Trust and Satisfaction with the National News Media," Sacred Heart University Polling Institute, September 23, 2009.

[42] Stefano Della Vigna and Ethan Kaplan, "The Political Impact of Media Bias," University of California at Berkeley, June 26, 2007. Found on World Wide Web at <http://elsa.berkeley.edu/~sdellavi/wp/mediabiaswb07-06-25.pdf> (accessed May 4, 2009).

[43]"Debate Transcripts," Commission on Presidential Debates. Found on World Wide Web at <http://www.debates.org/pages/debtrans.html> (accessed on August 4, 2009).

[44] Andrew Sullivan, "The New Face of America," *Sunday Times of London*, December 16. 2007.

[45] Mark Steyn, "Obama May Not Be So 'Post-Racial'," *Orange County Register*, June 21, 2008.

[46] Lawrence B. Goodheart, "The Ambivalent Anti-Semitism of Malcolm X," *Patterns of Prejudice* 28, no. 1 (January 1994): 10; Milton Himmelfarb, "Blacks, Jews, and Muzhiks," *Commentary* 42, no. 4 (October 1966); Peter Goldman, *The Death and Life of Malcolm X* (New York: Harper and Row, 1974), 16; Alan Shelton, "Malcolm X and the Jews," *Midstream* 42, no. 4 (May 1996: 20-23; Seth Forman, *Blacks in the Jewish Mind: A Crisis of Liberalism*, (New York: New York University, 1998): 70-71.

[47] Barack Obama, *Dreams From My Father* (New York: Three Rivers Press, 2004) 86, 197-199, 200; Peter Wallsten, "Obama's Life of Striking Contrasts," *Los Angeles Times*, March 24, 2008.

[48] Ben Shapiro, "Barack Obama Throws Grandma under the Bus," *Creators.com*. Found on World Wide Web at http://www.creators.com/opinion/ben-shapiro/barack-obama-throws-grandma-under-the-bus.html (accessed January 2, 2009).

[49]Jonathan Strong, "Documents Show Media Plotting to Kill Stories about Rev. Jeremiah Wright," *The Daily Caller*, July 20, 2010.

[50] Mike Glover, "Obama Disowns Pastor After All," *Associated Press,* April 30, 2008; Byron York, "Why Did the Press Ignore the Van Jones Scandal?," *Washington Examiner*, September 8, 2009; "Airbrushing Reverend Wright: Part II," *Powerlineblog.com*, March 27, 2008; Charles Krauthammer, "The Fabulist vs. the Saint," *Washington Post*, April 4, 3008; Mark Tapscott, "Obama, Democrats Got 88

Percent of 2008 Contributions by TV Network Execs, Writers, Reporters," *Washington Examiner,* August 27, 2010.

Read more at the Washington Examiner:
http://www.washingtonexaminer.com/opinion/blogs/beltway-confidential/Obama-Democrats-got-88-percent-of-TV-network-employee-campaign-contributions-101668063.html#ixzz0y72DdnV3

[51] Patrick J. Buchanan, "Address to the Republican Convention," August 17, 1992. Found on World Wide Web at <http://www.americanrhetoric.com/speeches/patrickbuchanan1992rnc.htm> (accessed on July 2, 2009).

[52] Steven Sark, "Right Wing Populist," *The Atlantic,* February 1996.

[53] Quoted in press release for Northwestern University's lecture series on the evangelical movement, October 4,2002; Christopher Hitchens, "Obama Does Not Represent the End of Obsession with Race," *Irish Times,* January 9, 2008.

[54] Online Focus, "A Republican No More," Public Broadcasting System, October 25, 1999; Sark, "Right-Wing Populist."

[55] Mark Silva, "Bob Jones University Dean Warms Up to Romney," *The Swamp,* October 16, 2007.

[56] "Obama and 'Them Jews': Not the Wright Stuff," *Foxnews.com,* June 12, 2009; Earl Ofari Hutchinson, "The Good Reverend Jeremiah Wright and 'Them Jews'," *Huffingtonpost.com,* June 13, 2009.

[57] Danny Hakim, "Spitzer Dropping His Driver's License Plan," *New York Times,* November 14, 2007; Marcia Kramer, "Just Call Him . . . Gov. Flip Flop," WCBS-TV, November 15, 2007; "Eliot Spitzer Driver's License Controversy, *Wikipedia.* Found on World Wide Web at http://en.wikipedia.org/wiki/Eliot_Spitzer_drivers_license_controversy#cite_note-19 (accessed October 2, 2009).

[58] 2007 National Survey of Latinos: As Illegal Immigration Issue Heats Up, Hispanics Feel a Chill," Pew Hispanic Center, December 13, 2007. Found on World Wide Web at http://pewhispanic.org/reports/report.php?ReportID=84 (accessed November 5, 2010; Harold Meyerson, "Recalling the Future," *American Prospect*, September 30, 2003.

[59] Swift Vets and POWs for the Truth. Found on World Wide Web <http://horse.he.net/~swiftpow/index.php> (accessed August 10, 2009).

[60] Domenico Montenaro, "Swift Boat: The Sequel," *MSNBC First Read*, July 11, 2007.

[61] "Obama: U.S. Troops in Afghanistan Must Do More than Kill Civilians," *Associated Press*, August 14, 2007.

[62] *Lexus Nexis Academic*. Search performed on "air-raiding villages" on June 15, 2009.

[63] "Obama's Margin of Victory: The Media," Media Research Center. Found on World Wide Web at <http://www.mrc.org/SpecialReports/2008/obama/ObamaMarginofVictory.pdf> (accessed June 15, 2009).

NOTES – Chapter 5

[1] Peter Berkowitz, "Bush Hatred and Obama Euphoria Are Two Sides of the Same Coin," *Wall Street Journal Online*, January 31, 2009; Stephan Thernstrom and Abigail Thernstrom, *America in Black and White: One Nation, Indivisible* (New York: Simon and Schuster, 1997), 67.

[2] Juan Williams, "Judge Obama on Performance Alone," *Wall Street Journal*, January 20, 2009.

[3] Tom Bevan, "Crying Racism," *Realclearpolitics.com*, September 8, 2009.

[4] Breitbart TV.com. Found on World Wide Web at <http://www.breitbart.tv/la-rep-obamacare-opponents-want-to-destroy-first-president-who-looks-like-me/> (accessed September 1, 2009); Marcia Kramer, "Rangel Plays Race Card, Says Obamacare the Victim," *WCBSTV.com*, September 3, 2009; David Harsanyi, "Why Can't We All Just Get Along," *Denver Post*, September 16, 2009.

[5] Jeffrey M. Jones, "Majority of Americans Say Racism Against Blacks Widespread," Gallup Organization, August 4, 2008.

[6] Byron York, "Why Did the Press Ignore The Van Jones Scandal?," *Washington Examiner*, September 8, 2009.

Notes

[7] Mary Mitchell, "Beck's Goal in Jones Case: Scare Whites," *Chicago Sun-Times*, September 8, 2009.

[8] Jim Abrams, "Lawmaker's 'You lie' Outburst Draws House Rebuke," *Associated Press*, September 16, 2009; James Rowley and Brian Faler, "Concerns of Black House Members Helped Spur Rebuke of Wilson," *Bloomberg News*, September 16, 2009; Harsanyi, "Why Can't We All"; Ben Feller, "Analysis: Many Tasks, 1 Speech," *Associated Press*, September 4, 2009; Janet Daley, "Jimmy Carter Plays the Race Card," *Telegraph.co.uk*, September 16, 2009.

[9] Leo E. Hendricks, "Unmarried Black Adolescent Father's Attitudes Toward Abortion, Contraception and Sexuality," *Journal of Adolescent Health Care*, 2, 1982: 199-203; CE Vincent et. al., "Abortion Attitudes in Poverty Level Blacks," *Seminars in Psychiatry*, 2, 1970: 309-317; Connecticut Mutual Life Report on American Values in the '80s: The Impact of Belief, Commissioned by Connecticut Mutual Life Insurance Co., Hartford, Connecticut (1981).

[10] Jeff Goldstein, "Provocateurism 8," *Proteinwisdom.com*. Found on World Wide Web at <http://proteinwisdom.com/?p=13152> (accessed on November 27, 2009).

[11] "Sotomayor Weathers First Week With High Approval," Quinnipiac University Poll, June 1, 2009; Jennifer Kelleher, "Hempstead School Unveils Barack Obama Elementary School," *Newsday*, February 4, 2009; Brett Tannehill, "Alabama County Creates Obama Holiday," National Public Radio, *All Things Considered* for December 30, 2008; *New York Times*/CBS News Poll: Obama's 100th Day in Office, April 22-26, 2008.

[12] Jeffrey M. Jones, "Obama's Approval Slide Finds Whites Down to 39 Percent Support," Gallup.com, November 24, 2009.

[13] Rex Nutting, "Net Wealth of Blacks has Disappeared," *Market Watch*, February 9, 2011.

[14] John Schmitt and Dean Baker, "What We're In For: Projected Economic Impact of the Next Recession," Washington D.C., Center for Economic Policy Research (January 2008); Reihan Salam, "Understanding Obama's Approval Rating," *National Review "Agenda" Blog*, November 25, 2009; Jeffrey M. Jones, "Obama's Approval Slide."

[15] Ron Brownstein, "The New Color Line," *National Journal*, October 10, 2009.

[16] "Georgia Lawmakers Fight Over Proposal Honoring Obama," *FOXNews.com*, March 21, 2009.

[17] James Taranto, "Invidious Statistics," *Opinionjournal.com*, April 29, 2009; New York Times/CBS News Poll: Obama's 100th Day in Office, April 22-26, 2008; "Blacks in Survey Say Race Relations No Better with Obama," *CNN.com*, June 25, 2009; "Voters Are Much Less Optimistic About Black-White Relations," Rasmussen Reports, October 6, 2010.

[18] "Public Opinion in Black and White: The More Things Change, the More They Stay the Same," National Association for the Advancement of Colored People, Washington, D.C., (August 2007); Abigail Thernstrom and Stephan Thernstrom, "Obama in Black and White," *National Review*, August 29, 2009.

[19] *Washington Post/Henry Kaiser Family Foundation Survey of African American Men*, Washington, D.C., (June 2006).

[20] Shelby Steele, "Why the GOP Can't Win With Minorities," *Opinionjournal.com*, March 16, 2009.

[21] *Trends in Political Values and Core Attitudes: 1987-2009*, Pew Research Center for the People and the Press, Washington D.C., May 21, 2009.

[22] David Billet, "The War on Philanthropy," *Commentary* (July/August 2009).

[23] John L. Jackson Jr., "Michael Jackson's Media Coverage Racist," Youtube.com video posted to column on *Chronicle of Higher Education* web site. Found on World Wide Web at <http://chronicle.com/review/brainstorm/index.php?id=1470> (accessed July 2, 2009).

[24] Incident Report 9005127, Cambridge Police Department, Cambridge, Massachusetts, July 14, 2009; Peter Wehner, "The President vs. The Police Officer," *Contentions,* July 24, 2009; Michael C. Moynihan, "Gates-Gate," *Weekly Standard*, August 3, 2009; Andrew Breitbart, "Obama's Accidental Gift on Race," *Realclearpolitics.com,* July 27, 2009.

[25] Michael C. Moynihan, "Gates-Gate."

[26] Henry Louis Gates Jr. entry on *Wikipedia.com* (accessed July 28, 2009); Vivek Viswanathan, "Du Bois Institute Opens in New Home," *Harvard Crimson*, November 23, 2005.

Notes

[27] Michael C. Moynihan, "Gates-Gate."

[28] Paul Street, *Barack Obama and the Future of American Politics* (Boulder, Colorado: Paradigm, 2008); John Blake, "Could an Obama Presidency Hurt Black Americans?" *CNNPolitics.com*, July 22, 2008.

[29] Glen Ford, "Black Agenda Report," (January 2008). Found on World Wide Web at <http://academic.udayton.edu/race/2008ElectionandRacism/Obama/obama24.htm> (accessed June 20, 2009).

[30] Shelby Steele, "Obama's Post-racial Promise," *Opinionjournal.com*, November 5, 2009.

[31] Steven Sailer, "White Guilt, Obamania, and the Reality of Race," *vdare.com*, January 2, 2007.

[32] Nia-Malika Henderson, "Blacks, Whites Hear Obama Differently," *Politico*, March 3, 2009.

[33] "Obama Mocks GOP, Jokes They Want Border Moat, *CBSNews*, May 10, 2011.

[34] Ron Sherer, "Obama's Nod to Al Sharpton: Asset or Liability for 2012 Reelection Bid?," *Christian Science Monitor*, April 6, 2011; John Stevens, "Obama Joins Michelle at Racially Charged White House Reception," *Daily Mail*, May 12, 2011.

Read more: http://www.dailymail.co.uk/news/article-1386032/Outrage-Michelle-Obama-welcomes-rapper-Common-White-House.html#ixzz1MjzzKn7V

[35] "Black Panther 'Civilian Security Force' On Patrol in Philly (And, Ivy League Intimidation)," Weekly Standard Blog, November 4, 2008; Hans Spakovsky, "Abusing the Civil Rights Act," *National Review*, February 11, 2011.

[36] Victor Davis Hanson, "What Happened to Our Post-racial President?," *National Review Online*, July 27, 2009.

[37] Stéphane Courtois, Nicolas Werth, Jean-Louis Panné, Andrzej Paczkowski, Karel Bartosek, Jean-Louis Margolin, Dr. Mark Kramer, Jonathan Murphy, Stephane Courtois, Jean-Louis Panne *The Black Book of Communism: Crimes, Terror, Repression* (Cambridge: Harvard University Press, 1999).

[38] Mona Charen, "Useful Idiots Caucus," *National Review,* April 9, 2009; Dennis Prager, "Time for Congressional Black Caucus to Disband?," *Realclearpolitics.com,* April 14, 2009.

[39] Jodi Cantor, "A Candidate, His Minister and the Search for Faith," *New York Times,* April 30, 2007.

[40] Scott Wilson, "Race a Dominant Theme at Summit," *Washington Post,* April 19, 2009.

[41] Steele, "Sotomayor and the Politics of Race."

NOTES – Chapter 6

[1] James Fallows, *More Like Us* (New York: Houghton Mifflin, 1989), 49.

[2] Barack Obama, *Dreams From My Father* (New York: Times Books, 1995), 55-56.

[3] "Co-Workers: Obama Inflated His Resume," *Sweetness and Light* blog. Found on world wide web at <http://sweetness-light.com/archive/did-obama-turn-down-a-wall-street-career> (accessed July 29, 2009).

[4] Richard Noyes, "Barack Obama and Bill Ayers: Stanley Kurtz Makes the Connection," Media Research Center, September 23, 2009; Stanley Kurtz, "Obama and Ayers Pushed Radicalism On Schools," *Wall Street Journal,* September 23, 2008; Stanley Kurtz, "Obama's Challenge," *National Review,* September 23, 2008; Dinitia Smith, "No Regrets for a Love Of Explosives," *New York Times Book Review,* September 11, 2009; Marcia Froelke Coburn, "No Regrets," *Chicago Magazine,* August, 2001.

[5] Noyes, "Barack Obama and Bill Ayers"; Kurtz, "Obama's Challenge."

[6] John Fund, "Obama's Liberal Shock Troops," *The Wall Street Journal*, July 12, 2008; Toni Foulkes, "Case Study: Chicago-The Barack Obama Campaign," *Social Policy,* October 18, 2004; Tim Novak and Fran Spielman, "Obama Helped Ex-Boss Get $1 Mil. From Charity," *Chicago Sun-Times,* November 11, 2007; Donors Forum Website. Found on world wide web at <ifs.donorsforum.org> (accessed June 10, 2008); Barackbook.com. Found on world wide web at <http://www.barackbook.com/Profiles/ACORN> (accessed December 24, 2009); Steven Malanga, "Organizer In Chief," *City Journal* (Summer 2008); P.J. Gladnick, "Will MSM Report on Obama Membership in Socialist New Party?," Newsbusters.com, October 8, 2008.

[7] "George Soros: The Man, The Mind and The Money Behind MoveOn," *Investor's Business Daily*, September 21, 2007.

[8] "Soomro Was Among Obama's Hosts in Pakistan," *The International News,* April 24, 2008; Jake Tapper, "Obama's College Trip," *ABCNews.com,* April 8, 2008.

[9] Andy McCarthy, "Suborned in the USA," *National Review Online*, July 31, 2009; Daniel Johnson, "The Kenya Connection," *New York Sun*, January 10, 2008.

[10] Andrew Breitbart, "On Race, 'No, He Can't'", *Realclearpolitics.com*, August 3, 2009.

[11] "HuffPost Blogger, College Prof: Release Birth Certificate," *Worldnetdaily.com,* August 2, 2009.

[12] Larry Johnson, "Second Posting, Obama Birth Certificate Controversy." Found on world wide web at <http://www.noquarterusa.net/blog/2009/07/27/2nd-posting-the-obama-birth-certificate-controversy> (accessed on July 29, 2009); McCarthy, "Suborned."

[13] Bret Stephens, "A President, Not a Symbol," *Wall Street Journal Online*, March 8, 2008.

[14] McCarthy, "Suborned"; Katherine Houreld, "Obama's Grandma Slams 'Untruths,'" *USA Today*, March 5, 2008.

[15] *Ibid.*; Jodi Cantor, "A Candidate, His Minister and the Search for Faith," *New York Times,* April 30, 2007.

[16] *Ibid.*; Jake Tapper, "The Emergence of President Obama's Muslim Roots," June 2, 2009; "Obama Tells *Al Arabiya* Peace Talks Should Resume," *Al Arabiya*, January 27, 2009; Tom Baldwin, "Barack Obama Tells Turkey the U.S. is Not at War With Islam," *Times of London*, April 7, 2009.

[17] "Most Voters Say News Media Wants Obama to Win," Pew Research Center for the People and the Press, Washington D.C., October 22, 2008; "Trust and Satisfaction with the National News Media," Sacred Heart University Polling Institute, Fairfield, Connecticut, September 23, 2009.

[18] "Steele: Obama Wasn't Vetted Because He's Black," CNNPolitics.com, May 22, 2009.

[19] "Remarks by the President at the White House Correspondents' Association Dinner, Washington Hilton, Washington D.C., May 9, 2009.

[20] "Partisan Gap in Obama Job Approval Widest in Modern Era," Pew Research Center for the People & the Press, Washington D.C., April 2, 2009; Jeffrey M. Jones, "Obama's Approval Most Polarized for First-Year President," Gallup.com, January 25, 2010; Jeffrey M. Jones, "Obama's Approval Ratings More Polarized in Year 2 Than Year 1," Gallup, February 1, 2011; Daily Presidential Tracking Poll, Rasmussenreports.com, June 5, 2009 and December 15, 2009.

NOTES – Chapter 7

[1] Jean Kaufman, "Reagan and Obama," *Weekly Standard*, October 10, 2009; Charles Krauthammer, *Democratic Realism* (Washington, D.C.: AEI Press, 2004).

[2] David Brooks, "Why the Europeans and the Arabs, Each in Their Own Way, Hate America and Israel," *Weekly Standard,* April 15, 2002; Dinesh D'Souza, *What's So Great about America* (Washington, D.C.: Regnery, 2002), 15.

[3] D'Souza, 20.

[4] Daniel Bell, *The Cultural Contradictions of Capitalism* (New York: Basic Books, Anniversary Addition, 1996); Irving Kristol, *Two Cheers for Capitalism* (New York: Signet, 1979).

[5] Edward W. Said, *Orientalism* (New York: Vintage, 1978); Howard Zinn, "The Power and the Glory: Myths of American Exceptionalism, *Bostonreview.com* (Summer 2005); Howard Zinn, *A People's History of the United States* (New York: Harper Perennial 2005), originally published in 1980; Ron Jacobs, "American Exceptionalism: A Disease of Conceit," *Counterpunch,* April 7, 2004. Found on world wide web at <http://www.counterpunch.org/jacobs07212004.html> (accessed July 9, 2009).

[6] "MSNBC's Buchanan Called Obama 'Exotic,'" *Mediamatters.org*, June 16, 2008.

[7] Jake Tapper, Sunlen Miller, Karen Travers, "Obama in Turkey Says U.S. Not at War With Islam," *ABCNews.com*, April 6, 2009; The White House, "Remarks by the President at the Summit of the Americas Opening Ceremony," April 17, 2009. Found on World wide web at <http://www.whitehouse.gov/the_press_office/Remarks-by-the-President-at-the-Summit-of-the-Americas-Opening-Ceremony> (accessed on June 2, 2009); The

White House, "News Conference by President Obama," April 2, 2009. Found on world wide web at <http://www.whitehouse.gov/the_press_office/News-Conference-by-President-Obama-4-02-09/> (accessed June 2, 2009); "Transcript: Obama addresses U.N. General Assembly."

[8] Robert Costa, "Bolton: 'A Post-American Speech by Our First Post-American President'," *"The Corner" blog of National Review Online,* September 23, 2009.

[9] Nick Dean, "Obama's Comment That Nations Are Defined by Bonds, Not Borders, Called 'Wishful Thinking'," *CNSNews.com,* May 24, 2010. Found on world wide web at http://www.cnsnews.com/news/article/66483 (accessed May 30, 2010).

[10] "Obama Sides With Mexico Against Arizona Immigration Law," *Newsmax.com,* May 19, 2010; Jim Hoft, "Top Obama Official: Feds Won't Process Illegals Referred by Arizona," *Gatewaypundit.firstthings.com,* May 24, 2010. Found on world wide web at http://gatewaypundit.firstthings.com/2010/05/top-obama-official-feds-wont-process-illegals-referred-by-arizona/ (accessed May 30, 2010).

[11] "Obama Sides With Mexico Against Arizona Immigration Law"; Hoft, "Top Obama Official."

[12] Mark Stevenson, "Mexico Acknowledges Abuse of Migrants," *San Francisco Examiner,* April 28, 2010.

[13] "Obama Sides With Mexico Against Arizona Immigration Law"; Hoft, "Top Obama Official."

[14] Dean, "Obama's Comment That Nations Are Defined by Bonds, Not Borders, Called 'Wishful Thinking'"; Jerry Markon and Michael D. Shear, "Justice Department Sues Arizona Over Immigration Law," *Washington Post,* July 7, 2010.

[15] "Transcript: Obama's Town Hall in China," *Washington Times,* November 16, 2009; Amnesty International USA, *2008 Annual Report for China.* Found on world wide web at <http://www.amnestyusa.org/> (accessed September 13, 2009); "China's Laws Kill Little Babies." Found on world wide web at <http://kassandraproject.wordpress.com/> (accessed September 13, 2009).

[16] The White House, "Remarks by President Obama and President Medvedev of Russia at New START Treaty Signing Ceremony and Press Conference," Prague Castle, Prague, Czech Republic, April 8, 2010, Washington, D.C.

[17] Harold Cruse, *The Crisis of the Negro Intellectual* (New York: Morrow, 1967), 344; Fred Siegel, *The Future Once Happened Here* (New York: Encounter Books, 1997).

[18] Seth Forman, "Obama's Authoritarian Multiculturalism," *American Thinker*, December 5, 2010.

[19] ABC News Poll, September 9-14, 2008. Found on world wide web at <www.pollingreport.com> (accessed on April 15, 2009); Susan Pincus, "Poll Analysis: U.S. and Israeli Jews Have Many Common Views," *Los Angeles Times*, April 19, 1998.

[20] "The Black and White of Public Opinion: Did the Racial Divide in Attitudes About Katrina Mislead Us?," The Pew Research Center for the People and the Press, October 31, 2005; Mark Krikorian, "Black & Tan Fantasy," *National Review*, May 6, 2002.

[21] *Statistical Abstract of the United States: 2008*, Economics and Statistics Administration, U.S. Census Bureau, Washington, D.C., 297, 323; "The Black and White of Public Opinion," Kaufmann Foundation for Entrepreneurship, Entrepreneurship Resource Center. Found on World wide web at <http://www.realclearmarkets.com/topic/entrepreneurship_center/> (accessed October 19, 2009).

[22] The White House, "Remarks by President Obama to the Turkish Parliament," April 6, 2009. Found on world wide web at <http://www.whitehouse.gov/the_press_office/Remarks-By-President-Obama-To-The-Turkish-Parliament/> (accessed on June 2, 2009).

[23] For more on the confluence of Obama's campaign and anti-Americanism see James Ceaser, "The Roots of Obama Worship," *Weekly Standard*, January 25, 2010; John Bolton, "The Post-American Presidency," *Standpoint* (July/August 2009).

[24] Sheldon Alberts, "No One Safe from Barbs as Obama Becomes Comic-in-Chief," *Canada.com*, May 10, 2009.

[25] "Why Does He Bash Us," *Powerlineblog.com*, April 5, 2009.

[26] "Transcript: 'This is Your Victory'," *CNNPolitics.com*, November 4, 2008.

[27] "Transcript: Obama Addresses U.N. General Assembly," *CNNPolitics.com*, September 23, 2009; Michael Gerson, "All about Obama," *Washington Post*, September 26, 2009.

[28] "President Obama's Address to the International Olympic Committee," *New York Times*, October 2, 2009; Ceasar, "Roots of Obama Worship."

[29] "Michelle Obama Takes Heat for Saying She's Proud of My Country for the First Time," *Foxnews.com*, February 19, 2008; Lauren Collins, "The Other Obama," *New Yorker*, March 10, 2008.

[30] "China: China's Growing Economic and Military Power," *WorldPublicOpinion.org*. Found on World wide web at <http://www.americans-world.org/digest/regional_issues/china/china2-5.cfm> (accessed on October 15, 2009).

[31] "Americans And The World Around Them: A Nationwide Poll," Zogby International, September 19, 2003; "Most Americans Proud of U.S. History, Say Other Nations Should Follow America's Lead," *Rasmussenreport.com*, July 2, 2008.

[32] "Obama: 'America is No Longer What It Once Was'," video posted at *Hotair.com*, August 7, 2008.

[33] Arthur M. Schlesinger, Jr., *The Politics of Hope and The Bitter Heritage* (Princeton, New Jersey: Princeton University Press, 2007).

[34] Barack Obama Speech, *notable-quotes.com*, November 3, 2008; Barack Obama Inaugural Address, *notable-quotes.com*, January 20, 2009; Kaufman, "Reagan and Obama."

NOTES – Chapter 8

[1] "U.S. Voters Disagree 3-1 with Sotomayor on Key Case, Quinnipiac University National Poll Finds, Most Say Abolish Affirmative Action," Quinnipiac University, June 3, 2009; Samuel Huntington, "One Nation, Out of Many," *American Enterprise* (September 24, 2004).

[2] Charles Krauthammer, "Obama's Ultimate Agenda," *Washington Post*, April 3, 2009.

[3] Charles Hurt, "Obama Fires a 'Robin Hood' Warning Shot," *New York Post*, October 16, 2008; William Douglas, "Obama Says McCain Flip-Flops by Opposing

Affirmative Action," *MiLatino.com*, July 28, 2008; Shelby Steele, "Sotomayor and the Politics of Race," *Wall Street Journal Online,* June 9, 2009; Jim Hoft, "Top Obama Official: Feds Won't Process Illegals Referred by Arizona," *Gatewaypundit.firstthings.com,* May 24, 2010. Found on world wide web at http://gatewaypundit.firstthings.com/2010/05/top-obama-official-feds-wont-process-illegals-referred-by-arizona/ (accessed May 30, 2010).

[4] Democratic National Committee, Vote 2010, *2010.BarackObama.com*, April 26, 2020; "Good Grief: Obama Compares His Socialist Agenda to "Slaves Sitting Around a Fire Singing Freedom Songs," *Weasel Zippers Blog.* Found on world wide web at <http://weaselzippers.us/2010/09/29/good-grief-obama-compares-his-socialist-agenda-to-slaves-sitting-around-a-fire-singing-freedom-songs/> (accessed on October 4, 2010).

[5] Huntington, "One Nation, Out of Many."

[6] Jacob Vigdor, "Choices To Make on Immigration Policy," *City Journal* (May 19, 2008).

[7] Jamie Glazov, "The Immigration Debate," *Frontpagemag.com,* October 5, 2007; Pew Hispanic Center/Kaiser Family Foundation 2002 National Survey Of Latinos, The Pew Hispanic Center & the Kaiser Family Foundation, December 17, 2002.

[8] Francis Fukuyama, "Immigrants and Family Values," *Commentary* (May 1993).

[9] W. James Antle, III, "Obama Urges Hispanics to Punish `Enemies,' Vote Democratic,", October 25, 2010.

[10] Amanda Carpenter, "Obama: Kids Should Learn Spanish," *Townhall.com,* July 9, 2009.

[11] Michael Scherer, "How Conservatives Will Try to Sink Sotomayor," *Time,* May 26, 2009; Stuart Taylor, "Sotomayor And Disparate Impact," *National Journal* (May 30, 2009); Stuart Taylor, "Identity Politics And Sotomayor," *National Journal* (May 23, 2009); Victor Davis Hanson, "The Diversity Mess," *Realclearpolitics.com*, June 4, 2009; Steele, "Sotomayor and the Politics of Race"; Stuart Taylor, "Justices Reject Sotomayor Position 9-0 -- But Bigger Battles Loom," *National Journal*, June 29, 2009.

[12] Hanson, "The Diversity Mess."

[13] National Vital Statistics Reports, "Births: Preliminary Data for 2007," 57, No, 12, March 18, 2009, Centers for Disease Control, Washington, D.C; Richard Fry and Jeffrey F. Passel, "Hispanic Children: A Majority are U.S. Born Off-Spring of Immigrants," Pew Hispanic Center, Washington, D.C., May 28, 2009; Heather MacDonald, "Seeing Today's Immigrants Straight," *City Journal* (Summer 2006); *Changing Patterns of Nonmarital Childbearing in the United States*, Centers for Disease Control, Washington D.C., Number 18, May 2009; Kay Hymowitz, "Burying the Lead," *City Journal*, May 29, 2009; Sam Roberts, "Study Reveals Changes Among Second Generation Hispanics," *New York Times*, May 28, 2009.

[14] *The 2004 National Survey of Latinos: Politics and Civic Participation*, Pew Hispanic Center/Kaiser Family Foundation, July, 2004.

[15] Jonathan Derbyshire, "Conversation between Jonathan Derbyshire and Kwame Anthony Appiah," *Prospect*, November 23, 2008.

[16] Jonathan Weisman, "Post-Partisan Promise Fizzles," *Wall Street Journal*, August 18, 2009.

[17] Charles M. Blow, "Black in the Age of Obama," *New York Times*, December 4, 2009.

[18] Seth Forman, "Krugman Misleads On Government Spending, Economic Growth," *Weekly Standard,* October 15, 2010.

[19] George Gilder, *The Israel Test* (New York: Richard Vigilante Books, 2009). Found in Mona Charen, "Gilder Throws Down a Gauntlet," *National Review Online*, July 31, 2009; Dennis Cauchon, "Reliance on Uncle Sam Hits a Record," *USA Today,* April 26, 2011; Sarah Murray, "About 1 in 7 in U.S. Receive Food Stamps," *Wall Street Journal,* May 3, 2011; U.S. Bureau of Labor Statistics.

[20] Philip Kennicott, "Obama as Joker: Racial Fear's Ugly Face," *Washington Post,* August 6, 2009.

NOTES – Chapter 9

[1] "Why Are Health Care Opponents Racist?," *The Political Inquirer,* August 11, 2009; Paul Krugman, "The Town Hall Mob," *New York Times*, August 6, 2009; "Support for Congressional Health Care Reform Falls to New Low," *Rasmussenreports.com*, August 11, 2009.

[2] Shelby Steele, "Obama and Our Post-Modern Race Problem," *Opinionjournal.com*, December 30, 2009.

[3] Charles Krauthammer, "Obama: A Dazzling Gatsby," *Washington Post*, September 1, 2008.

[4] Marc Ambinder, "Bill Clinton . . . Well, He Just Puts Everything on the Table. Read It," *The Atlantic*, December 14, 2007.

[5] Nathan Glazer, "Notes on the State of Black America," *The American Interest* (July-August, 2010).

[6] "Voters Are Much Less Optimistic About Black-White Relations," Rasmussen Reports, October 6, 2010.

[7] Thomas Sowell, "An Old Newness," *National Review*, April 29, 2008.